MORALITY
IN ACCOUNTING

MORALITY
IN ACCOUNTING

Ahmed Riahi-Belkaoui

Q

QUORUM BOOKS
Westport, Connecticut • London

Library of Congress Cataloging-in-Publication Data

Riahi-Belkaoui, Ahmed
    Morality in accounting / Ahmed Riahi-Belkaoui.
      p.   cm.
    Includes index.
    ISBN 0-89930-729-9 (alk. paper)
    1. Accounting—Moral and ethical aspects.   I. Title.
HF5657.R5   1992
174′.9657—dc20   92-7485

British Library Cataloguing in Publication Data is available.

Library of Congress Catalog Card Number: 92-7485
ISBN: 0-89930-729-9

First published in 1992

Quorum Books, 88 Post Road West, Westport, CT 06881
An imprint of Greenwood Publishing Group, Inc.

Printed in the United States of America

The paper used in this book complies with the
Permanent Paper Standard issued by the National
Information Standards Organization (Z39.48–1984).

10 9 8 7 6 5 4 3 2 1

44.46

10-27-93

To Hédi J. and Janice M. Belkaoui

Contents

Preface

The accounting profession is involved in the production and/or the verification of accounting information, deemed vital to users' decision making and to an efficient working of capital markets and national economies. The complete reliance on the resulting accounting information derives from the belief held by the general public about the high moral standards used by accountants in the accomplishment of their duties. Therefore morality in accounting is the crucial factor that helps accounting professionals maintain their high and prestigious occupations and their perceived high level of integrity. This book examines morality in accounting by exploring the conventional view about the facets of this morality as well as the deficiencies, distortions, and even fallacies that still affect some of these facets. To accomplish this task this book covers, in six chapters, five aspects of morality in accounting: (1) fairness, (2) ethics (with issues and cases), (3) honesty, (4) social responsibility, and (5) truth. A good appreciation of the morality issues in accounting is instrumental to a better use and reliance on accountants and accounting data.

The book should be of interest to practitioners, educators, and public policy officials with interest in the general issues of morality in accounting, as well as graduate and undergraduate students in accounting ethics and public-interest accounting courses.

Many people helped in the development of this book. Eric Valentine and Katie Chase of Quorum Books are true professionals and have my deepest gratitude. My thanks go to the individuals and organizations that gave me permission to reprint their excellent material as well as to University of Illinois at Chicago students Kalliopi Karabatsos, Latonja L. Brown, and Catherine Serra for their capable assistance.

1

Fairness as a Concept of Justice in Accounting

Fairness judgments are taken for granted in accounting although their clear meaning is not well specified. Two generally accepted meanings concern the idea of neutrality in preparation and presentation of financial reports and the idea of justice in outcome. While both notions play a useful role in accounting, the expansion of the notion of fairness to deal with distribution considerations links it to alternative philosophical concepts more compatible with moral concepts of justice. Basically, fairness may be viewed as a moral concept of justice subject to three different interpretations of the notions of distributive justice. Accordingly, the objective of this chapter is to expand the accounting discussion of fairness by introducing the main philosophical concepts of distributive justice in the accounting contest. The end result is the possibility to view and compare the concept of fairness through different distributive justice frameworks.

FAIRNESS IN ACCOUNTING

Fairness as Neutrality in Presentation

Fairness is best understood in the professional accounting literature and pronouncements as an expression of the neutrality of the accountant in the preparation of financial reports.[1] The first suggestion of the use of fairness in accounting was made by D. R. Scott in 1941 when he listed it as a principle of accounting and stated: "Accounting rules, procedures, and techniques should be fair, unbiased and impartial. They should not serve a special interest."[2] Since then, the fairness concept has become an implicit ethical norm. In general, the fairness concept implies that accounting statements have not been subject to undue influence or bias. Fairness implies that the preparers of accounting information have acted in good faith and employed ethical business practices and sound accounting judgment in the presentation, production, and auditing of accounting results.

Fairness is a value statement that is variously applied in accounting. James Patillo, who made fairness the subject of a book, ranks it as a basic standard to be used in the evaluation of other standards because it is the only standard that implies "ethical considerations."[3] He states:

From contrasting the connotation of justice, truth, and fairness, the current social concept of fairness is selected as the basic standard by which to measure the propriety of accounting principles and rules which purports to be the means of attaining the objective. Fairness to all parties, therefore, is formulated to be the single basic standard of accounting, that criterion or test which all accounting propositions must reflect before being included in the accounting structure.[4]

The importance of fairness was also evident when C. T. Devine gave preserving equity among conflicting groups a central place among accounting concerns.[5] And in spite of contentions that fairness is subjective, ambiguous, and therefore cannot serve as a basis for developing accounting theory[6,7] it has become one of the basic objectives of accounting. A first evidence of this importance is the reference by the American Institute of Certified Public Accountants' (AICPA) Committee on Auditing Procedures to the criteria of "fairness of presentation" as conformity with generally accepted accounting principles, disclosure, consistency, and comparability.[8] In an unqualified report, "present fairly" connotes compliance with generally accepted accounting principles and generally accepted auditing standards. The reference to a true and fair view in auditors' reports, under laws on the English pattern, is similar to the U.S. connotation. It implies that the auditor, by being fair, has complied with protocol largely of his own creation.[9] Under both laws however, the term fairness is given dominance although not well specified. R. C. Chambers attributes the situation to the loose rein of the law. He states: "The vagueness of the law may be attributed to the belief of legislators or of lawyers that the terms used in the statutes are terms of art, peculiar to accounting and accountants, which should properly be left to accountants to elucidate."[10]

Without mentioning fairness explicitly, Baruch Lev advocated a concept of equity as equality of opportunity in the sense of an equal access to information relevant for asset valuation.[11] Absence of equity implies systematic and significant information asymmetries leading to adverse private and social consequences in the form of high transaction costs, thin markets, low liquidity, and decreased gains from trade. Operationally, Lev suggests the decrease of information asymmetries by a search for those specific information items that are at the disposition of some informed investors while not of others, favoring thereby the interests of the less informed over those of the more informed.

The equity criterion as espoused by Lev and others in this section are forms of fairness in presentation aimed at decreasing information asymmetries between various classes of investors and financial statement users to ensure an equal endowment of information. It is very much in line with the argument that equality of opportunity, as opposed to equality of actual outcomes, is the sole principle of justice guiding government decisions.[12] It is also appealing to those who may intuitively see a link between increasing equality of opportunity and equality of outcomes,[13] and to those who assume that the ex-ante equality of opportunity concept conflicts less with efficiency incentives than do the egalitarian ex-post concepts of equity.[14]

Fairness as Justice in Outcome

The view of fairness as neutrality in presentation of an equality of opportunity is not without its critics. Paul Williams characterized it as an evaluation process with the following two attributes: (1) that the evaluator is aware of the condition that any consequences of his or her actions will be judged as fair or unfair, and (2) that the evaluation attempts to adopt a perspective of impartiality.[15] Williams argued that given the concern in accounting with efficiency and the link between efficiency and distribution, distributive judgments are fairness judgments.[16] Therefore, fairness derives also from a concept of distributive justice. The problems of distribution have almost been ignored in the conventional view of fairness as neutrality in presentation as a matter beyond the scope of their concern. The concern was with merely the final production and disclosure of accounting results rather than their distribution.

There are, however, three notable exceptions in the accounting literature that have shown concern with distributive questions:

The first exception emanates from the social accounting concern with accounting for externalities and reporting some forms of social report. A first example includes Scott's view of the social role of accounting in the resolution of conflicting social interest: "The compromise of conflicting interests is a process of valuation. It accomplishes social organization and results in a distribution of economic incomes. Value and distribution constitute a simple problem and accounting theory is especially and peculiarly a treatment of that problem."[17]

A second example includes the various calls for the role of social accounting in some form of rectification of society's ills.[18] It is best stated by H. Schreuder and K. V. Ramanathan as follows: "In the context of traditional economic analysis, the issue boils down to a distributional problem, namely the apportionment in a society of the costs and benefits of economic activity. Economists have long recognized that such distributional issues cannot be addressed without taking a normative position."[19]

Fairness in the social accounting literature becomes a matter of the distribution of social responsibility in general and social responsiveness as the capacity of a corporation to respond to social pressures. Thus, corporate social responsiveness, as an expression of fairness, goes beyond the moral and ethical connotation of social responsibility to the managerial process of response. The response to be fair involves the identification, measurement, and disclosure, where necessary, of the social costs and benefits created by the economic activities of the firm, as well as the adequate responses to these problems.

The second exception emanates from advocates of the political economy of accounting, and the critical and Marxist approach to accounting.[20] They advocate a political economy approach that recognizes power and conflict in society and the effects of accounting reports on the distribution of income, wealth, and power in society.

The third exception emanates from the positive theory of accounting view that accounting can be used to optimally resolve conflicts over resource allocation to a limited set of participants.[21] Fairness in this context is ultimately in the shareholders' interest.[22]

FAIRNESS AS A MORAL CONCEPT OF JUSTICE

For fairness to be perceived as a moral concept of justice, parallels must be made to the main theories of distributive justice, namely J. A. Rawls', A. M. Nozick's, and A. Gerwith's theories of justice.

Rawls' Contribution

Rawls' Theory of Justice

The goal of Rawls' theory of justice is to develop a moral theory about justice in the form of principles to apply to the development of the basic structure of society, and that presents a direct challenge to utilitarianism.[23] As an egalitarian theory, its main contention is the distribution of all economic goods and services equally except where an unequal distribution would actually work to everyone's advantage, or at least would benefit the worst-off society. Using what he calls the "Kantian concept of equality," Rawls starts by comparing life to a game of chance where nature bestows on each individual a generation, a culture, a social system, a family, and a set of personal attributes that determines his or her happiness. Accepting this random allocation is viewed as unjust and a set of just institutions is required. To establish just institutions, Rawls suggests that individuals step behind a "veil of ignorance" that eliminates any knowledge about potential positions and benefits under a given set of principles. Then, to reach a social contract, they must choose from this original position principles of justice leading to the just society. From this original position and under the veil of ignorance, individuals will choose two principles of justice:

First: each person is to have an equal right to the most extensive basic liberty compatible with a similar liberty for others. Second: social and economic inequalities are to be arranged so that they are both (a) reasonably expected to be to everyone's advantage, and (b) attached to positions and offices open to all.[24]

Rawls maintains that the two principles are lexicographically ordered, the first one over the second. He states:

Now it is possible, at least theoretically, that by giving up some of their fundamental liberties men are sufficiently compensated by the resulting social and economic gains. The general conception of justice implies no restrictions on what sort of inequalities; it only requires that everyone's position be improved. . . . Imagine . . . that men forgo certain political rights when the economic returns are significant and their capacity to influence the course of policy by the exercise of these rights would be marginal in any case. It is this kind of exchange which the two principles as stated rule out; being arranged in serial order they do not permit exchanges between basic liberties and economic and social gains.[25]

The first principle shows that emphasis placed by Rawls on liberty and the precedence of liberty over the second principle of justice. Liberty can only be restricted when it is formulated as follows: "The principles of justice are to be ranked in lexical order and therefore, liberty can be restricted only for the sake of liberty. There are two cases: (a) a less restrictive liberty shared by all, and (b) a less than equal liberty must be acceptable to those citizens with the lesser liberty."[26]

The second principle of justice, which Rawls labeled the difference principle, contains a second lexicographic ordering of the welfare of the individuals from lowest to highest, where the welfare of the worst-off individual is to be maximized first before proceeding to higher levels. In its most general form, the difference principle states:

In a basic structure with no relevant representatives, first maximize the welfare of the worst-off representative, minimize the welfare of the second worst-off man, and so on until the last case which is, for equal welfare of all the preceding n–1 representatives, maximize the welfare of the best-off representative man. We think of this as the lexical difference principle.[27]

These two principles show a democratic conception that eliminates those aspects of the social world that seem arbitrary from a moral point of view. This does not necessarily eliminate economic inequality. Rawls justifies some difference in income first: as incentives to attract people in certain positions and motivate them to perform; and as a guarantee that certain public-interest positions will be filled. To implement Rawls' theory, the idea of "basic structure" may be "a constitutional democracy," which preserves equal basic liberties, with a government that promotes equality of opportunity and guarantees a social minimum and a market-based economic system. Rawls suggests that this social minimum be established before allowing the rest of the total income to be settled by the price system. It is to be settled by special payments for sickness and unemployment and monetary transfer systems such as negative income tax. Rawls, however, gives little attention to the identification of the worst-off representative. He offers only two alternatives: (1) to choose a particular social position, say that of the unskilled worker, and then to count as the least advantaged all those with the average income of this group, or less; or (2) to focus on the relative income and wealth with no reference to social position—that is, all persons with less than half of the median income and wealth may be taken as the least advantaged segment.[28] With regard to redistribution, Rawls finds large inequalities to be permissible if lowering them would make the working class even worse-off. Basically, with the raising of expectations of the more advantaged, the situation of the worst-off is continuously improved. Inequalities will tend to be leveled down by the increasing availability of educated talent and ever-widening expectations. However, Rawls calls for the establishment of social minimums through various transfers and redistributive mechanisms. But would Rawls' difference principle assure an adequate level of the necessary goods and services? There are a lot of disagreements on this issue.[29]

Derek Phillips joins the opposite chorus:

The major reason for this concerns Rawls' emphasis on incentives. With the difference principle . . . an unequal distribution of wealth and income is justified if and only if it will maximize benefits to the least advantaged segments within a society. But if, as Rawls assumes, these inequalities must be rather large, then it seems likely that the actual benefits — even if maximized — will not be sufficient to provide an adequate level for the least advantaged segment, they will fail to do so for those persons who require extra medical care, protection and other basic goods. This is a consequence of the fact . . . that the difference principle makes no allowances for the particular needs of especially disadvantaged individuals."[30]

While better criteria still need to be developed to resolve these issues, Gerwith asserts that what is needed is a drastic redistribution of wealth and an effective exercise of the fundamental rights to freedom and well-being.[31] Basically, Rawls and Gerwith disagree on how the needs of the disadvantaged are to be met. While Rawls is willing to accept an unequal distribution of economic rewards, if it benefits the least advantaged, Gerwith maintains that the wealthy have an obligation to assist the disadvantaged.

Fairness in Accounting According to Rawls

Rawls' contract theory—a theory of just social institutions—may be offered as a concept of fairness in accounting. Applied to accounting, it suggests first the potential reliance on the veil of ignorance in all the situations calling for an accounting choice eventually to yield solutions that are neutral, fair, and socially just. Second, it also suggests the expanded role of accounting in the creation of just institutions and the definition of the social minimum advocated by Rawls. This role, as also espoused by advocates of accounting, will lead to the elimination of those aspects of the social world in general, and the accounting world in particular, that seem arbitrary from a moral point of view. This view of fairness would be most welcome to advocates of social accounting. As stated by Williams:

Rawlsian principles also may prove to be a useful set of premises for speculation about alternative accounting systems. For example, one plausible reason for the slow theoretical development of social accounting, at least in the United States, could be the constraining effect of conventional accounting premises about character and legitimacy of institutions, both public and private. Accounting scholars with interests in social accounting are certainly free to generate and test hypotheses about measuring and reporting, in Rawlsian, or any other, institutional setting.[32]

Nozick's Contribution

Nozick's Theory of Justice

While Rawls is interested in the justice of one or another pattern of distribution, Nozick is interested in the process through which distribution comes about.[33] He first argued that Rawls' theory of justice violates people's rights, and consequently cannot be morally justified; that it ignores people's entitlements and is, like most other theories of justice, patterned. Patterned theories of justice imply that a distribution is to vary along some natural dimension, weighted sum of natural dimensions, or lexicographic ordering of natural dimensions.[34] Examples of such distributions include those based on need, merit, or work. Nozick maintains: "To think that the task of a theory of justice is to fill in the blank in each according to his ——— is to be predisposed to search for a pattern; and separate treatment from each according to his ——— treats production and distribution as two separate and independent issues."[35]

Nozick argues that such theories of justice, based on the patterned and end-state principles, violate people's rights and exclude recognition of an entitlement principle of distributive justice, whereby individuals are entitled to their possessions as long as they acquired them by legitimate means, including voluntary transfers, exchanges, and cooperative productive activity. Nozick's theory focuses on the importance of historical principles, in the sense that a distribution is just or not depending on how it came about. He justifies his theory as follows:

1. A person who acquires a holding in accordance with the principle of justice in acquisition is entitled to that holding.

2. A person who acquires a holding in accordance with the principle of justice in transfer, from someone else entitled to that holding, is entitled to the holding.
3. No one is entitled to a holding except by (repeated) applications of 1. and 2.[36]

The principles involve, respectively, the question of original acquisition of holdings, and the rectification of injustices in holdings. Nozick introduced a proviso, however, to ensure that an individual's entitlements do not result in a net loss in what remains for other persons to use. Nozick's theory is then a theory of justice in holdings. It is a very special kind of theory of distributive justice, as Nozick emphasizes:

The term "distributive justice" is not a neutral one. Hearing the term "distribution," most people presume that some thing or mechanism uses some principle or criterion to give out a supply of things. . . . However, we are not in the position of children who have been given portions of pie by someone who now makes last-minute adjustments to rectify careless cutting. There is no central distribution, no person or group entitled to control all the resources, jointly deciding how they are to be doled out. What each person gets, he gets from others who give it to him in exchange for something, or as a gift. In a free society, diverse persons control different resources, and new holdings arise out of the voluntary exchanges and actions of persons. There is no more a distribution of shares than there is a distribution of mates in a society in which persons choose whom they shall marry. The total result is the product of many individuals' decisions which the different individuals involved are entitled to make.[37]

Although some criteria remain to be used, Nozick's theory has been criticized for its failure to recognize the right to well-being. The question generally asked is: Is it just to tie the socioeconomic standing of other family members entirely to the moral acceptability of historical process through which the breadwinner has acquired his or her holdings? Those answering "no" argue that it may appear to anyone involved with a sense of justice and concerned about some family members reducing their standard of living radically, when, in other cases, correction is required because of someone else's unjust acquisition; and feeling something morally unsatisfactory about some people being very well compared to others.[38]

Fairness in Accounting According to Nozick

The use of the economic man theory in accounting and the decision usefulness criterion used in empirical accounting research link fairness and distributive justice to a free market mechanism. Accounting is viewed as essential to the efficient running of an organization, and the mere reaching of efficiency is presumed to make everybody better off in possession of their just share.[39] Fairness to the positivists and the rationality theorists is linked to an efficient market that allows a just transfer to shareholders.

It is essentially a libertarian theory of distribution a la Nozick, based on a principle of justice in acquisition and in transfer. This concept of distributive justice with its reliance on a free market mechanism does not allow for dealing adequately with fairness as a distributive function, because it is assumed to fail the discussion of the social obligations of humans to each other, perpetuate past violations of principles of acquisition and transition, and distort the meaning of well-offness in a world of scarcity.[40] The reliance on the market mechanism, the absence of a moral language to discuss the social obligations, as well as the absence of a concept of redistributive justice are the fans of the cited failures of the libertarian theory of justice. In addition, the growing importance of meritocracy in the context of a basically market system has created problems for a Nozickean theory of justice. The conflicting rules of distribution are not well accepted in our contemporary culture. Most often, members of the organization demand to receive what they justly deserve.

Under the tutoring of the school system, and reinforced by other meritocratic organizations, a person has been socialized to feel that he or she ought to get what has been earned and to be protected from the vagaries and irrationalities of the market. Basically, stakeholders and other shareholders may not be satisfied by the conventional reporting emphasis on returns to shareholders. For example, labor may feel that the profit generated dictates a different distribution than the one dictated by justice in holding and transfer, and a reporting system emphasizing the "mere" just distribution is warranted.

Gerwith's Contribution

Gerwith's Theory of Justice

The goal of Gerwith's theory of justice was to provide a rational justification for moral principles to objectively distinguish morally right actions and institutions from morally wrong ones.[41] The necessary content of morality is in actions and their generic features. The actions are distinguished in terms of two categorical features: voluntariness and purposiveness. Given the importance of action as the necessary and universal matter of all moral and other practical precepts, Gerwith presents his doctrine of the structure of actions in three main steps:

First, every agent implicitly makes evaluative judgments about the goodness of his purposes and hence about the necessary goodness of the freedom and well-being that are necessary conditions of his acting to achieve his purposes. Second, because of this necessary goodness, every agent implicitly makes a deontic judgment in which he claims that he has rights to freedom and well-being. Third, every agent must claim these rights for the sufficient reason that he is a prospective agent who has purposes he wants to fulfill, so that he logically must accept the generalization that all prospective agents have rights to freedom and well-being.[42]

The rights to freedom and well-being are seen as generic, fundamental, and universal. As a result Gerwith asserts that every agent logically must acknowledge certain generic obligations:

Negatively, he ought to refrain from coercing and from harming his recipients; positively, he ought to assist them to have freedom and well-being whenever they cannot otherwise have the necessary goods and he can help them at no comparable loss to himself. The general principle of these obligations and rights may be expressed as the following precepts addressed to every agent: Act in accord with the generic rights of your recipients as well as yourself. I call this the Principle of Generic Consistency (PGC) since it combines the formal consideration of rights to the generic features or goods of action.[43]

Gerwith calls the PGC the supreme moral principle, as it requires the agents not to interfere with the freedom and well-being of others. It remains that the PGC has both direct and indirect application. The direct application concerns the requirement for agents to act in accord with rights to freedom and well-being of all other persons. The indirect application concerns the requirement that institutional arrangements must express or serve the freedom and well-being of all other persons.

The indirect application involves specifically social rules and arrangements to be implemented in a static and dynamic phase. The static phase generates rules to protect an existing equality of generic rights, while the dynamic phase calls for redistributive justice to eliminate inequalities through a "supportive state." The social rules between two extremes are as follows: (1) a certain libertarian extreme that would defend the existing distribution of wealth, arising presumably from just acquisition, and (2) an egalitarian extreme that calls for a drastic redistribution to be guided solely by the aim of maximally benefiting those who are the least advantaged. Both extremes appear deficient:

The former extreme does not recognize the independent right to well-being, including additive goods, on the part of those whose initial position in life subjects them to serious advantages. The latter extreme does not recognize the independent right to freedom as applied in the production of valued commodities and the consequent earnings in income. Thus the two extremes overlook, respectively, the claims of severe economic need and the claims of worthiness as based on voluntary effort and accomplishment.[44]

Naturally the two extremes are Nozick's and Rawls' positions, as they are seen as ignoring the independent right to well-being and the independent right to freedom.

Fairness in Accounting According to Gerwith

Gerwith's theory of justice may be offered as a concept of fairness in accounting. Applied to accounting, it suggests the primary of the concerns for the rights of freedom and well-being of all persons affected by the activities of the firm and for the creation of institutional and accounting arrangements to guarantee these rights. These arrangements call for some form of rectification through the creation of a "supportive system" and specific social rules to be followed by organizations and members within the organization. Accounting may be called on to facilitate a drastic redistribution of wealth and an effective exercise of the fundamental rights to freedom and well-being of the stakeholders in organizations. Gerwithian principles may prove to be a useful set of premises for speculation about the merit of value-added reporting. This supports the emphasis in value-added reporting to report the total return to all members of the "production team": shareholders, bondholders, suppliers, labor, government, and society. Not one of these members is relegated to the position of "disadvantaged" as in other concepts of distributive justice, as they are all given a place of importance in the measurement, reporting, and allocation of the total return of the firm. Basically the Gerwithian principles applied to fairness in accounting include a recognition of the rights of all those affected by the activities of the organization and as stated by Gerwith himself:

a recognition of the rights of others, a positive concern for their having the objects of these rights, and a positive regard for them as persons who have rights or entitlements equal to his own as well as the rational capacity to reflect on their purposes and to control their behavior in light of such reflection.[45]

It calls for action that is voluntary and purposive to affirm an egalitarian universalist moral principle. As Marx's "man makes its own history," the role of action toward making moral judgments applies to accounting making efficiency and distribution judgments that protect the generic rights of all the recipients of accounting information. Accounting will create its own history of a moral agent in the marketplace, an agent concerned by the rights of the recipients of accounting information. The merits of application of the principle of generic consistency of the concept of fairness in accounting derives from its capacity of presenting the accountant with rationally grounded answers to each of the three questions of moral philosophy:

1. The distributive question of which persons' interests ought to be favorably considered is answered by calling for the respect of the generic rights of all recipients and for the equality of the rights of all prospective purpose agents.
2. The substantive question of which interests ought to be favorably considered is answered by focusing on the primacy of freedom and well-being.
3. The authoritative question of why should anyone be moral in the sense of taking favorable account of other people's interests is justified by the reason of avoiding self-contradiction. Basically an action that violates the PGC principle cannot be rationally justified.[46]

CONCLUSIONS

While fairness has been generally associated in accounting and auditing with a connotation of either neutrality in presentation or justice in outcome, it may, borrowing from theories of distributive justice and its expansion to considerations of distribution, play a moral role in accounting. That moral dimension of fairness in matters of distribution may easily be associated with the market for entitlements of Nozick, or the reliance on a veil of ignorance concept and the creation of just institutions of Rawls, or as a guarantor and implementor of the rights to freedom and well-being of all persons affected by the activities of the firm and a basis for the creation of institutional and accounting arrangements to guarantee these rights of Gerwith. A communitarian perspective of fairness is presented in the Appendix to this chapter.

NOTES

1. Financial Accounting Standards Board (FASB), *Statement of Financial Accounting Concepts No 1: Objectives of Financial Reporting by Business Enterprises* (Stamford, Conn.: FASB, 1978).

2. D. R. Scott, "The Basis of Accounting Principles," *The Accounting Review* (December 1941), p. 341.

3. James W. Patillo, *The Foundation of Financial Accounting* (Baton Rouge: Louisiana State University Press, 1965), p. 11.

4. Ibid., pp. 60–61.

5. C. T. Devine, "Research Methodology and Accounting Theory Formation," *The Accounting Review* (July 1960), pp. 387–399.

6. H. E. Arnett, "The Concept of Fairness," *The Accounting Review* (April 1967).

7. M. Moonitz, *The Basic Postulates of Accounting,* Accounting Research Study No 1 (New York: AICPA, 1961).

8. American Institute of Certified Public Accountants, *Report of the Committee on Auditing Procedures* (New York: AICPA, 1963).

9. E. L. Kohler, "Fairness," *Journal of Accountancy* (December 1967), pp. 58–60.

10. R. C. Chambers, *Securities and Obscurities: A Case for Reform of the Law of Accounts* (Sydney, Australia: Gower Press, 1973), pp.18–19.

11. Baruch Lev, "Toward a Theory of Equitable and Efficient Accounting Policy," *The Accounting Review* (January 1988), p. 3.

12. K. Joseph and J. Sumption, *Equality* (London: Rowan and Littlefield, 1979).

13. A. M. Okum, *Equality and Efficiency: The Big Tradeoff* (Washington, D.C., 1975).

14. Lev, "Toward a Theory of Equitable and Efficient Accounting Policy," p. 4.

15. Paul F. Williams, "The Legitimate Concern with Fairness," *Accounting, Organizations and Society* (March 1987), p. 171.

16. Ibid., p. 176.

17. Scott, "The Basis of Accounting Principles," p. 248.

18. Ahmed Belkaoui, *Socio-Economic Accounting* (Westport, Conn.: Greenwood Press, 1973).

19. H. Schreuder and K. V. Ramanathan, "Accounting and Corporate Accountability: An Extended Comment," *Accounting, Organizations and Society* (Fall 1984), p. 407.

20. D. J. Cooper and M. J. Sherer, "The Value of Corporate Accounting Reports: Arguments for a Political Economy of Accounting," *Accounting, Organizations and Society* (Fall 1984), pp. 207–232.

21. M. C. Jensen and W. H. Meckling, "Theory of the Firm: Managerial Behavior, Agency Costs and Ownership Structure," *Journal of Financial Economics* (October 1976), pp. 305–362.

22. R. L. Watts and J. L. Zimmerman, "Towards a Positive Theory of the Determination of Accounting Standards," *The Accounting Review* (January 1978), pp. 112–134.

23. J. A. Rawls, *A Theory of Justice* (Cambridge, Mass.: Harvard University Press, 1971).

24. Ibid., p. 67.

25. Ibid., pp. 62–63.

26. Ibid., p. 250.

27. Ibid., p. 83.

28. Ibid., p. 64.

29. Brian Barry, *The Liberal Theory of Justice* (Oxford: Oxford University Press, 1973).

30. Derek L. Phillips, *Toward a Just Social Order* (Princeton, N.J.: Princeton University Press, 1986), p. 354.

31. A. Gerwith, *Reason and Morality* (Chicago: University of Chicago Press, 1978), p. 313.

32. Williams, "The Legitimate Concern with Fairness," p. 184.

33. A. M. Nozick, *Anarchy, State and Utopia* (New York: Basic Books, 1974).

34. Ibid., p. 156.

35. Ibid., pp. 159–160.

36. Ibid., p. 160.

37. Ibid., pp. 149–150.

38. Phillips, *Toward a Just Social Order*, p. 348.

39. Williams, "The Legitimate Concern with Fairness," p. 184.

40. Ibid., p. 181.

41. Gerwith, *Reason and Morality*.

42. Ibid., p. 48.

43. Ibid., p. 153.

44. Ibid., pp. 312–313.

45. Ibid., pp. 137–148.

46. Ibid., p. 150.

BIBLIOGRAPHY

Adams, J. S. "Inequity in Social Exchange." In Leonard Berkowitz (ed.), *Advances in Experimental Social Psychology*, New York: Academic Press, 1965.

Arnett, H. E. "The Concept of Fairness." *The Accounting Review* (April 1967).

Barry, Brian. *The Liberal Theory of Justice.* Oxford: Oxford University Press, 1973.

Belkaoui, Ahmed. *Socio-Economic Accounting.* Westport, Conn.: Greenwood Press, 1973.

Blau, Peter M. and Otis Dudley Duncan. *The American Occupational Structure.* New York: John Wiley, 1976.

Chambers, R. C. *Securities and Obscurities: A Case for Reform of the Law of Company Accounts.* Sydney, Australia: Gower Press, 1973.

Cooper, D. J. and M. J. Sherer. "The Value of Corporate Accounting Reports: Arguments for a Political Economy of Accounting." *Accounting, Organizations and Society* (Fall 1984), pp. 207–232.

Deutsche, Morton. "Equity, Equality and Need: What Determines Which Value Be Used as a Basis of Distributive Justice?" *Journal of Social Issues* 31, no. 3, (1975).

Devine, C. T. "Research Methodology and Accounting Theory Formation." *The Accounting Review* (July 1960), pp. 387–399.

Financial Accounting Standards Board, *Statement of Financial Accounting Concepts No. 1: Objective of Financial Reporting by Business Enterprises.* Stamford, Conn.: FASB, 1978.

————. *Statement of Financial Accounting Concepts No. 2: Objective of Financial Reporting by Business Enterprises.* Stamford, Conn.: FASB, 1980.

Gambling, T. *Societal Accounting.* Chicago: University of Chicago Press, 1978.

Gerwith, A. *Reason and Morality.* Chicago: University of Chicago Press, 1978.

Homans, Georges C. *Social Behavior: Its Elementary Forms.* New York: Harcourt Brace Jovanovich, 1965.

Ijiri, Y. "On the Accountability-Based Conceptual Framework of Accounting," *Journal of Accounting and Public Policy* (Summer 1983).

Jasso G. and P. H. Rossi. "Distributive Justice and Earned Income." *Journal of Accountancy* (December 1967).

Jensen, M. C. and W. H. Meckling, "Theory of the Firm: Managerial Behavior, Agency Costs and Ownership Structure." *Journal of Financial Economics* (October 1976), pp. 305–362.

Joseph, K. and J. Sumptions. *Equality* (London: Rowman, 1979).

Kohler, E. L. "Fairness." *Journal of Accountancy* (December 1967), pp. 58–60.

Lee, T. A. *Contemporary Financial Reporting: Issues and Analysis.* London: Thomas Nelson and Sons, 1976.

Lev, Baruch. "Toward a Theory of Equitable and Efficient Accounting Policy." *The Accounting Review* (January 1988), pp. 1–92.

Moonitz, M. *The Basic Postulates of Accounting,* Accounting Research Study No. 1 (New York: AICPA, 1961).

Miller, David. *Social Justice.* Oxford: Clarendon Press, 1976.

Nozick, R., *Anarchy, State and Utopia.* New York: Basic Books, 1974.

Okum, A. M. *Equality and Efficiency: The Big Tradeoff.* Washington, D.C.: Littlefield, 1975.

Patillo, James W. *The Foundation of Financial Accounting.* Baton Rouge: Louisiana State University Press, 1965.

Phillips, Derek L. *Toward a Just Social Order.* Princeton, N.J.: Princeton University Press, 1986.

Rawls, J. A., *A Theory of Justice*. Cambridge, Mass.: Harvard University Press, 1971.

Rubinstein, David. "The Concept of Justice in Sociology." *Theory and Society* 17 (1988/1989).

Schreuder, H. and K. V. Ramanathan. "Accounting and Corporate Accountability: An Extended Comment." *Accounting, Organizations and Society* (Fall 1984), pp. 405–415.

Scott, D. R. "The Basis of Accounting Principles." *The Accounting Review* (December 1941).

Tinker, A. M., B. D. Merino, and M. D. Neimark. "The Normative Origins of Positive Theories: Ideology and Accounting Thought." *Accounting, Organizations and Society* (Spring 1982), pp. 167–200.

Watts, R. L. and J. L. Zimmerman. "Towards a Positive Theory of the Determination of Accounting Standards." *The Accounting Review* (January 1978), pp. 112–134.

Williams, Paul F. "The Legitimate Concern with Fairness." *Accounting, Organizations and Society* (March 1987).

Wolff, Robert Paul. *Understanding Rawls*. Princeton, N.J.: Princeton University Press, 1977.

Appendix: The Legitimate Concern with Fairness: A Comment*

JUNE PALLOT

Victoria University of Wellington, New Zealand

Abstract

This paper comments on what appear to be more basic concerns underlying Williams' article (Williams, P. F., The Legitimate Concern with Fairness, *Accounting, Organizations and Society* (1987) pp. 169–179). It is suggested that fairness under accountability and fairness in distribution stem from different ethical frameworks and different, though complementary, assumptions about society. Some preliminary suggestions are then made as to how a communitarian perspective might be introduced alongside a predominantly individualistic one in accounting.

In drawing our attention to fairness as a legitimate concern for accounting academics as well as practitioners, Paul Williams makes two significant attacks on mainstream accounting research. Firstly, building on Ijiri's (1983) editorial, he argues the importance of an accountability perspective relative to a decision usefulness perspective for external financial reporting, suggesting that a constraining principle (accountability) cannot be subsumed under a facilitating principle (decision usefulness). He further points out the inability of the decision usefulness framework to both evaluate and explain accounting data as well as its tendency to ignore the simultaneity of efficiency and distributive effects. Secondly, Williams questions the "value free" stance of mainstream accounting research, calling for a more explicit recognition of fairness. Since Ijiri raised the issue of fairness but seemed unprepared to consider the full range of possibilities that such a notion has as a goal for accounting, Williams elaborates on what might be at stake, drawing on theories of justice proposed by Nozick, Rescher and Rawls.

Given mounting dissastisfaction with positivistic accounting research (see for example Chua, 1986; Lavoie, 1987) and the investigation of conceptions of justice and fairness by a number of disciplines in recent years (for reviews see Cohen, 1986), calls for a return to ethical approaches in accounting seem particularly timely. Since Williams' article seems to have stimulated surprisingly little discussion to date, comments are made here in an attempt to clarify and extend the very pertinent points he has raised. It is suggested that fairness under accountability and fairness in distribution stem from different ethical frameworks and different, though complementary, assumptions about society. Judging from his lengthy critique of Nozick, Williams appears to have resolved the issue of different frameworks for himself but, because his underlying assumptions have not been made entirely explicit, he has not elaborated on all that was at stake in the Ijiri editorial. By expanding on what appear to this reader to be the underlying assumptions, it is hoped that further discussion might be stimulated. To initiate yet further consideration of the issues, some preliminary suggestions are also made as to how a com-

---

*The author wishes to thank colleagues at Victoria University for their support and two anonymous reviewers for their comments on an earlier draft of this paper.

Source: June Pallot, "The Legitimate Concern with Fairness: A Comment" *Accounting, Organizations and Society,* 16, no. 2 (1991), pp. 201–208. Reprinted with permission.

munitarian perspective might be introduced alongside a predominantly individualistic one in accounting.

ALTERNATIVE ETHICAL FRAMEWORKS

If we adopt the position that fairness is the transcendent principle in accounting,[1] we face the question of what exactly is meant by "fairness". Williams distinguishes justice (i.e. fairness) in procedures from justice in outcomes. He does not, however, appear to make the Aristotelian distinction between commutative (exchange) justice and distributive justice. He advocates an accountability perspective because it "contains fairness as an inherent property" (p. 175). Yet his primary concern seems to be with distributive justice. Accountability, however, is primarily a question of exchange justice as witnessed in Ijiri's concern about a fair flow of information between accountor and accountee. Greater accountability is the *quid pro quo* for greater power or control over resources; hence, for example, the particular concern about accountability in the public sector. It is suggested here that accountability (at least as conventionally viewed in accounting literature and in Ijiri's editorial) and distribution are allied with different assumptions about society and different ethical frameworks each of which adopts a different attitude to the question of fairness. These alternative frameworks can also be seen to represent different views of human nature.[2] Whilst there is no necessary connection between ontological and methodological assumptions on the one hand and political and ethical values on the other, there is a strong tendency for them to be associated (see for

example Bloor, 1982).

Two primary views of society can be detected in the literature of the humanities and social sciences.[3] The first — which we might call an individualist model — views society as a collection of separate and equivalent individuals who interact with one another on a largely contractual basis. The model emphasizes rationality, impartiality and adjudicative justice. The second — which we might call an organic model — sees people as members of a community held together by common values. The emphasis is on face-to-face relations, mediation and social harmony. Within the individualist model it is possible to distinguish between moral individualism and sociological individualism. Moral individualism argues that people are autonomous and have a capacity for moral choice which cannot be reduced to the performance of given roles. Sociological individualism assumes that persons are not connected by intrinsic social bonds; society is therefore merely an aggregate of individuals. The different views of society can be aligned with different ethical frameworks — utilitarianism, rights-based approaches and civic humanism.

Utilitarianism, at least as adopted by neoclassical economics, mainstream accounting research and the decision usefulness perspective (on its own or combined with a "social welfare" objective of allocative efficiency) tends towards sociological individualism. Whilst attempts have been made to build moral values into utility functions — usually to the point of making utility tautological — the approach tends to steer clear of issues of fairness where possible, preferring to concentrate on concepts like efficiency. For example, in the neoclassical paradigm, exchanges are conceived of in terms of individual

---

[1]The stance is different from that of Scott (1941) who equated truth with a scientific or objective connotation and contended that the truth concept would eventually replace justice or fairness and hence would become the transcendent "principle" of accounting.

[2]Schwartz (1986) for example sees this as a "battle" between the view of human nature as selfish and competitive (the Hobbesian tradition) and the view of human nature as altruistic and cooperative (the Rousseauian tradition). Even if people can be observed to be behaving selfishly most of the time, the question is whether this is matter of unalterable biology or is a result of social institutions, including theories of human nature. If the latter, then it is relevant for social institutions and sciences (which include accounting) to address moral concerns.

[3]Perhaps most well-known is Tonnies' (1897) distinction between *Gesellschaft* and *Gemeinschaft*.

utility and the concern both parties might have in ensuring the bargain is a *fair* one seems to be ignored.

Rights-based approaches are more closely aligned with moral individualism. The debate between utilitarians and rights based theorists, stimulated by Rawls' *Theory of Justice*, seems to have been decided firmly in favour of the latter (Gutmann, 1985). Accounting researchers who shift from decision usefulness to accountability appear to be following this trend. In doing so, however, they remain firmly rooted in the individualist paradigm for accountability, with its emphasis on rights, contracts and two party exchanges is an individualist model. The notion of fairness[4] is one of commutative justice.

It is possible for the notion of accountability to be extended beyond a narrow two-party contract to social responsibility accounting in which other parties such as employees, consumers and even society at large are considered. Even in models for corporate social responsibility accounting, however, there is usually an emphasis on contracts, albeit it a series of contracts. The underlying assumption of the reporting entity as a sort of individual with rights to privacy and private property is pervasive despite attempts (for example, in value added reporting) at alternative entity theories.

Accountability models based solely on rights and contracts seem incomplete. Sandel (1984) points out that the rights-based theorists themselves have come under attack from proponents of a communitarian model in which ethical values are based on shared understandings and notions of a shared common life. Untidy though it may be, it would appear that a complete framework needs to accommodate both individualist and communitarian perspectives. Benn & Gaus (1983), for example, identify the individualist viewpoint as the dominant model in liberal societies but find that some of society's practices and related modes of reasoning cannot be integrated into the model, notable examples being the moral claims of the public interest (individualists have difficulty explaining why this is effective rhetoric in liberal societies) and the value of participation in public life. They conclude that when liberals find that the individualist model fails to express adequately their intuitions about the relations of individuals in society, they turn to a second, organic model. Macneil (1986) argues that people are separate individuals but at the same time require other human beings even to exist physically and psychologically, the upshot being that they constantly alternate between selfish and self-sacrificing behaviours.[5] Failure to recognize this duality, Macneil argues, renders much social analysis fundamentally useless. The "failure of most utilitarian models to incorporate the social aspect and of much Marxist dogma to adequately accept human separateness as a fact" is seen by him to prevent either from coming to grips with the issues bedevilling social sciences such as economics.

Whilst the *concern* about distributive justice may stem from an organic perspective,[6] distribution itself can be carried out in accordance with either predominantly individualist or predominantly communitarian values. Individual and communitarian models may emphasize different material principles of distributive justice. Whilst individualism tends to favour merit, entitlement, desert and contribution to production, communitarian approaches tend to place more emphasis on such principles as need and equality. Empirical studies in psychology (e.g. Leventhal, 1976; Stake, 1983) have found that equality is more often used to promote interpersonal harmony (a communitarian value) whereas desert is used to elicit and maintain high individual per-

---

[4]It is also this notion of fairness that is meant when accounting refers to "fair" value.

[5]Koestler (1975) describes the tension between self assertive and self transcending tendencies in his concept of holons which can be viewed from "above" or "below" within a hierarchical system.

[6]Mueller (1976, p. 396) suggests that a difference in views of the state as either a union of individuals engaged in *quid pro quo* exchange or as an organic entity constitutes the natural conceptual boundary between the allocative and redistributive functions of government and between positive and normative public choice theory.

formance.

Exactly how different ethical frameworks will affect accounting will depend on the values and assumptions held by those able to influence the accounting policy making process. Accounting reflects predominant social values but in doing so also reinforces them. It has the potential to reinforce alternative values and assumptions. Hopwood (1984, p. 179) suggests that accounting by "shaping the realm of the visible" can have a major impact on the directions of change considered desirable. Whilst some might feel that recognition of communitarian principles in an accounting policy making process that is dominated by individualistic business interests is improbable, there are sufficient social changes afoot to suggest it may yet be possible. Firstly, the individualistic assumptions underlying economics have been challenged in the public policy arena in favour of an "I-and-We" paradigm (Etzioni, 1988). Secondly, it has been observed that women are more strongly inclined toward communitarian values than men (see French, 1985).[7] If this is the case, then ethical assumptions may shift as women gain increasing access to the accounting policy making process. Thirdly, the pursuit of harmonization in international accounting exposes individualistic cultures to more communitarian ones. Although the tendency seems to be for dominant cultures to take over smaller or weaker ones, the exposure to other cultures may yet influence ethical assumptions in accounting, in the way that less individualistic values of Japanese culture have had an impact on approaches to organizational management.

What principles of justice are adopted may also vary according to what type of goods we are concerned with. There are at least three sets of goods the distribution of which are relevant concerns in accounting. The distribution of each of these in turn impacts upon the distribution of the others. The first of these concerns is the distribution of *wealth* and *income*. Almost every accounting policy choice affects the amount appropriated by management and thus the amount available for distribution to outside parties. Many accounting policy choices have inter-period effects which influence whether present or future parties will be better off. Insofar as distribution is in accordance with predetermined agreements such as stated dividend policies, profit-sharing arrangements, debt convenants or public utility rate regulations, determination of accounting income will also affect distribution of resources amongst external parties. Furthermore, accounting may also legitimate, and thus perpetuate, the pattern of distribution it portrays. The second concern in accounting is the equitable distribution of *information* (see for example Lev, 1988). A third concern is the distribution of *power*, including the power to influence the accounting policy making process itself.

Different material principles of distributive justice may apply to different goods. For example, effort or contribution may be appropriate for income. The relative need of current and future citizens could be a basis for determining accounting policies, such as depreciation or current cost accounting in government, which have intergenerational effects. Accounting policy makers could debate the merits of entitlement as a basis for the distribution of wealth. Need may be appropriate for determining the distribution of information whilst equality might be an appropriate principle for the distribution of power.

Combining models of society and combining material principles of justice, whilst messy, is nevertheless necessary, a point which Williams seems to recognize when he steers away from Rawls' attempt to establish universal principles towards Rescher's intuitionist theory. "That there is [for accounting rule making bodies] more than one basis for answering a legitimate claim can be a practical principle for deciding on legitimate rules in the absence of strict legal

---

[7]Tonnies (*op. cit.*) associated women with a *Gemeinschaft* orientation. The generally accepted finding in psychology experiments is that men are more likely to distribute resources according to a principle of equity whilst women are more likely to distribute equally (for reviews see Kahn & Gaeddart, 1985; Major & Deaux, 1982).

mandates or in opposition to pressures to adhere to some ideological norm" (p. 185).

TOWARD A COMMUNITARIAN PERSPECTIVE IN ACCOUNTING

If communitarian values are to be given visibility alongside individualist ones in accounting, how is this to be achieved? The first step is to give greater prominence to distributive justice within the objectives of accounting (for example in "Conceptual Framework" projects) recognizing, as Williams does for accountability, that this does not mean that fairness will prevail in the presence of power differentials. Williams gives ample evidence of the importance of distributional issues to accounting and little more needs to be added except to reiterate that an accountability perspective in itself will not automatically deal with distributive justice, and note that interperiod and intergenerational justice need to be considered as well as justice amongst claimants at a point in time. Concerns about the distributive function of accounting can be viewed, not so much as an adjunct to accountability, but as the accounting equivalent of a strong body of communitarian sentiment which would like to see the balance between individualist and organic views of society, and in particular between productivity and social harmony, restored.

Secondly, fairness in *presentation* would seem to require that if there is more than one underlying set of values and assumptions in society, more than one should be given visibility within the financial reports themselves. One way in which communitarian values could be given more visibility is the development of new accounting concepts. For example, we could develop a concept of assets based on common property (the right not to be excluded from use) alongside our present notions of assets based solely on private property (the right to exclude others except in return for value received). The New Zealand Society of Accountants (1987) moves in this direction with its concept of "community assets" to cover government managed

facilities which are infrastructural (e.g. highways, drainage and lighting systems), cultural (e.g. museums, public libraries) or environmental (e.g. scenic reserves, historic monuments). Community assets are deliberately distinguished from state assets, the private property of government entities. The term "community" seems preferable to the American notion of "infrastructure" assets with its technical, rather than social, connotations. Kamenka (1982) shows that the emotive connotations of the term "community" have been mobilized throughout history in attempts to bring about social change.

Whilst private property has been viewed as necessary for efficiency and wealth maximization (see for example Posner, 1986, chapter 3), common property can be viewed as necessary for the furtherance of other values. For example, in the civic humanist tradition, Self (1985, pp. 187–188) argues that:

> [There is a] case for regarding some public services as being fundamental to the concept of citizenship ... One important index to the welfare of any society is the quality and safety of its "public domain" — the streets, parks, community buildings etc., which provide the meeting places for a vital common life. The quality of the public domain does not show up in figures of economic growth. Its deterioration in high growth countries is eloquent testimony to the erosion of the norms of citizenship by private acquisition. Without shared citizenship, economic development will eventually become pointless and self destructive.

The development of new accounting concepts might also help prevent established accounting concepts from extending their domain. The development of a notion of community assets might serve as a foil to increasing "privatization" in a world where not only are public assets, ranging from telecommunications networks to forests and water supply, being placed in the hands of private corporations, but there are also concerted attempts to establish private property rights in what were previously considered public goods such as knowledge and clean air. Even family relationships have been viewed in terms of rights and contracts with children being referred to as "commodities" (e.g. Posner, 1985, chapter 5).

Pallot (1990) suggests some practical advantages of having a concept of community assets, including the ability to give different concepts different accounting treatments, improved analysis of financial position and fairer measurement of management performance. There are also several less immediately apparent reasons why accounting might be improved by developing a notion of community assets. For example, Macpherson (1978) believes that a system of private property, when combined with the liberal system of market incentives and rights of free contract, leads to and supports a concentration of ownership and a system of power relations between individuals and classes which negates the equal effective right of all individuals to use and develop their capacities. By broadening the property concept to include common property, Macpherson believes that the conflict between the liberal property right and the ethical goal of free individual development can be reconciled. He goes on to suggest that as society moves towards a fully automated productive system the economic problem that has been central to liberal democracy will become a purely political problem — one of democratic control over the uses to which the amassed capital of a society is put (one might add that an increasing proportion of resources will be knowledge and information). He sees that this problem can be tackled with the concept of property as a right not to be excluded but that it cannot be handled with the narrower concept of property as an exclusive right.

A notion of common property may also be a pre-condition for examining issues of intergenerational equity such as the depletion of natural resources. A notion of private property, which gives the present owner the right to destroy the property, cannot adequately handle such matters (Barry, 1977). A concept of "community assets" here could parallel the new concept of the "common heritage of mankind" which is emerging in the literature of international law and politics (see for example Kiss, 1985; Joyner, 1986). Accounting, by developing a notion of "community assets", might reinforce this emerging trend towards longer term considerations.

Again, such developments could act as a foil to the attempts by dominant groups in society to "privatize" the world.

Armed with a concept of common property, it may be possible to develop a different view of accountability than is generally envisaged in accounting research and in agency theory. In a somewhat neglected article, Chen (1975) moves towards this in her model of social and financial stewardship. She suggests that all property is fundamentally owned by the whole of society (in other words, at base, all property is common property). Private ownership is contingent on the fulfilment of Man's duty to use and administer it, not exclusively for private purposes, but to serve the needs of the whole of society. When owners delegate some of their property rights to agents, the agent assumes a stewardship responsibility. On these premises Chen builds a framework for external reporting in which management's performance is evaluated in terms of both profit (secondary stewardship responsibility, financial reports) and social objectives (primary stewardship, responsibility social reports). Whilst she does not consider the public sector, it would seem that in the case of "community assets", society and the owner are one and the same such that primary and secondary stewardship responsibilities merge and objectives are solely social objectives. This sort of accountability framework is fundamentally different from those where the starting assumption is one of private property and social responsibility accounting is seen as a matter of accounting for social costs and benefits viewed as externalities. In a world where a commitment to shared values, rather than the pursuit of self interest, was the norm, accountability might be seen as a voluntary obligation in the public interest rather than a mechanism for constraining self seeking behaviour and protecting rights.

CONCLUDING REMARKS

This paper fully supports Williams' concern with fairness. It is hoped that additional points about more fundamental assumptions underlying views of accountability and distributive justice will stimulate further discussion on alternative concepts of fairness in accounting. Lest it be thought (as Williams suspects accountants of thinking) that only a decision usefulness perspective gives accounting a sufficiently large role in society, it may be appropriate to respond with a quote from Michael Walzer:

> Distributive justice is a large idea. It draws the entire world of goods within the reach of philosophical reflection. Nothing can be omitted; no feature of our common life can escape scrutiny. Human society is a distributive community. That's not all it is, but it is importantly that: we come together to share, divide and exchange (1983, p. 3).

Explicit acknowledgement of a communitarian perspective alongside the presently individualistic one in accounting may be an important first step in developing new approaches to the issues of accountability and distributive justice.

BIBLIOGRAPHY

Barry, B., Justice Between Generations, in Hacker, P. M. S. & Raz, J. (eds), *Law, Morality and Society* (Oxford: Clarendon Press, 1977).

Benn, S. I. & Gaus, G. F., The Liberal Conception of the Public and Private, in Benn, S. I. & Gaus, G. F., *Public and Private in Social Life* pp. 31–65 (London: Croom Helm, 1983).

Bloor, D., Durkheim and Mauss Revisited: Classification and the Sociology of Knowledge, *Studies in the History and Philosophy of Science* (December 1982) pp. 267–297.

Chen, R., Social and Financial Stewardship, *The Accounting Review* (July 1975) pp. 533–543.

Chua, W. F., Radical Developments in Accounting Thought, *The Accounting Review* (October 1986) pp. 601–632.

Cohen, R. L. (ed.), *Justice: Views from the Social Sciences* (New York: Plenum Press, 1986).

Etzioni, A., *The Moral Dimension: Towards a New Economics* (New York: Free Press, 1988).

French, M., *Beyond Power: On Women, Men and Morals* (New York: Summit Books, 1985).

Gutmann, A., Communitarian Critiques of Liberalism, *Philosophy and Public Affairs* (1985) pp. 308–322.

Hopwood, A., Accounting and the Pursuit of Efficiency, in Hopwood, A. & Tomkins, C., *Issues in Public Sector Accounting* (Oxford: Philip Allan Publishers, 1984).

Ijiri, Y., On the Accountability-Based Conceptual Framework of Accounting, *Journal of Accounting and Public Policy* (Summer 1983) pp. 75–81.

Joyner, C. C., Legal Implications of the Concept of the Common Heritage of Mankind, *International and Comparative Law Quarterly* (January 1986) pp. 190–199.

Kahn, A. S. & Gaeddart, W. P., From Theories of Equity to Theories of Justice: The Liberating Consequences of Studying Women, in O'Leary, V. E., Unger, R. K. & Wallston, B. S. (eds), *Women, Gender and Social Psychology* pp. 129–148 (Hillsdale, N.J.: Earlbaum, 1985).

Kamenka, E., *Community as a Social Ideal* (London: Edward Arnold, 1982).

Kiss, A., The Common Heritage of Mankind: Utopia or Reality?, *International Journal* (Summer 1985) pp. 185–211.

Lavoie, D., The Accounting of Interpretations and the Interpretation of Accounts: The Communicative Function of the Language of Business, *Accounting, Organizations and Society* (1987) pp. 579–602.

Lev, B., Toward a Theory of Equitable and Efficient Accounting Policy, *The Accounting Review* (January 1988) pp. 1–22.

Leventhal, G. S., The Distribution of Rewards and Resources in Groups and Organizations, in Walster, E. & Berkowitz, L. (eds), *Advances in Experimental Social Psychology* pp. 211–239 (Morristown, N.J.: General Learning Press, 1976).

Macneil, I. R., Exchange Revisited: Individual Utility and Social Solidarity, *Ethics* (April 1986) pp. 567–593.

Macpherson, C. B. (ed.), *Property: Mainstream and Critical Positions* (Toronto: University of Toronto Press, 1978).

Major, B. & Deaux, K., Individual Differences in Justice Behaviour, in Greenberg, J. & Cohen, R. I. (eds), *Equity and Justice in Social Behaviour* pp. 43–76 (New York: Academic Press, 1982).

Mueller, D. C., Public Choice: A Survey, *Journal of Economic Literature* (1976) pp. 395–433.

New Zealand Society of Accountants, *Statement of Public Sector Accounting Concepts* (Wellington: Council of the N.Z. Society of Accountants, 1987).

Pallot, J., The Nature of Public Assets: A Response to Mautz, *Accounting Horizons* (June 1990).

Posner, R. A., *Economic Analysis of Law*, 3rd Edn (Boston: Little Brown, 1985).

Rawls, J., *A Theory of Justice* (Cambridge: Harvard University Press, 1971).

Rescher, N. *Distributive Justice* (Indianapolis: Bobbs-Merrill, 1966).

Sandel, M. (ed.), *Liberalism and its Critics* (Oxford: Basil Blackwell, 1984).

Schwartz, B., *The Battle for Human Nature: Science, Morality and Modern Life* (New York: Norton, 1986).

Scott, D. R., The Basis for Accounting Principles, *The Accounting Review* (December 1941) pp. 341–349.

Self, P., *Political Theories of Modern Government* (London: George Allen and Unwin, 1985).

Stake, J. E., Factors in Reward Distribution: Allocation Motive, Gender and Protestant Work Ethic Endorsement, *Journal of Personality and Social Psychology* (February 1983) pp. 410–418.

Tonnies, F., *Gemeinschaft and Gesellschaft* (Leipzig: H. Buske, 1897). English Translation by Loomis, C., *Community and Society* (New York: Harper, 1963).

Walzer, M., *Spheres of Justice* (New York: Basic Books, 1983).

Williams, P. F., The Legitimate Concern with Fairness, *Accounting, Organizations and Society* (1987) pp. 169–189.

2

Ethics in Accounting

Accountants find themselves performing tasks daily in an environment governed by a complex set of rules, principles, and practices. In performing their tasks they are asked to take a certain role. A role is best described as follows:

The concept of a role is . . . one which enters in the sociologist's account of a social interaction. It is needed in describing the repeatable patterns of social relations which are not mere physical facts and which are structured partly by the rules of acceptable behavior in the society in question.[1]

In performing their roles, accountants face formal or legal rules of behavior but also moral elements created by specific situations. By accepting certain roles, accountants accept at the same time the resulting obligations and moral responsibilities of roles, or as F. H. Bradley puts it: "There is nothing better than my station and its duties, nor anything higher or more truly beautiful."[2] It implies that there are ethics behind "my station and duties" that need to be accounted for. By ethics, it is meant the concern with the moral judgments involved in making moral decisions about what is morally wrong and right or morally good and bad. This assumes the existence of moral standards that affect our human well being,[3] are not established or changed by decisions of authoritative bodies,[4] are intended to override the self-interest,[5] and are based on impartial considerations.[6,7]

Various categories of ethical perspectives or modes of ethical thinking are applicable to accounting. They are reviewed next before a discussion of the implementation, teaching, and research of ethics in accounting.

ETHICAL PERSPECTIVES

Utilitarian Ethics

Utilitarian ethics or utilitarianism as an approach to resolving moral issues is also known as consequentialism. The approach considers an action as being morally right or wrong based solely on the consequences that result from performing it. The right action is the one that brings the best consequences, or the greatest amount of utility.

The implicit assumption is that the costs and benefits of an action are measurable on a common numerical scale and can be added and subtracted from each other.[8] The interests to consider when choosing an action are the nonegoist and altruistic approaches that consider the most utility for all the persons affected by the action.[9]

The advantages of utilitarian ethics are related to:

- *The goal of morality:* "It asserts that morality is important because the performance of right actions leads to the general satisfaction of human desires."[10]
- *The process of moral reasoning:* "The consequentialist at least offers a relatively clear procedure for finding out what is the right thing to do: list the alternatives, ascertain their probable consequences, and evaluate the consequences in light of their implications for everyone affected."[11]
- *Flexibility and exceptions:* "We simply need to recognize the special cases in which there is good reason to believe that the consequences of following the traditional moral rule are worse than the consequences of making an exception."[12]
- *Avoiding rule conflict:* "From the consequentialist perspective, the existence of a conflict in rules is a signal that we are dealing with one of those exceptional circumstances in which we cannot simply follow even the soundest of rules."[13]

The difficulties with utilitarianism relate to:

- *The objection from special obligations:* "It fails to take into account our special moral obligations to people with whom we have a special relation."[14]
- *The objection from rights:* "[It] does not take into account the existence of individual rights in deciding on moral issues."[15]
- *The objection from justice:* "By only paying attention to one factor, the consequentialist has left out other important moral factors, such as justice, that need to be weighed."[16]

In addition, there are serious problems of measurement in the sense that some benefits and costs are interactable to measurement,[17] many benefits and costs of an action cannot be reliably predicted and measured,[18] and there is a lack of clarity on what is to count as a benefit and what as a cost.[19,20]

Deontological Ethics

Deontological ethics as an approach to resolving moral issues is also known as rule-based morality. The approach considers an action as morally right if it conforms with a proper moral rule. An action that violates the rule but results in beneficial actions is still considered wrong. The sources of the rule could be either theological in the sense that the actions are stipulated as moral by a religion, or societal in the sense that they are the result of a social consensus as to whether they are right or wrong.

Because of the limitations of these two sources, criteria have been adopted based on either the consequences of adopting a particular set of moral rules, or our supposed faculty of moral intuition.[21] First, this rule consequentialism differs from the act consequentialism adopted by utilitarianism because it states that, in effect, "the rightness of a particular action lies in its conformity with the proper moral rule; the properness of the moral rule, in turn is based on the value of the consequences of it being followed."[22] Second, the intuitionist approach holds that our special faculty of moral intuition tells us which actions have the inherent properties of being morally right.

Rule-based moralists can accommodate most of the weaknesses of utilitarianism. The weaknesses correspond to the strengths of utilitarianism.

The Notion of Fittingness

Because of the strengths and limitations of both utilitarianism and deontological ethics, a suitable compromise would be ideal.[23] One compromise suggested by W. W. May is to use aspects of both approaches.[24] An alternative to both utilitarianism and deontological ethics is offered by the notion of fittingness. Fittingness, from the ancient Greek concept of *kathokonda,* may be used to evaluate the morality of actions by a reference to whether they are appropriate and proper with the *ethos* shared by the individual and the society. Martin Heidegger speaks of ethos as comprised of "freely accepted obligations and traditions," of "that which concerns free behavior and attitudes," and of "the shaping of man's historical being."[25] The ethos defines the fitting response, the arena for moral discourse and action. Compared to the other views of ethics the notion of fittingness proposes a dramatic shift. As Calvin Schrag states:

This shift is a shift away from the primacy of theological inquiry (what is the end of man in terms of his nature-conferred essence?), the primacy of deontological inquiry (what is the unconditional duty of man?) and the primacy of utilitarian inquiry (what is the greatest good for the greatest number?). The question "How does one perform a fitting response?" is, we submit, more originative than inquiry about ends, duties and the good. It is only by addressing this question that ends duties, and the good achieve a context for definition.[26]

The notion of fittingness places the individual in a context of responsibility and responsiveness to the ethos in which are gathered the social and political concerns of the society around him or her. To Reinhold Niebuhr, the fitting action is part of the ethics of responsibility.[27] How others reacted to a previous act and how they will react to a similar act determines a responsible act. The responsible act must interpret the old reactions and fit itself in the new reactions. Fittingness becomes the criteria for evaluating moral choice. As stated again by Schrag: "The language of morality is the language of responsiveness and responsibility and if there is to be talk of 'an ethics' in all this it will need to be an ethics of the fitting response."[28]

MORAL DEVELOPMENT

To uncover the general interpretive framework that a person brings to moral problems, moral judgment research attempts to examine the reasons individuals give for their decisions when faced with a variety of moral dilemma situations. The approach rests on L. Kohlberg's research in cognitive development.[29] The thesis is that individuals progress from lower stages of development to higher stages unless deprivations for opportunities for social interaction are used to retard their development. Accordingly, Kohlberg identified three general levels of moral thought, with each level consisting of two stages. Each stage of moral development constitutes a unique way of defining a given moral dilemma and of evaluating critical issues related to the moral situation under consideration.[30] Each stage of moral development explicates how judgments are made and why a particular judgment was made.

The six stages identified by Kohlberg are as follows.[31]

Preconventional level

Stage 1: Internal Compulsion and Power. The physical consequences of actions determine their goodness or badness. Avoidance of punishment and unquestioning deference to power are valued in their own right. Basically punishment and obedience constitute the basis of moral order.

Stage 2: Simple Interpersonal Exchange and Need Satisfaction. Right actions satisfy one's own needs, and occasionally the needs of others, when reciprocity is present. Basically, instrumentalism and relativism constitute the basis of moral order.

Conventional level

Stage 3: Maintaining Positive Interpersonal Relationships. Good behavior is what pleases or helps others and is approved by them. Conformity to stereotypical images of what is common or natural behavior wins approval by others. Basically, interpersonal concordance constitutes the basis of moral order.

Stage 4: Maintaining Social Order. Right behavior consists of doing one's duty, showing respect for authority, and maintaining the social order for its own sake. Basically law and order constitute the basis of moral order.

Postconventional level

Stage 5: Intuitive Individualism and Humanism. Right actions are defined by general individual rights and standards agreed upon by society. Outside what is agreed upon by society, the right is a matter of personal values and opinions. Basically, the social contract constitutes the basis of moral order.

Stage 6: Individual Conscience. Right is defined by the decision of conscience in accord with self-chosen ethical principles of justice, equality, and dignity of human beings. Basically, ethics and principles constitute the basis of moral order.

J. R. Rest developed the Defining Issues Test (DIT) to gauge moral judgment development and determine the subject's stage of moral reasoning.[32] The DIT is an objective measure composed of six moral dilemmas, each one describing a situation with competing social claims. The output of the test is a "P" (for principled) score. It is "interpreted as the relative importance a subject gives to principled moral considerations in making a decision about moral dilemmas."[33] It indicates what percent of a subject's thinking is at a principled level (i.e., levels 5 and 6 in Kohlberg's model).

The accounting studies relied on the DIT to assess the moral reasoning of accounting subjects. The first study by M. B. Armstrong compared accounting practitioners (CPAs) to a broad section of college students, college graduate students, and adults.[34] The practitioners' "P" score was lower than those of college students, college graduate students, and adults. These results are indeed disturbing: "These results initiate that the CPA respondents appear to have reached the moral maturation level of adults in general, instead of maturing even to the level of college students, much less to the level of college graduates. In other words, their college education may not have fostered continued moral growth."[35]

The second study by St. Pierre et al. examined the ethical development of seniors in ten different disciplines representing business and nonbusiness majors.[36] Accounting majors and the other business disciplines scored lower than the students in the three nonbusiness majors. The results also raise disturbing questions:

Given that the majors outside the College of Business performed better in the DIT (statistically higher, except for Finance) and that the norm groups for college seniors in general performed better than the College of Business seniors, what can we say about the efforts of the profession in the ethics area? Does the moral atmosphere of the business school affect our majors' ethical development? Are the nonbusiness majors exposed to an educational atmosphere or socialization process that is conducive to ethical development? A question that is even more basic focuses on the type of individual selecting business as a field study. Is it possible that, due to self-selection, those entering the business discipline are Stage 4 personality types and will function at that level regardless of the socialization process?[37]

A more important question is whether or not students entering the accounting field are Stage 4 and will stay at that stage given the absence of teaching ethics in the accounting curriculum, and the absence of moral socialization process in the practice of accounting. It may also explain the findings that accounting students showed strong adherence to social norms and values.[38] That is very characteristic of Stage 4 personality types. These results argue for major changes in the accounting curriculum and practice to instill higher moral principles in those choosing the accounting discipline.

IMPLEMENTATION OF ETHICS IN ACCOUNTING

Codes of Ethics

One way of implementing ethics in accounting is to use the deontological view of ethics and use a code of ethics for each of the professions of accounting. Each of the main accounting professions in the United States has in fact a code of ethics. The codes of ethics for management accountants and internal auditors are shown in Exhibits 2.1 and 2.2. In 1988 the AICPA issued a new code of professional conduct that has a more positive tone than the previous one. It contains Principles of Professional Conducts that are enforceable through the Rules of Performance and Behavior and through the interpretation of the various senior-level committees of the AICPA: Ethics, Accounting and Auditing, Accounting and Review Services, Taxes, and Management Advisory Services.

The Principles cover the following areas:

1. *Responsibilities of Members:* In carrying out their responsibilities as professionals, members should exercise sensitive professional and moral judgments in all their activities.

2. *The Public Interest:* Members should accept the obligation to act in a way that will serve the public interest, honor the public trust, and demonstrate commitment to professionalism.

3. *Integrity:* To maintain and broaden public confidence, members should perform all professional responsibilities with the highest sense of integrity.

4. *Objectivity and Independence:* A member should maintain objectivity and be free of conflicts of interest in discharging professional responsibilities. A member in public practice should be independent in fact and appearance when providing auditing and the other attestation services.

5. *Due Care:* A member should observe the profession's technical and ethical standards, strive continually to improve competence and the quality of services, and discharge professional responsibility to the best of the member's ability.

6. *Scope and Nature of Services:* A member in public practice should observe the Principles of the Code of Professional Conduct in determining the scope and the nature to be provided.

Exhibit 2.1
Standards of Ethical Conduct for Management Accountants

Management accountants have an obligation to the organizations they serve, their profession, the public, and themselves to maintain the highest standards of ethical conduct. In recognition of this obligation, the National Association of Accountants has promulgated the following standards of ethical conduct for management accountants. Adherence to these standards is integral to achieving the *Objectives of Management Accounting.*[1] Management accountants shall not commit acts contrary to these standards nor shall they condone the commission of such acts by others within their organizations.

COMPETENCE
Management accountants have a responsibility to:
■ Maintain an appropriate level of professional competence by ongoing development of their knowledge and skills.
■ Perform their professional duties in accordance with relevant laws, regulations, and technical standards.
■ Prepare complete and clear reports and recommendations after appropriate analyses of relevant and reliable information.

CONFIDENTIALITY
Management accountants have a responsibility to:

■ Refrain from disclosing confidential information acquired in the course of their work except when authorized, unless legally obligated to do so.
■ Inform subordinates as appropriate regarding the confidentiality of information acquired in the course of their work and monitor their activities to assure the maintenance of that confidentiality.
■ Refrain from using or appearing to use confidential information acquired in the course of their work for unethical or illegal advantage either personally or through third parties.

INTEGRITY
Management accountants have a responsibility to:
■ Avoid actual or apparent conflicts of interest and advise all appropriate parties of any potential conflict.
■ Refrain from engaging in any activity that would prejudice their ability to carry out their duties ethically.
■ Refuse any gift, favor, or hospitality that would influence or would appear to influence their actions.
■ Refrain from either actively or passively subverting the attainment of the organization's legitimate and ethical objectives.
■ Recognize and communicate professional limitations or other constraints that would preclude responsible judgment or successful performance of an activity.
■ Communicate unfavorable as well as favorable information and professional judgments or opinions.

■ Refrain from engaging in or supporting any activity that would discredit the profession.

OBJECTIVITY
Management accountants have a responsibility to:
■ Communicate information fairly and objectively.
■ Disclose fully all relevant information that could reasonably be expected to influence an intended user's understanding of the reports, comments, and recommendations presented.

RESOLUTION OF ETHICAL CONFLICT

In applying the standards of ethical conduct, management accountants may encounter problems in identifying unethical behavior or in resolving an ethical conflict. When faced with significant ethical issues, management accountants should follow the established policies of the organization bearing on the resolution of such conflict. If these policies do not resolve the ethical conflict, management accountants should consider the following course of action:

■ Discuss such problems with the immediate superior except when it appears that the superior is involved, in which case the problem should be presented initially to the next higher managerial level. If satisfactory resolution cannot be achieved when the problem is initially presented, submit the issues to the next higher managerial level.
   If the immediate superior is the chief executive officer, or equivalent, the acceptable reviewing authority may be a group such as the audit committee, executive committee, board of directors, board of trustees, or owners. Contact with levels above the immediate superior should be initiated only with the superior's knowledge, assuming the superior is not involved.
■ Clarify relevant concepts by confidential discussion with an objective advisor to obtain an understanding of possible courses of action.
■ If the ethical conflict still exists after exhausting all levels of internal review, the management accountant may have no other recourse on significant matters than to resign from the organization and to submit an informative memorandum to an appropriate representative of the organization.

Except where legally prescribed, communication of such problems to authorities or individuals not employed or engaged by the organization is not considered appropriate.

[1] National Association of Accountants. *Statements on Management Accounting: Objectives of Management Accounting,* Statement No. 1B, New York. N.Y., June 17, 1982.

Source: Reprinted by permission of The National Association of Accountants, *Statements on Management Accounting: Objectives of Management Accounting*, Statement No. 1C, New York, N.Y., June 17, 1982.

Exhibit 2.2
The Institute of Internal Auditors, Inc. Code of Ethics

THE INSTITUTE OF INTERNAL AUDITORS
CODE OF ETHICS

PURPOSE: A distinguishing mark of a profession is acceptance by its members of responsibility to the interests of those it serves. Members of The Institute of Internal Auditors (Members) and Certified Internal Auditors (CIAs) must maintain high standards of conduct in order to effectively discharge this responsibility. The Institute of Internal Auditors (Institute) adopts this *Code of Ethics* for Members and CIAs.

APPLICABILITY: This *Code of Ethics* is applicable to all Members and CIAs. Membership in The Institute and acceptance of the "Certified Internal Auditor" designation are voluntary actions. By acceptance, Members and CIAs assume an obligation of self-discipline above and beyond the requirements of laws and regulations.

The standards of conduct set forth in this *Code of Ethics* provide basic principles in the practice of internal auditing. Members and CIAs should realize that their individual judgment is required in the application of these principles.

CIAs shall use the "Certified Internal Auditor" designation with discretion and in a dignified manner, fully aware of what the designation denotes. The designation shall also be used in a manner consistent with all statutory requirements.

Members who are judged by the Board of Directors of The Institute to be in violation of the standards of conduct of the *Code of Ethics* shall be subject to forfeiture of their membership in The Institute. CIAs who are similarly judged also shall be subject to forfeiture of the "Certified Internal Auditor" designation.

STANDARDS OF CONDUCT

I. Members and CIAs shall exercise honesty, objectivity, and diligence in the performance of their duties and responsibilities.

II. Members and CIAs shall exhibit loyalty in all matters pertaining to the affairs of their organization or to whomever they may be rendering a service. However, Members and CIAs shall not knowingly be a party to any illegal or improper activity.

III. Members and CIAs shall not knowingly engage in acts or activities which are discreditable to the profession of internal auditing or to their organization.

IV. Members and CIAs shall refrain from entering into any activity which may be in conflict with the interest of their organization or which would prejudice their ability to carry out objectively their duties and responsibilities.

V. Members and CIAs shall not accept anything of value from an employee, client, customer, supplier, or business associate of their organization which would impair or be presumed to impair their professional judgment.

VI. Members and CIAs shall undertake only those services which they can reasonably expect to complete with professional competence.

VII. Members and CIAs shall adopt suitable means to comply with the *Standards for the Professional Practice of Internal Auditing*.

VIII. Members and CIAs shall be prudent in the use of information acquired in the course of their duties. They shall not use confidential information for any personal gain nor in any manner which would be contrary to law or detrimental to the welfare of their organization.

IX. Members and CIAs, when reporting on the results of their work, shall reveal all material facts known to them which, if not revealed, could either distort reports of operations under review or conceal unlawful practices.

X. Members and CIAs shall continually strive for improvement in their proficiency, and in the effectiveness and quality of their service.

XI. Members and CIAs, in the practice of their profession, shall be ever mindful of their obligation to maintain the high standards of competence, morality, and dignity promulgated by The Institute. Members shall abide by the *Bylaws* and uphold the objectives of The Institute.

Adopted by Board of Directors, July 1988.

The focus on ethical modes for the implementation of ethics in accounting is strongly recommended by the profession and associated units. For example, the National Commission on Fraudulent Financial Reporting recommends that public companies develop and enforce written codes of corporate conduct.[39] This view of the strengths of ethical codes in implementing ethics is not shared by the academic literature. Various limitations are raised about codes of ethics:[40]

1. Codes of ethics make the rules the central focus of morality.[41] Being ethical means simply following the rules rather than having a moral character.
2. Ethical codes are either too vague or too detailed, making them difficult to apply.[42]
3. Ethical codes can make it easier for individual to hide behind rules as an excuse for making appropriate decisions.[43]
4. Ethical codes can be enforced by punitive and coercive actions because they are similar to laws and regulations rather than ethics.[44]
5. Ethical costs may be used by professions to limit the supply of practitioners and to restrict competition.[45]

In reality ethical codes in accounting have had limited effect in stemming the trade of white-collar crimes and serve mainly as a symbolic exercise. Witness the following comment:

The effects of ethics codes on accounting appear limited. Readers of AICPA and state society newsletters see periodic listings of code violators. Most appear to be CPAs in small firms, and their offenses seem to be rather unequivocal. Frequently, their membership or license is stripped following conviction in the courts for fraud or conspiracy. The tougher, "borderline" cases appear less often, and large practitioners seem almost never to be involved in violations. It may be, then, that ethics codes play a minor role in structuring the limits of practice. They also lend themselves to violation in spirit because they are subject to broad interpretation. This, perhaps, explains why they are ineffective as enforcement devices for borderline cases.[46]

How Do We Discipline the Accounting Profession?

General Forms of Discipline

The press has a tendency to emphasize the role of the accounting profession in some of the more flagrant and unethical business practices. Some may argue that the ethical standards in our society are relatively low, which should explain the role accountants have played in some business scandals. In addition, the profession's commitment to the general public and to the protection of the public interest is not exactly part of the accountant's environment. D. F. Linowes argues the same point as follows:

What is needed is an environment which establishes an attitude on the part of the practitioner so that he personally practices his profession using his best technical judgment, supported by the counsel and guidance of his peers, and constantly striving toward his appropriate role in society.[47]

Unfortunately, there are few guidelines in the accounting profession concerning which clients accountants are to serve or what services they are expected to render. In some cases, the government or the courts intervene to pinpoint the kinds of services expected. Due to this lack of identification of their role, accountants wind up serving various masters. One consequence has been the frequent use of footnotes to avoid making hard and fast professional judgments. One solution would be to define the mission of the accounting profession. Linowes offers some questions:

Are we experts in internal information systems? If so, should we be integral parts of the field of behavioral science? Are we solely independent verifiers of the results of an organization's activities? Are we market-research experts, systems designers, energy-utilization experts, tax advisers, or are we all of these things? If we are all of these things, is it reasonable to expect that one set of standards can serve so many diverse functions?[48]

Obviously, no one accountant or one set of standards can effectively serve all these functions. Some form of discipline is required. Several forms are possible:

1. CPAs may need to develop adequate specialization in one or several areas before exercising any functions in those areas.
2. Adequate literature could be developed to guide CPAs in all these functions.
3. The AICPA could be reorganized into specialized sections that could serve as a forum for new ideas, creative thinking, and specific ethical guidelines.
4. Continuing education by the profession and/or academia would be necessary to ensure the best performance of all specialized professional services.
5. CPA firms could be organizationally restructured to differentiate and integrate various functions more efficiently. Each unit — whether an audit department, a tax department, or a management advisory services department — would be assured a minimum level of independence.
6. The sanctions provided under the licensing laws are injunctive in nature because they are restricted to suspensions or revocations of rights to practice. Stronger medicine may be needed, as the following remark suggests:

   Redress for civil damages or punishments for criminal acts relating to malpractice must be sought under the civil liability and criminal laws that are designed for application to a much wider range of activities than that of professionals.[49]

7. Practitioners may have to be motivated to adhere to the high ideals of professionals. These ideals are best defined as follows:

Those who are inclined to ascribe a much higher level of altruism to the motives of professionals have long insisted that the essence of professionalism is to put the public's interest ahead of self interest. A dedication to serving others is regarded as essential to laying claim to being a professional, and a profession has an obligation to be concerned about substandard behavior whether or not it is actionable under the law.

The question is: Would the threat of punishment for wrongdoing be necessary to motivate practitioners to adhere to the high ideals of professionals? Can morality and good behavior be legislated? If so, how? These questions must be faced by the accounting profession. As a first step, two reports have been published by the United States and Canada, respectively: the Cohen Report and the Adams Report. Each is examined next.

The Cohen Report: United States

In 1974 the American Institute of Certified Public Accountants' Commission on Auditors' Responsibilities (usually known, from the name of its chairman, as the Cohen Commission) was established, with the following objective:

To develop conclusions and recommendations regarding the appropriate responsibilities of independent auditors. It should consider whether a gap may exist between what the public expects or needs and what auditors can and should reasonably expect to accomplish. If such a gap exists, it needs to be explored to determine how the disparity can be resolved.[50]

The Commission eventually released its report, referred to here as the Cohen Report, which concluded that there is a gap between the performance of auditors and the expectations that users of financial statements have of auditors. The Report proposed that this gap be narrowed by making fundamental changes in the auditor's role and by educating users about some of their unrealistic expectations. It may be useful to examine some of the highlights of the Report as it speaks to each of the following technical issues: the independent auditor's role in society, forming an opinion about financial presentations, reporting on significant uncertainties in financial presentations, clarifying responsibility for the detection of fraud, corporate accountability and the law, the boundaries and extension of the auditor's role, and the auditor's communication with users.

The Independent Auditor's Role in Society. The Cohen Report describes the auditor as an intermediary in an accountability relationship and as the third party in the relationship between the issues covered in financial statements and users who rely on these statements. The auditor's primary responsibility is considered to be to the users of his or her work. The Report attempts to correct the fallacious beliefs held by users that auditors are responsible for the actual preparation of financial statements or that a report prepared by an auditor indicates that a business is sound. The direct responsibility for financial statements is placed on management; the auditor's responsibility is to audit the information and to express an opinion about it.

Forming an Opinion about Financial Presentations.   The Cohen Report considers the difficulties that arise when one is asked to analyze the meaning of the phrase in the auditor's report "present fairly . . . in conformity with generally accepted accounting principles." The Report suggests that the emphasis on "fairness" be removed. The essence of the auditor's responsibility is not to judge the fairness of the information that is presented but to determine whether the judgments made by management in the selection and application of accounting principles are appropriate or inappropriate. As a result, the Report calls for guidance for auditors in *three* areas: (1) evaluating the appropriateness of accounting in areas for which there are no detailed accounting principles; (2) evaluating the appropriateness of selection when alternative accounting principles are acceptable; and (3) evaluating the cumulative effects of accounting principles.

Reporting on Significant Uncertainties in Financial Presentations.   The Commission made two main recommendations: First, it proposed the elimination of the "subject to" qualification of the auditor's opinion. The "subject to" qualification is generally issued when a material uncertainty exists and its subsequent resolution may substantially affect the financial condition of the firm. Three reasons were given for the proposed elimination of the "subject to" qualification: (1) it requires auditors to be both reporters and interpreters of uncertainties; (2) the "subject to" concept is ambiguous; and (3) its absence may be interpreted as meaning that the company faces no uncertainties. Following the Cohen Commission's recommendation, the Auditing Standards Board of the AICPA decided to retain the "subject to" qualification. However, in November 1980, the Canadian Institute of Chartered Accountants terminated the use of the "subject to" qualification.

Second, the Commission proposed the addition of a new note on uncertainties to highlight significant uncertainties as well as to give users enough information to make their own evaluations of uncertainties and their potential effects on future operations.

Clarifying Responsibility for the Detection of Fraud.   Given that detection of fraud is ranked as the most important objective of an audit, the Commission stated that an audit should be designed to provide users of financial statements with reasonable assurance that the financial statements are not affected by fraud and that management is accountable for material amounts of corporate assets. To do so, the standards of professional skill and care should be:

- A systematic approach to investigating the reputation and integrity of a company and its management before accepting a new engagement or a continuing engagement.

- Approaching an audit with an open mind about the integrity and good faith of management—neither assuming that management is dishonest nor taking management's integrity and good faith for granted; if auditors have serious doubts about the management's honesty, integrity, or good faith that cannot be resolved satisfactorily, they should consider resigning.
- Taking into account unusual circumstances or relationships that may predispose management to commit frauds.
- Maintaining an understanding of a client's business and industry.
- Extending the study and evaluation of internal control beyond that now required.[51]

Corporate Accountability and the Law. The Cohen Commission suggested that the auditors must be able to approach the detection and disclosure of illegal or questionable acts by management within a defined and agreed-on-framework. Two recommendations form the basis of this framework:

1. Companies should adopt a policy on corporate conduct and monitor compliance with such a policy.
2. The auditor's report should review compliance with the corporate-conduct policy; the auditor's report could include a conclusion about such compliance. When discovering illegal or questionable acts, the auditor should consider them without regard to the conventional concepts of materiality.

The Boundaries and Extension of the Auditor's Role. The Cohen Commission suggested that the audit function should be broader than the traditional association of auditing with financial statements. The Commission recommended that the auditor's role be extended to permit the auditor to express an opinion on internal accounting control as part of the audit. It also recommended that the audit be viewed as a function to be performed during a particular set of financial statements. Furthermore, the Commission recommended that the audit function should be expanded to cover information of an accounting and financial nature that management has a responsibility to report, provided that the auditor's competence is relevant to the verification of the information and that the information is produced by the accounting system. Three steps are deemed necessary to facilitate this extension of the role of auditors:

- The auditors' study and evaluation of the internal control over the accounting system should be expanded to allow them to conclude whether the controls over each significant part of the accounting system provide reasonable assurance that the system is free of material weaknesses.
- Management should publish a report on the condition of the controls over the accounting system as well as its response to the auditors' suggestions for the correction of the weaknesses.

- The auditors should report on whether they agree with management's description of the company's controls and should describe any material uncorrected weaknesses not disclosed by management.[52]

The Auditor's Communication with Users.   The Cohen Commission found the present auditor's standard report unsatisfactory and in need of a thorough revision. The Commission's examples of yesterday's auditors' report and today's auditors' report appear in Exhibits 2.3 and 2.4. Both reports are deemed ideal for revision to clarify the present intended measuring, and to add important aspects of the audit function that are not covered explicitly at present. On that basis, the Commission suggested the preparation of an "illustrative" report for the future, shown in Exhibit 2.5. In addition, the Commission proposed that a separate management report be made along the lines of Exhibit 2.6.

The Education, Training, and Development of Auditors.   The Commission deplored the schism that has developed between academic and practicing accountants. It also suggested that formal accounting education does not provide students with a sense of professional identity. The solution recommended was an educational program similar to that for the legal profession, which would consist of a four-year undergraduate and a three-year graduate program in a professional school of accountancy.

The Process of Establishing Auditing Standards.   The Commission recommended that the present Auditing Standards Executive Committee be replaced by an Auditing Standards Board within the AICPA. The auditing standards would then incorporate a statement of the independent auditor's role and include the recommendations made by the Commission.

Regulating the Profession to Maintain the Quality of Audit Practice.   The system of regulation of the public accountant profession involves practitioners, the development and promulgation of technical and ethical standards, the design and implementation of quality control policies and procedures, and the establishment of an effective disciplinary system to penalize departures from standards established by the law, Securities and Exchange Commission (SEC) regulation, or the profession. The Commission found that the present regulatory structure of the profession was adequate. It felt, however, that an improvement might result if the following recommendations were implemented:

- Secrecy should be removed from disciplinary actions and from the penalties imposed.
- Action on alleged violations of professional ethics should not be deferred pending the outcome of litigation, except when the accused demonstrates that the litigation is directly related to the changes.
- To reduce nuisance suits against auditors, courts should be given greater discretionary authority to assess costs against unsuccessful plaintiffs.[53]

Exhibit 2.3
Yesterday's Auditors' Report

Certificate of Chartered Accountants

New York
March 12, 1903

To the Stockholders of the United States Steel Corporation:

We have examined the books of the United States Steel Corporation and its subsidiary companies for the year ending December 31, 1902, and certify that the Balance Sheet at that date and the Relative Income Account are correctly prepared therefrom.

We have satisfied ourselves that during the year only actual additions and extensions have been charged to the Property Account; that ample provision has been made for Depreciation and Extinguishment, and that the item of Deferred Charges represents expenditures reasonably and properly carried forward to operations of subsequent years.

We are satisfied that the valuations of the inventories of stocks on hand as certified by the responsible official have been carefully and accurately made at approximate cost; also that the cost of material and labor on contracts is fair and reasonable.

Full provision has been made for bad and doubtful accounts receivable and for all ascertainable liabilities.

We have verified the cash and securities by actual inspection or by certificates from the depositories, and are of opinion that the stock and bonds are fully worth the value at which they are stated on the Balance Sheet.

And we certify that in our opinion the Balance Sheet is properly drawn up so as to show the true financial position of the corporation and its subsidiary companies, and that the Relative Income Account is a fair and correct statement of the net earnings for the fiscal year ending at that date.

Karabatsos & Co.

In addition, the Commission deemed the development of some form of statutory limitation of monetary damages essential to the continued healthy existence of the public accounting profession. Other recommendations included the use of court-appointed experts to make impartial expertise available during complex litigation and the granting of "safe harbors" when auditors must assume new responsibilities or significantly extend old ones.

The Adams Report: Canada

In 1977 the Board of Governors of the Canadian Institute of Chartered Accountants (CICA) created the Special Committee to Examine the Role of the Auditor (usually known, from the name of its chairman, as the Adams Commission), with the following charge:

Exhibit 2.4
Today's Auditors' Report

Accountants' Report

New York
February 11, 19x5

To the Directors and Stockholders of the General Motors Corporation:

We have examined the Consolidated Balance Sheet of General Motors Corporation and consolidated subsidiaries as of December 31, 19x4, and 19x3, and the related Statements of Consolidated Income and Changes in Consolidated Financial Position for the years then ended. Our examination was made in accordance with generally accepted auditing standards, and accordingly included such tests of the accounting records and such other auditing procedures as we considered necessary under the circumstances.

   In our opinion, these financial statements present fairly the financial position of the corporation and its consolidated subsidiaries as of December 31, 19x4 and 19x3, and the results of their operations and the changes in their financial position for the years then ended, in conformity with generally accepted accounting principles consistently applied.

Scherazade & Co.

Exhibit 2.5
Tomorrow's Auditors' Report?

Report of Independent Auditors

The accompanying consolidated balance sheet of XYZ Company as of December 31, 19x6, and the related Statements of Consolidated Income and Changes in Consolidated Financial Position for the year ended, including the notes, were prepared by XYZ Company's management, as explained in the report by management.

   In our opinion, these financial statements, in all material respects, present the financial position of XYZ Company as of December 31, 19x6, and the results of its operations and changes in financial position for the year then ended in conformity with generally accepted accounting principles appropriate under the circumstances.

   We audited the financial statements and the accounting records and documents supporting them in accordance with generally accepted auditing standards. Our audit included a study and evaluation of the company's accounting system and the controls over it. We obtained sufficient evidence through a sample of the transactions and their events reflected in the financial statement amounts and an analytical review of the information presented in the statements. Under the circumstances, we believe our auditing procedures were adequate to support our opinion.

Exhibit 2.5 (continued)

Based on our study and evaluation of the accounting system and the controls over it, we concur with the description of the system and controls in the report by management. [or: Based on our study and evaluation of the accounting system and the controls over it, we believe the system and controls have the following uncorrected material weaknesses not described in the report by management: . . . ; or other disagreements with the description of the system and controls in the report by management; or a description of uncorrected material weaknesses found if there is no report by management.] Nevertheless, in the performance of most control procedures, errors can result from personal factors. Also, control procedures can be overridden or circumvented by collusion. Furthermore, projection of any evaluation of internal accounting control to future periods is subject to the risk that changes in conditions may cause procedures to become inadequate and the degree of compliance with them to deteriorate.

We reviewed the process used by the company to prepare the quarterly information released during the year. Our reviews were conducted each quarter [or times as explained. Any other information reviewed, such as replacement cost data, would be identified.] Our reviews consisted primarily of inquiries of management, analysis of financial information, and comparison of that information to information and knowledge about the company obtained during our audits and were based on our reliance on the company's internal accounting control system. Any adjustments or additional disclosures we recommended are reflected in the information.

We reviewed the company's policy statement on employee conduct, described in the report by management, and reviewed and tested the related controls and internal audit procedures. Although no controls or procedures can prevent or detect all individual misconduct we believe the controls and internal audit procedures have been appropriately designed and applied.

We met with the Audit Committee [or the Board of Directors] of XYZ Company sufficiently often to inform it of the scope of our audit and to discuss any significant accounting or auditing problems encountered and any other services provided to the company [or indication of failure to meet or insufficient meetings or failure to discuss pertinent problems.]

Kalliopi & Co.
Certified Public Accountants

---

to review recent reports and developments affecting the role of the auditor and to recommend:

- Policies that are an appropriate response by the Canadian CA (Chartered Accountant) profession to those reports and developments.
- Action by appropriate CICA committees and other bodies regarding those policies.[54]

To justify possible departures from the Cohen Report, the Adams Report began by identifying the following differences between the Canadian and U.S. environments:

Exhibit 2.6
Proposed Separate Management Report

Report by Management

We prepared the accompanying consolidated balance sheet of XYZ company as of December 31, 19x6, and the related statements of consolidated income and changes in consolidated financial position for the year ended, including the notes. The statements have been prepared in conformity with generally accepted accounting principles appropriate under the circumstances, and include amounts that are based on our best estimates and judgments. The financial information in the remainder of this annual report [or other document] is consistent with that in the financial statements.

The company maintains an accounting system and controls over it to provide reasonable assurance that assets are safeguarded against loss from unauthorized use or disposition and that the financial records are reliable for preparing financial statements and maintaining accountability for assets. There are inherent limitations that should be recognized in considering the potential effectiveness of any system of internal accounting control. The concept of reasonable assurance is based on the recognition that the cost of a system of internal control should not exceed the benefits derived and that the evaluation of those factors requires estimates and judgments by management. The company's system provides such reasonable assurance. We have corrected all material weaknesses of the accounting and control systems identified by our independent auditors, Test Check & Co., Certified Public Accountants. [or: We are in the process of correcting all material variances . . . ; or We have corrected some of the material weaknesses but have not corrected others because we believe that correcting them would cost more than it is worth.]

The functioning of the accounting system and controls over it is under the general oversight of the Board of Directors [or the Audit Committee of the Board of Directors]. The members of the Audit Committee are associated with the company only by being directors. The system and controls are reviewed by an extensive program of internal audits and by the company's independent auditors. The Audit Committee [or the Board of Directors] meets regularly with the internal auditors and the independent auditors and reviews and approves their fee arrangements, the scope and timing of their audits, and their findings.

The company's legal counsel has reviewed the company's position with respect to litigation, claims, assessments, and illegal or questionable acts; has communicated that position to our independent auditors; and is satisfied that it is properly disclosed in the financial statements.

The company has prepared and distributed to its employees a statement of its policies prohibiting certain activities deemed illegal, unethical, or against the best interests of the company. (The statement was included in the 19xx annual report of the company; copies are available on request.) In consultation with our independent auditors, we have developed and instituted additional internal controls and internal audit procedures designed to prevent or detect violations of those policies. We believe that policies and procedures provide reasonable assurance that our operations are conducted in conformity with the law and with a high standard of business conduct.

[*If applicable:* The Board of Directors of the Company in March 19xx engaged

Exhibit 2.6 (continued)

Super, Sede & Co., Certified Public Accountants, as our independent auditors to re-place Test Check & Co. following disagreements on . . . . Test Check & Co. agrees with that description of disagreements.]

Hedi R.B.
Chief Financial Officer

---

1. Unlike in the United States, the relationship in Canada between the Chartered Ac-countant profession and various levels of government is not an adversary one but one of cooperation and support.
2. There is a more litigious climate in the United States due to the following reasons:
   a. Unlike in the United States, courts in Canada, as a general rule, award what are referred to as "party and party" costs to the successful defendant against the unsuccessful plaintiff.
   b. There is no absolute right to a jury trial in Canada.
   c. The United States has more liberal discovery rules, making it possible for any person to be examined under oath.
   d. In general, contingent fees are not permitted in Canada.
   e. The rules for bringing class actions are much more liberal in the United States than in Canada.

The contents of the Adams Report focus on the following technical issues: the independent auditor's role, enterprises subject to audit, the detection of fraud, illegal and questionable acts, the auditor's standard report, indepen-dence of auditors, and regulation of the profession.

The Independent Auditor's Role. The Adams Commission viewed add-ing credibility to financial information as the primary function of auditors. Their legal liabilities extend to a wider audience, although there seems to be a gap between what the public expects and what the auditors are doing. Servicing all these new users has created a challenge when it is not clear which group's views and information needs are permanent. Given this new climate, the Commission recommended an extension of "qualified privilege" and its codification into statute, and defined "qualified privilege" as the pro-vision of legal frankness by auditors as long as it is not maliciously inspired. The Commission also recommended a study of what responsibilities audit committees should be required or encouraged to assume. However, the Commission was careful to test the extension of the auditor's role in cost-benefit considerations. The audit committee should review the entire annual report, and the board of directors should consider the audit committee's rec-ommendation and be responsible for the approval of the complete annual report. Unlike the Cohen Report, the Adams Report recommended an ex-tension of the audit of nonprofit corporations to include the economy, efficiency, and effectiveness of the enterprise operations, referred to as the "value-for-money audit."

Enterprises Subject to Audit. The Adams Commission recommended that all enterprises with public accountability be audited. Public accountability exists when a firm has widely held securities, significant social and economic impact, and/or the use of significant amounts of funds from the general public.

The Detection of Fraud. The Adams Commission emphasized that it is the auditor's responsibility to make a reasonable search to discover material misstatement that can arise from errors or fraud and recommended attention to the following areas:

* The establishment of an effective client-investigation program.
* The importance of having an adequate understanding of the client's business.
* Alertness for conditions that may suggest an increased likelihood of management fraud.
* Standards with respect to auditor's reliance on opinions and work of experts, whether outside parties or within the enterprise; this should include consideration of whether there are circumstances in which a report by the experts should accompany the financial statements.
* The accounting treatment and disclosure of related party transactions and the responsibility of auditors with respect to them.[55]

Illegal and Questionable Acts. The Commission recommended that any enterprise required to have an audit also set forth a code of corporate conduct in its bylaws. The enterprise's lawyers would advise the audit committee of any breaches in the law or the enterprise's code of conduct that might come to their attention. The duty of the accounting profession would be to establish the auditor's role and responsibilities concerning illegal and questionable acts by clients.

The Auditor's Standard Report. The Commission recommended that the auditor's standard report be changed to more clearly express the auditor's message. Users of financial statements would have to be educated concerning the function of auditors and the meaning of their report. Similarly, attention to the following matters was recommended:

1. Auditors may have to state whether proper accounting records have not been or were not kept.
2. Auditors may have the responsibility of commenting on whether or not the accounting principles applied by management are the most appropriate.
3. Reporting on uncertainties is a management responsibility; it may require a note disclosing all material uncertainties and their impact on earnings and the financial position.
4. "Subject to" opinion should be eliminated.

Independence of Auditors. The Commission considered the fundamental objectives of independence rules to be: (1) protecting the substance of the auditor's independence; (2) ensuring that a reasonable observer would consider such independence to have been protected; and (3) ensuring that auditors are not permitted to use their inside knowledge of client affairs for their own personal advantage.

With regard to audit fees, the Adams Commission did not believe that audit fees from clients were a serious threat to auditor independence. However, the Commission did recommend that an amendment to the rules of professional conduct be developed, requiring that when fees from one client exceeded a given percentage of an auditor's gross fee, the auditor should take the necessary steps to remove the apparent threat to audit objectivity.

With regard to sources of strain on independence and pressures on staff to reduce time and costs, the Commission made the following recommendations:

1. To encourage enterprises to move their fiscal year end to the natural year end.
2. To include public accounting firms' bidding practices in the process of professional-practice review.
3. To include an explicit statement in companies' press releases (or other releases) of preliminary earnings, warning that results are subject to revision on examination by independent auditors.
4. To review with the audit committee the audit deadlines, especially in view of the reliability of internal control.

With regard to management advisory services, the Commission made two recommendations:

1. To require auditors providing other services to clients to act in a consulting and not a decision-making role.
2. To require auditors to inform the audit committee of the nature of fees and other services provided by the auditors.

Regulation of the Profession. The Adams Commission acknowledged the importance of protecting the public interest by requiring a consistently high standard in the services provided by public accountants. To ensure this high standard, the Commission made several recommendations:

1. To develop a single set of standards of qualification, performance, and discipline of practitioners.
2. To establish or expend lay representations on professional standard-setting bodies and their committees.
3. To consider the need for a class of paraprofessionals to perform, under supervision, the less demanding important tasks at present included in the work performed by students.

Accountants and Organizational Politics

Both financial and managerial accountants, as members of organiza-tions, compete over resources, energy, information, and influence, either as individuals or as members of a coalition.[56] Any conflict over means or ends calls for the use of power.[57] The use may be nonpolitical or political.[58] It is nonpolitical if it involves sanctioned means for sanctioned ends. Political use of power involves moving outside the formal authority, established pro-cedures, and role descriptions. Political use of power is intended to influence other organizational members and defeat policy changes that can affect their own interests.[59] Not only is the traditional authority/responsibility linkage broken with the use of political power, but Machiavellian techniques may emerge such as "situational manipulation," "dirty tricks," and "back-stabbing."[60] According to Cavanagh et al., "there is, then, a need for a nor-mative theory of organizational politics that addresses ethical issues directly and from the standpoint of the exercise of discretion."[61] They developed a model that integrates three kinds of ethical theories: utilitarianism (which evaluates behavior in terms of its consequences), theories of moral rights (which emphasize the entitlements of individuals), and theories of justice (which emphasize the distributional effects of actions or policies). It is very much applicable for an ethical analysis of the political behavior of account-ants within organization in those cases not covered by the code of ethics. The model is not necessarily unique. For example, instead of utilitarian eth-ics, deontological ethics could have been used. Similarly, a specific theory of justice could be used as the best norm of justice and fairness: justice accord-ing to Rawls, Nozick, or Gerwith.

THE TEACHING AND RESEARCH OF ACCOUNTING ETHICS

The call for accounting ethics was strongly made by the *Report of the National Commission on Fraudulent Financial Reporting* (the Treadway Commission). The Commission argued that "the independent public ac-countant's responsibility and accountability to the public requires a much broader exposure to ethics. Business schools should include ethics discus-sions in every accounting course."[62] It also recommends that "business and accounting curricula should emphasize ethical values by integrating their de-velopment with the acquisition of knowledge and skills to help prevent, de-tect, and deter fraudulent financial reporting."[63] The American Accounting Association Committee on the Future Structure, Content, and Scope of Ac-counting Education notes that "professional accounting education . . . must . . . instill the ethical standards and the commitment of a professional."[64]

The teaching of ethics courses in business schools is on the increase.[65] Au-diting appears to be the only accounting course where there is a significant integration of ethics and accounting.[66] Various reasons may explain this situation: (1) the textbook coverage of ethical and fraudulent financial reporting is minimal and focuses largely on reviewing the Code of Professional Ethics of the AICPA, forcing the accounting educators to devote a lot of resources to cover ethics in their courses;[67] (2) business schools foster a climate where there is not a good understanding of ethics, business school professors rely heavily on the economic concept of Pareto optimality, and ethics issues are considered "soft" and unscientific;[68] (3) there is a belief that accounting faculty cannot solve the moral and ethical problems of the accounting profession.[69] Cheryl Lehman warns, however, about four possible misinterpretations in the advocacy for accounting ethics:

First, we do not suggest that ethics are desirable because they will ensure survival of the system. There is a danger that educators will justify ethical practices as a public relations strategy (i.e., a practice to be followed because it increases goodwill and profits). This would clearly distort the fundamental meaning of ethics and would perpetuate accounting ethics as an oxymoron — a self-contradiction — because an accounting culture reifying ethics for profits does not harmonize with the concept of ethics.

Second, we do not purport that the problematic consequences of unethical behavior are the detriments to business referred to earlier (e.g., increased competition for clients in the securities market). Rather, we wish to highlight the broad deleterious effects on the environment, the sacrifice of human lives, the suffering of employees as the outcomes of unethical behavior (e.g., Hooker Chemical's waste disposal in Love Canal, Nestlé's international promotion of powdered milk, the use of asbestos by Manville's employees).

A third misinterpretation would be to conclude that the task of educators is merely to prompt individuals to be more ethical. Education in ethics must go beyond the study of good deeds versus rapacious acts of individuals — a redefinition of inquiry into the subject is needed. Educators and students should be questioning the institutionalization of inequalities that empower some groups over others; they need to explore political constraints regarding ethics and challenge accepted hierarchies of power and control, and they should investigate the role of accounting in social conflicts.

The fourth possible misreading, related to the preceding points, concerns the political and regulatory arena. We do not view regulation as captured and beneficial only to some interest: rather, regulatory mechanisms are potentially useful for promoting moral values. We fail to usurp their potential by continuing to teach accounting and business (i.e., economic issues) as if they were separate from sociopolitical issues; this is neither desirable or possible.[70]

The last argument about teaching ethics in accounting courses is made indirectly by S. E. Loeb as follows: "Accounting is a pluralistic profession — consisting of many segments. Ethical dilemmas occur in all segments of accounting."[71]

Examples of ethical dilemmas in financial and cost accounting are shown in Exhibits 2.7, 2.8, and 2.9. The teaching of ethics in accounting can help the student feel more confident later when confronting an ethical dilemma

Exhibit 2.7
Examples of Ethical Dilemmas in Financial Accounting

Opportunities to Exploit Judgment and Estimation Biases

1. Abuse of doctrine of conservatism in either direction.
2. Use of percentage-of-completion method when future costs are excessively difficult to estimate.
3. Estimation of uncollectible receivables.
4. Capitalizing expenditures with questionable future economic benefits.
5. Propriety of expected service lives, cost allocation methods, and residual values.
6. Measurement of goodwill.
7. Judgments on whether investments have experienced a decline in market value that is other than temporary.
8. Likelihood judgments for loss contingencies.
9. Assurance of benefit of net operating loss carryforward.
10. Whether a long-term contract is "completed."
11. Adequacy of capitalized costs for self-constructed plant assets.
12. Ability and intent to refinance short-term debt.
13. Appropriateness of equity method.
14. Substance of creative financing arrangements – debt or equity.
15. Borderline cases involving capital versus revenue expenditure.
16. Appropriateness of discount rates in present value applications.
17. Reasonableness of current versus noncurrent classifications.
18. Appropriateness of market values in applying the lower-of-cost-or-market rule to inventories.
19. Appropriateness of estimates used in pension reporting.
20. Use of tax method of depreciation for financial reporting in order to avoid reporting deferred income taxes.
21. Existence of significant right of return for sales.

Opportunities to Exploit Pronouncement Latitude or Absence of Relevant Pronouncements

1. Conforming to the letter of a pronouncement while concealing the substance of a transaction.
2. Biased interpretation of disclosure requirements where sensitive information is involved.
3. Disclosure or nondisclosure of poststatement events.
4. Income statement classifications, especially operating versus nonoperating income.
5. Deemphasizing unfavorable items by reporting them as prior-period adjustments or extraordinary items.
6. Capitalization tests for leases in light of possible management incentives for off-balance sheet financing.
7. Structuring stock option plans to appear noncompensatory or to delay expense recognition.
8. Assessing whether a stock dividend is "small" or "large."
9. Appropriateness of straight-line amortization of bond discount or premium in lieu of effective interest method.

Exhibit 2.7 (continued)

Opportunities to Exploit Weak Internal Control

1. Presence of excessive errors, possibly obscuring fraud or Foreign Corrupt Practices Act violations.
2. Presence of excessive errors, possibly obscuring transactions that are questionable but not clearly fraudulent.
3. Existence of "special purpose" cash funds.
4. Proper accounting for items not commonly emphasized in accounting courses, such as debt issue costs.
5. Compensating balance arrangements with banks.
6. Losses on abandonment of assets.
7. Manipulation of cost of goods sold through inadequate inventory controls.
8. Ambiguity of items charged to miscellaneous expense.
9. Classification of employee as "contract laborers."

Opportunities to Obscure the Substance of Related Party Transactions

1. Sale-leaseback transactions with related parties.
2. Classification of debt versus equity, particularly in small businesses.
3. Fair valuation of assets contributed by shareholders of partners.
4. Constructive dividends.
5. Below-market borrowing by related parties.
6. Presence of significant "receivables" from related parties.
7. Recording of receivables and revenues for owner use of enterprise.
8. Actual availability of reported assets for use in the operation of the business.
9. Reasonableness and disclosure of owner-manager compensation.
10. Appropriateness of the reporting entity in a complex structure of investor-investee relationships. (This is especially important in an advanced course.)

Source: Reprinted with permission from *Journal of Accounting Education*, 7, no. 1, E. Scribner, and M. P. Dillaway, "Strengthening the Ethics Content of Accounting Courses," pp. 54–55, copyright 1989, Pergamon Press plc.

in practice. A first goal is to teach the student the various roles of ethics that the different accounting associates have promulgated and the mechanisms for enforcing these roles. Other goals of teaching ethics in general and accounting ethics in particular include: "stimulating the moral imagination,"[72] "recognizing ethics issues,"[73] "eliciting a sense of moral obligations,"[74] "developing analytical skills,"[75] "tolerating — and reducing — disagreement and ambiguity."[76]

The teaching of ethics in accounting falls on the shoulders of accounting academics. The presumption is that some academic accountants are guided by explicit or implicit ethical codes. In fact, the Committee on Academic Independence of the American Accounting Association (AAA) concluded that there is a need for an AAA code of ethics for academic accountants.[77] Yet a

Exhibit 2.8
Framework for Analyzing Behavioral and Ethical Issues

Accounting Topic

Mathematical Technique

	Behavioral Issues		**Ethical Issues**	
Topic	*Long-Run*	*Short-Run*	*Black/White*	*Grey*
A. Cost Allocation	Effect on use of allocated services (e.g., computer support services).	Conflict between responsibility accounting system and arbitrary allocation.	Excessive cost allocation to "cost plus" contracts.	Closing down segments of business which are not meeting allocated costs.
B. Absorption vs. Direct costing	Incentives to over-produce to generate favorable volume variance.	Managers focus on short-term accounting numbers instead of long-run economic viability of the firm.	Falsifying ending inventory numbers to change reported income.	Produce greater amounts of inventory to generate a favorable volume variance.
C. Budgeting	Political process of negotiating budgets.	Incentives to spend all items budgeted.	Underestimating expected activity in order to reduce the amount of fixed cost assigned to the manager's budget.	Issue of presenting optimistic or unrealistic budgets.
D. Divisional Performance Measures (ROI)	Neglecting expenditures on maintenance.	Neglecting investment in R&D.	Falsifying numbers (e.g., keeping sales open after the period).	Rejecting investments which are greater than the company's required rate of return but which lower the divisional ROI.
E. Special Decisions	Outsourcing decisions motivated by desire to avoid Overhead Costs for labor intensive products.	Effect on pride in work if product is not made as a whole unit.	Possible conflict of interest in some subcontracting.	Responsibility to other stakeholders (e.g., workers, community).
F. Capital Budgeting	Conflict between accounting returns and economic returns on investment decisions.	Nonquantitative elements ignored (e.g., manager's previous track record).	Presenting large project as a series of smaller expenditures in order to circumvent company policy.	Changing assumptions to make project attractive (e.g., length of life or discount rate).
G. Variance Analysis	Neglect of non-counted items (e.g., product quality).	The effect on long-run motivation of comparing performance against unrealistic perfection standards.	Falsifying or giving incomplete explanations for significant variances.	Rejecting a rush order which creates unfavorable cost variances for the department but increases overall firm profitability.

Source: J. R. Cohen and L. W. Pant, "Ethics in the Classroom," *Management Accounting* (August 1989), p. 21. Reprinted with permission.

study by Terry Engle and Jack Smith on the ethical standards of accounting academics seems to indicate that a significant minority of faculty are probably violating normative standards of ethical conducts, as prescribed by their peers.[78] Note some of the interesting results shown in Exhibit 2.10. Some of the results raise the question of whether there should be a code of ethics for academic accounting for both teaching and research, if they want to deal with ethical issues in both areas. A case can be made for a code of ethics for academic accountants required to teach ethics. Based on Frankel's work,[79] Loeb restated and adapted five functions that a code of ethics for academic accountants may perform:

1. Giving an accounting professor a recognized set of standards that can be employed when he or she encounters an ethical dilemma;
2. Providing a set of standards that society can call upon an accounting professor to meet;
3. Providing a set of standards that can be used in the training of accounting doctoral students;
4. Providing a set of standards that possibly will raise the stature of accounting academia; and
5. Providing a set of standards that could be used if disagreements arise between accounting academics and other individuals.[80]

A case can also be made for a code of ethics for accounting research.[81] Other disciplines have developed such a code. Exhibit 2.11 shows the topics covered in the APA (American Psychological Association),[82] the ASA (American Sociological Association),[83] and the AMA (American Marketing Association).[84]

With the acceptance of both codes of ethics for teaching and research in accounting, academics may be more inclined to teach ethics in either an integrative approach, where ethics will be included in all the accounting courses, or a pervasive method, where ethics will be taught in a single course.[85] Some still may question whether accounting academics, even with the presence of codes, can teach accounting ethics. Witness the following comment by Grimstad:

To teach ethics it is necessary to have a historical perspective, a broad understanding of societal forces and a philosophical orientation. The accounting teacher who in his own educational background and professional training may not have acquired these outlooks is not likely to explore the "whys" of ethical standards or to question their validity.[86]

Reasons for not teaching ethics in general include the following:

1. Pluralistic presuppositions pervading Western civilization incline us to accepting many differing views. A history of ethics or an introductory course in ethics re-

Exhibit 2.9
Professional Dilemmas

> *A company code was the leading alternative to an occupational code.*

1. Expectations of management v. Internalized professional values (and/or Professional judgment)

1-1 Management asks an accountant to prepare for its use one or more financial analyses which will reflect favorably on a past decision or one which is planned. Based on available data, only analyses which in the accountant's judgment are misleading or dubious will meet the requirement, such as full costing analyses where only incremental costs are relevant *(Rationalization of Management Action)*.

1-2 An accountant whose views on the matter are known to management is asked to sign a document he believes contrary to the interests of minority shareholders *(Minority Interest)*.

1-3 An accountant is asked to analyze data which he has reason to doubt would be available to the company other than through ethically questionable means. It is unlikely that he could *prove* his suspicions *(Suspicious Acquisition of Data)*.

1-4 Management insists upon external reporting policies widely viewed by the accountants as designed to "bury" information highly important to major users of the reports (for example, in regard to divisional or product-line reporting). The accountants doubt, however, that management's approach would violate established reporting requirements *(Accounting Manipulation)*.

1-5 Advised by legal counsel that it may do so, management withholds from a party with whom it is negotiating a contract certain information which a company accountant regards as genuinely material to the transaction *(Legally Approved Concealment)*.

1-6 Independently of regulated reporting, management publicly materially misrepresents, in an accountant's judgment, matters relating to the company's financial condition. The accountant registers objection through normal channels, but no corrective action is taken *(Public Misrepresentation)*.

1-7 A junior accountant feels that, notwithstanding management's letter of representation, a material fact concerning the company's financial condition has been withheld from the independent accountant *(Nondisclosure to Auditor)*.

2. Expectations of management v. Expectations of other major reliant parties

2-1 Management and the independent audit committee of the board of directors differ as to the nature and extent of accounting information to be shared with the committee, under its mandate *(Disclosure to Audit Committee)*.

52

2-2 The policies of an accountant's present employer as to confidentiality are less restrictive than those of a former one, a competitor. Management expects the accountant to provide information about the former employer which, under the latter's policies only, is confidential *(Continuing Confidentiality).*

2-3 Management asks a senior accountant to change accounting treatments to reduce the risk of reporting results which, on their face, would violate bond indenture, or other contractual, requirements. He thinks that pertinent changes might be accepted by the firm's independent accountant, but is concerned about his responsibility to (for example) the bondholders *(Accounting Solution).*

2-4 An accountant is asked by management to act contrary to express company policy on a given matter. While plausible business reasons are given, the accountant has reason to doubt that such an exception would be acceptable to all major parties legitimately interested in the matter *(Requested Violation of Policy).*

3. *Internalized professional values v. Professional career objectives*

3-1 A high-ranking accountant has been offered an outstanding professional opportunity by another company. It is unlikely that his employer could replace him really satisfactorily, on a timely basis *(Employment Dilemma).*

3-2 An accountant comes upon information about a likely rival for advancement within the company which, from management's point of view, would reflect adversely upon the other accountant. Trying objectively to decide whether to report it to management, the accountant is not satisfied that the information *should* damage his colleague's standing *(Employee Rivalry).*

4. *Other conflicts*

4-1 Expectations of management v. Personal Values

An accountant is asked to develop transfer-pricing and/or other analyses in support of transnational operating policies he opposes as contrary to legitimate interests of "host" countries *(Incompatible Values).*

4-2 Internalized professional values v. Operating practicalities

A cost accountant finds that factory foremen, or others upon whom he depends heavily for important operating data, expect certain deviations from proper record keeping. He is concerned about their potential cumulative effect *(Offensive Operating Practicalities).*

Source: T. K. Sheldahl, "Ethical Dilemmas in Management Accounting," *Management Accounting* (January 1988), p. 36.

53

Exhibit 2.10

Attitudes about Ethical Behavior and Warranted Sanctions (Response Percentages, $n = 245$)

	Totally Ethical (No Sanctions)	Slightly Unethical (No Sanctions)	Moderately Unethical (Discussion)	Moderately to Extremely Unethical (Severe Reprimand)	Extremely Unethical (Dismissal)
Research Activities					
1. Plagiarizing research.	1%	1%	2%	27%	69%
2. Submitting a manuscript to two or more journals in violation of journal policy.	6	28	42	19	5
3. Falsifying documentation for research grants.	1	1	4	35	59
4. Falsifying research data.	1	0	2	24	73
5. Not giving graduate student(s) coauthorship on publications when the student(s) contributions justified coauthorship.	2	6	31	48	13
6. Inappropriately giving a colleague a coauthorship status.	4	22	39	33	2
7. Presenting the same research to more than one regional or annual meeting (against meeting policy).	6	26	47	18	3
Travel Activities					
8. Padding an expense account,	0	4	27	50	19
9. Attending a meeting at university expense and not substantively participating (most of the time spent sight-seeing, etc.).	2	15	50	29	4
Outside Employment					
10. Neglecting university responsibilities due to outside employment.	2	2	43	41	12
11. Using university equipment for personal activities.	2	13	44	35	6

	22%	38%	27%	12%	1%
Relationships with Publishers					
12. Selling complimentary textbooks to a used book salesperson.	0	3	4	34	59
13. Accepting a bribe (e.g., money, sex) from a publisher for a textbook adoption.	3	13	32	44	18
14. Adoption of a texbook in return for assets donated to the accounting department by the publisher.	6	20	46	23	5
Student-Related Activities					
15. Favoring a particular firm(s) in employment advice to students because grants, employment, etc. have been accepted from the firm by the faculty member.					
16. Using student assistants for personal work (e.g., running errands).	4	20	47	24	5
17. Cancelling office hours excessively.	5	9	64	19	3
18. Accepting sex for grades.	0	0	1	6	93
19. Accepting money or gifts for grades.	0	0	1	6	93
20. Dating a student in his or her class.	8	8	33	41	10
21. Dating a student not in his or her class who is an accounting major.	23	21	29	23	4
22. Dating a student not in his or her class who is not an accounting major.	50	20	15	11	4
23. Allowing lecture notes to become outdated.	7	16	57	18	2
24. Allowing a relative or friend in class and giving them preferential treatment.	0	5	35	48	12

Exhibit 2.10 (continued)

	Totally Ethical (No Sanctions)	Slightly Unethical (No Sanctions)	Moderately Unethical (Discussion)	Moderately to Extremely Unethical (Severe Reprimand)	Extremely Unethical (Dismissal)
Student-Related Activities—Continued					
25. Allowing a student assistant to grade nonobjective exams and/or written assignments that require significant judgment.	10%	16%	44%	27%	3%
26. Cancelling classes when the faculty member is not ill and has no other university related commitments.	3	7	40	43	7
27. Conducting university responsibilities under the influence of drugs or alcohol.	1	1	13	44	41
28. Using outdated text to avoid the effort necessary to revise notes, etc.	1	10	52	35	2
Other Activities					
29. Falsifying activity reports that are utilized by his or her institution for raises, promotion, or tenure evaluations.	0	3	12	50	35

Source: Terry J. Engle, and Jack L. Smith, "The Ethical Standards of Accounting Academics," *Issues in Accounting Education* (Spring 1990), pp.12–14. Reprinted with permission.

Exhibit 2.11
Topics Covered in APA, ASA and AMA Codes

APA*	ASA*	AMA*
1. Ethical evaluation of study	1. Objectivity in research	*For research users, practitioners, and interviewers:***
2. Responsibility for ethics	2. Integrity in research	1. Separation of research and sale of goods or services
3. Informed consent	3. Rights of privacy and dignity	2. Subject's anonymity
4. Honest relationship with subject	4. Personal harm	*For research practitioners:*
5. Subject's right to decline	5. Confidentiality of data	1. Misrepresentation of research
6. Fair agreement with subject	6. Presentation of findings	2. Dissemination of research information
7. Physical and mental harm to subject	7. Misuse of data	3. Competitive clients
8. Debriefing	8. Research collaboration	*For research users:*
9. Undesirable consequences and the investigator's responsibility	9. Disclosure of financial support	1. Dissemination of conclusions
10. Subject's right to privacy	10. Distortion of findings	2. Plagiarism
	11. Disassociation from unethical research	*For field interviewers:*
	12. Interpretation of ethical principles	1. Confidentiality of data
	13. Applicability of principles	2. Personal use of data
		3. Adherence to instructions
		4. Multiple assignments

*APA = American Psychological Association, ASA = American Sociological Association, and AMA = American Marketing Association.

**Research users are the clients who sponsor the research studies, research practitioners are in charge of conducting the research studies, and interviewers contact the subjects.

Source: Reprinted with permission from *Journal of Accounting Education*, Fall, D. E. Keys and J. A. Hendricks, "The Ethics of Accounting Research: Some Crucial Issues," p. 79, copyright 1984, Pergamon Press plc.

veals many different ethical theories, each with its own advantages and disadvantages. A person remains uninformed ethically until he understands several such theories. To teach one of these while excluding others is feared as indoctrination.

2. U.S. Constitutional guarantees of freedom of opinion require us to respect each individual's rights to his own explanation of ethical ultimates as long as his acts do not harm others. To wade through the peculiarities, complexities, inadequacies, and falsities of the views of each of several persons trying to cooperate in solving a practical problem would add enormous difficulties to those inherent in the problem itself. Attention to them can be not only a waste of time but can dredge up fundamental disagreements preventing cooperative solution altogether.

3. The truth about value ultimates cannot yet be found by looking for them. Some day we may know; but today disputes among professional philosophers persist without expectation that they will be settled soon. Each of several alternative theories has recognizable merits, but no theory is yet available having all such merits.

4. People usually believe that they know what is right and wrong in particular situations even when they cannot explain why. Hence knowledge of ethical theory is not necessary for solving ethical problems.

5. Persons enjoying freedom from earlier ethical systems, whether prescriptive or explanatory, have little interest in adopting another one just because it has changed, possibly up-dated, presuppositions. If the onerous task of tracing the rightness and wrongness of particular decisions to their ultimate theoretical foundations is unnecessary, then we not only can but should avoid it and get on with more urgent matters.[87]

Others present a qualified assessment. For example, A. P. Mayer-Sommer and S. E. Loeb suggest that academic educators should have a strong "theory of practice" and a good understanding of the uncertainties inherent in the actual practice of accounting to be able to effectively teach accounting ethics.[88] Loeb also suggests consideration be given to the training of accounting faculty assigned to teach ethics or the training of ethicists to teach accounting ethics.[89] The appointment of ethics committees and consultants in public accounting firms could be a constructive first step (see the Appendix to this chapter).

CONCLUSIONS

Ethics in accounting is fundamental to the credibility and reputation of the integrity of the accounting profession and discipline. While individual accountants may be tempted to define their ethics in utilitarian terms, the presence of codes of ethics in accounting, as well as various rules of conduct, point to a deontological view favored by the profession and the discipline. From some of the discussions in the chapter it appears that the profession and the discipline ought to adopt a view of ethics of accounting that (1) rests in a notion of fittingness to an accounting ethos, comprised of freely accepted obligations and traditions and in which are gathered the social and political concerns of society, and that favors the language of responsiveness and responsibility; (2) favors the moral development and moral reasoning of accountants to a level that is defined by a conscience in accord with self-chosen ethical principles of justice, equality, and dignity of human beings, and (3) calls for the adoption of accounting ethics in both education and research in accounting.

The work of accountants carries real responsibilities. Their words and actions in rendering opinions relate not only to the technical competency but also to the moral standards and the code of ethics governing the profession. To abide by the strictest of ethical codes, accountants ought to have their own "Hippocratic Oath." The following suggested oath may be a beginning:

I will to the best of my ability exercise due care in the performance of my work. Where judgment is involved, I will consider dispassionately and objectively all demonstrable facts and determinants necessary to express an informed and unbiased opinion. I will present fairly all financial information in accordance with generally accepted accounting principles consistently applied, and will render no false or misleading statements. Whatever I do in the practice of my art, I will do for the benefit of those who seek my services and will commit no voluntary acts, of corruption or mischief. I will hold in strict confidence all matters whose revelation be injurious to others, nor will I knowingly suggest counsel that would be deleterious. I will keep myself informed of current developments so that I may know and apply the most competent principles, procedures, and standards. With simple dignity and with sincere humility, I will rejoice in my profession. May it be granted to the courage and foresight to keep inviolate this Oath and to enjoy life and the practice of my art, respected by all men in all times.[90]

NOTES

1. D. Emmet, *Rules, Roles, and Relations* (Boston: Beacon Press, 1966), p. 15.

2. F. H. Bradley, *Ethical Studies* (Indianapolis: Bobbs-Merrill, 1951), p. 136.

3. H. L. A. Hart, *The Concept of Law* (London: Oxford University Press, 1966), pp. 84–85.

4. Kurt Baier, *The Moral Point of View* (New York: Random House, 1965), pp. 83–90.

5. Michael Scriven, *Primary Philosophy* (New York: McGraw Hill, 1966), pp. 232–233.

6. R. B. Brandts, *Ethical Theory* (Englewood Cliffs, N.J.: Prentice Hall, 1959), p. 250.

7. Manuel G. Velasquez, *Business Ethics: Concepts and Cases* (Englewood Cliffs, N.J.: Prentice Hall, 1982), pp. 10–11.

8. Henry Sidguiche, *Methods of Ethics*, 7th ed. (Chicago: University of Chicago Press, 1962), p. 413.

9. John Stuart Mill, *Utilitarianism* (Indianapolis: Bobbs-Merrill, 1957), p. 22.

10. Baruch Brady, *Ethics and Its Applications* (San Diego: Harcourt, Brace, Jovanovich, 1983), p. 16.

11. Ibid., p. 16.

12. Ibid., p. 17.

13. Ibid., p. 18.

14. Ibid., p. 19.

15. Ibid., p. 19.

16. Ibid., p. 20.

17. Michael D. Bayles, "The Price of Life," *Ethics*, 89, no. 1 (October 1978), pp. 20–34.

18. G. E. Moore, *Principia Ethica,* 5th ed. (Cambridge: Cambridge University Press, 1956), p. 146.

19. A. MacIntyre, "Utilitarianism and Cost-Benefit Analysis: An Essay on the Relevance of Moral Philosophy to Bureaucratic Theory," in Kenneth Syre (ed.), *Values in the Electric Power Industry* (Notre Dame, Ind.: University of Notre Dame Press, 1977).

20. Velasquez, *Business Ethics,* pp. 49–50.

21. Brady, *Ethics and Its Applications,* p. 28.

22. Ibid., p. 28.

23. Ibid., p. 31.

24. W. W. May, "How to Resolve an Ethical Issue," in *Ethics in the Accounting Profession* (New York: Touche Ross, 1985), pp. 32–33.

25. Martin Heidegger, *An Introduction to Metaphysics*, trans. Ralph Manheim (New York: Doubleday, 1959), p. 13.

26. Calvin O. Schrag, *Communicative Praxis and the Space of Subjectivity* (Bloomington: Indiana University Press, 1986), pp. 203–204.

27. R. Niebuhr, *The Responsible Self* (New York: Harper and Row, 1963), pp. 60–107.

28. Schrag, *Communicative Praxis,* p. 204.

29. L. Kohlberg, "Stage of Moral Development," in *Moral Education* (Toronto: University of Toronto Press, 1971).

30. J. R. Rest, D. Coper, R. Coder, J. Masanz, and D. Anderson, "Judging the Important Issues in Moral Dilemma: An Objective Test of Development," *Development Psychology,* 10 (1974), pp. 451–501.

31. Kohlber, "Stages of Moral Development."

32. J. R. Rest, *Development in Judging Moral Issues* (Minneapolis: University of Minnesota Press, 1979).

33. J. R. Rest, *Revised Manual for the Defining Issues Test* (Minneapolis: University of Minnesota Press, 1979), p. 52.

34. M. B. Armstrong, "Moral Development and Accounting Education," *Journal of Accounting Education*, 5, no. 1 (1987), pp. 27–44.

35. Ibid.

36. Kent E. St. Pierre, Eileen S. Nelson, and A. L. Gablin, "A Study of Ethical Development of Accounting Majors in Relation to Other Business and Nonbusiness Disciplines," *The Accounting Educators' Journal* (Summer 1990), pp. 23–35.

37. Ibid., p. 30.

38. N. Aranya, E. I. Meir, and A. Ilan, "An Empirical Examination of the Stereotype Accountant Based on Holland's Theory," *Journal of Occupational Psychology,* 5, no. 1 (1978), pp. 139–145.

39. National Commission on Fraudulent Financial Reporting, *Report of the National Commission on Fraudulent Financial Reporting,* 1987.

40. E. Scribner, and M. P. Dillaway, "Strengthening the Ethics Content of Accounting Courses," *Journal of Accounting Education* (Spring 1989), pp. 41-55.

41. A. MacIntyre, *After Virtue* (Notre Dame, Ind: University of Notre Dame Press, 1981), p. 112.

42. P. T. Heyne, *Private Keepers of the Public Interest* (New York: McGraw Hill, 1968), p. 47.

43. Ibid., p. 55

44. Ibid., p. 53.

45. M. Larson, *The Rise of Professionalism* (Berkeley: University of California Press, 1981), p. 28.

46. Scribner and Dillaway, "Strengthening the Ethics Content of Accounting Courses," pp. 49-50.

47. D. F. Linowes, "How Do You Discipline a Profession?" in Sidney Davidson (ed.), *The Accounting Establishment in Perspective* (Chicago: Arthur Young & Company, 1979), p. 146.

48. Ibid., p. 149.

49. W. E. Olson, in ibid. p. 157.

50. The Commission on Auditors' Responsibilities, "Report, Conclusion, and Recommendations" (New York: Commission on Auditors' Responsibilities, 1978), p. 3.

51. P. D. Jackson, "The *Cohen Report,*" *The Canadian Chartered Accountant Magazine* (June 1977), pp. 48-50.

52. Ibid., p. 49.

53. Ibid., p. 51.

54. The Special Committee to Examine the Role of the Auditor, "Report," *The Canadian Chartered Accountant Magazine* (April 1978), p. 37.

55. Ibid., p. 45.

56. D. J. Hickson, C. R. Hinnings, C. A. Lee, R. E. Schneck, and J. M. Pennings, "A Strategic Contingencies Theory of Intraorganizational Power," *Administrative Science Quarterly,* 19 (1971), pp. 216-229.

57. J. Pfeffer, "Power and Resource Allocation in Organizations," in B. Staw and G. Salanicks (eds.), *New Directions in Organizational Behavior* (Chicago: St. Clair Press, 1977), pp. 235-266.

58. V. E. Schein, "Individual Power and Political Behaviors in Organizations: An Inadequately Explored Reality," *Academy of Management Review,* 2 (1977), pp. 235-266.

59. A. M. Pettigrew, *The Politics of Organizational Making* (London: Tavistock, 1973).

60. Gerald F. Cavanagh, D. J. Moberg, and M. Velasquez, "The Ethics of Organizational Politics," *Academy of Management Review,* 6, no. 3 (1981), pp. 363-374.

61. Ibid., p. 364.

62. National Commission on Fraudulent Financial Reporting, p. 83.

63. Ibid., p. 82.

64. American Accounting Association Committee on the Future Structure, Content and Scope of Accounting Education, "Future Accounting Education: Preparing

for the Expanding Profession," *Issues in Accounting Education* (Spring 1986), p. 179.

65. W. M. Hoffman, and J. M. Moore, "Results of a Business Ethics Curriculum Survey Conducted by the Center of Business Ethics," *Journal of Business Ethics,* 1 (1982), pp. 81–83.

66. J. R. Cohen, "Ethics and Budgeting," *Management Accounting* (August 1988), pp. 29–31.

67. J. C. Wyer, "Fraudulent Financial Reporting: The Potential for Educational Impact," *Report of the National Commission on Fraudulent Financial Reporting* (1987), p. 108.

68. L. T. Hosmer, "The Other 338: Why a Majority of Our Schools of Business Administration Do Not Offer a Course in Business Ethics," *Journal of Business Ethics,* 9 (1985), pp. 17–22.

69. R. M. Carver, Jr. and T. E. King, "Attitudes of Accounting Practitioners Towards Accounting Faculty and Accounting Education," *Journal of Accounting Education* (Spring 1986), pp. 31–43.

70. Cheryl R. Lehman, "Accounting Ethics: Surviving Survival of the Fittest," *Advances in Public Interest Accounting,* 2 (1988), pp.79–80.

71. S. E. Loeb, "Teaching Students Accounting Ethics: Some Crucial Issues," *Issues in Accounting Education* (Fall 1988), pp. 316–329.

72. D. Callahan, "Goals in the Teaching of Ethics," in D. Callahan and S. Bok (eds.), *Ethics Teaching in Higher Education* (New York: Plenum Press, 1980), p. 64.

73. Ibid., p. 65.

74. Ibid., p. 66.

75. Ibid., p. 67.

76. Ibid.

77. American Accounting Association, Committee on Academic Independence, *Report of the Committee on Academic Independence of the American Accounting Association* (Sarasota, Fla.: American Accounting Association, 1981).

78. Terry J. Engle, and Jack L. Smith, "The Ethical Standards of Accounting Academics," *Issues in Accounting Education* (Spring 1990), pp. 7–29.

79. M. S. Frankel, "Professional Codes: Why, How, and With What Impact?" *Journal of Business Ethics* (February/March 1989), pp. 109–115.

80. Loeb, "Teaching Students Accounting Ethics," p. 125.

81. D. E. Keys, and J. A. Hendricks, "The Ethics of Accounting Research: Some Crucial Issues" *Journal of Accounting Education* (Fall 1984) p. 125.

82. American Psychological Association, Committee on Ethical Standards, "Ethical Principles in the Conduct of Research with Human Participants," *American Psychologist* (January 1973), pp. 79–80.

83. American Sociological Association, Committee on Professional Ethics," Towards a Code of Ethics for Sociologists," *The American Sociologist* (November 1968), pp. 316–318.

84. D. W. Twedt, "Why a Marketing Research Code of Ethics," *Journal of Accounting* (October 1963), pp. 45–50.

85. C. R. Grimstad, "Teaching the Ethics of Accountancy," *Journal of Accountancy* (July 1964), pp. 82–85.

86. Ibid., p. 84.

87. Archie J. Bahn, "Teaching Ethics Without Ethics to Teach," *Journal of Business Ethics,* 1 (1982), pp. 46–47.

88. A. P. Mayer-Sommer and S. E. Loeb, "Fostering More Successful Professional Socialization Among Accounting Students," *The Accounting Review* (January 1981), pp. 125–136.

89. Loeb, "Teaching Students Accounting Ethics," p. 327.

90. Lincoln G. Kelly, "The Value to the Individual Professional Man of a Strict Adherence to his Code of Ethics," *Journal of Accountancy* (November 1983), pp. 142–143.

SELECTED READINGS

Armstrong, M. B., "Moral Development and Accounting Education." *Journal of Accounting Education*, 5, no. 1 (1987), pp. 27–44.

Callahan, D. "Goals in the Teaching of Ethics." in D. Callahan and S. Bok (eds.), *Ethics Teaching in Higher Education.* (New York: Plenum Press, 1980, pp. 61–80.

Grimstad, C. R., "Teaching the Ethics of Accountancy." *Journal of Accountancy* (July 1964), pp. 82–85.

Loeb, S. E., "Codes of Ethics and Self-Regulation for Non-Public Accountants: A Public Policy Perspective." *Journal of Accounting and Public Policy* (Spring 1984), pp. 1–8.

———. "Teaching Students Accounting Ethics: Some Crucial Issues." *Issues in Accounting Education* (Fall 1988), pp. 316–329.

——— and J. P. Bedingfeld. "Teaching Accounting Ethics." *The Accounting Review* (October 1972), pp. 811–813.

Scribner, E. and M. P. Dillaway, "Strengthening the Ethics Content of Accounting Courses," *Journal of Accounting Education* (Spring 1989), pp. 41–55.

St. Pierre, Kent E., Eileen S. Nelson, and A. L. Gablin. "A Study of Ethical Development of Accounting Majors in Relation to Other Business and Nonbusiness Disciplines." *The Accounting Educators' Journal* (Summer 1990), pp. 25–35.

Appendix: Ethics Committees and Consultants in Public Accounting Firms?

Stephen E. Loeb

Stephen E. Loeb is Professor and Chairman of Accounting and Ernst & Young Alumni Research Fellow at the University of Maryland at College Park.

The ethical milieu of public accounting has become increasingly complex. Casler indicates that when in 1905 the American Accounting Association of Public Accountants (the original name of the American Institute of Certified Public Accountants (AICPA)) adopted its first ethical standards, only two "were adopted."[1] This is in sharp contrast to the current environment in which a public accountant works.

Other professions—law and medicine for example—also practice in a complex ethical milieu. Research suggests that these two professions are perhaps better preparing students in their professional schools for the ethical complexities of practice.[2] Additionally, as will be discussed later in this paper, hospital ethics committees and ethics consultants have evolved to assist medical practitioners and the institutions in which they work to deal with ethical issues and/or dilemmas.

In a recent editorial in *The Journal of the American Medical Association*, Edmund D. Pellegrino, M.D., at the time Director of the Kennedy Institute of Ethics, Georgetown University, states that

> In democratic, educated, and morally heterogeneous societies like ours, the intuitive and idiosyncratic way of making ethical choices is no longer tenable.... The physician's decisions must now be justified to patients and their families, one's colleagues, and the courts. As a result, every physician requires a more formal and systematic knowledge of ethical analysis and must know how to use the advice of ethics consultants wisely and well.[3]

Pellegrino's comments are addressed to the field of medicine; however, his message is likely relevant to the public accounting pro-

fession. As noted above, the environment of public accounting has become ethically complex (examples of such complexity are discussed later in this paper). Further, the report of the National Commission on Fraudulent Financial Reporting (Treadway Commission) recommends increased coverage of ethics (1) in business courses as well as accounting courses at colleges and universities, (2) on examinations for professional certificates, and (3) in continuing education courses for accountants as well as individuals associated with public corporations.[4] These recommendations are likely in part a recognition of these complexities. The use of ethics committees and/or consultants in public accounting firms may, in fact, provide a more systematic approach to ethical issues and/or dilemmas that public accounting firms may encounter.

I wish to acknowledge the assistance of various practitioners, state society executives, and a physician, with whom I discussed the topic of this paper. Also, I benefited from the comments of Robert K. Mautz, Jack M. Taylor, and an anonymous reviewer on earlier drafts of this paper.

[1]Darwin J. Casler, *The Evolution of CPA Ethics: A Profile of Professionalization*, Occasional Paper No. 12, Bureau of Business and Economic Research, Graduate School of Business (Administration, Michigan State University, East Lansing, Michigan, 1964, p. 5.

[2]See, for example, Stephen E. Loeb, "Teaching Students Accounting Ethics: Some Crucial Issues," *Issues in Accounting Education*, Fall 1988, p. 317 for a brief discussion of some of this research.

[3]Edmund D. Pellegrino, "Clinical Ethics: Biomedical Ethics at the Bedside," *The Journal of the American Medical Association*, August 12, 1988, p. 837.

[4]National Commission on Fraudulent Financial Reporting, *Report of the National Commission on Fraudulent Financial Reporting*, October 1987, pp. 15, 16, 82-86.

Source: Stephen S. Loeb, "Ethics Committees and Consultants in Public Accounting," *Accounting Horizons* (December 1989), pp. 1–10. Reprinted with permission.

This paper briefly reviews the institutional framework of public accounting and compares it to the institutional framework of medical practice. It is within such frameworks that the ethical issues and/or dilemmas are considered and resolved by each profession. Examples of some of the ethical problems and complexities that exist in public accounting are then reviewed. Next, a discussion of ethics committees and ethics consultants in medicine is presented. The implications of the medical profession's experience with ethics committees and consultants are then considered in relation to the public accounting profession.

INSTITUTIONAL FRAMEWORKS

Institutionally, public accounting is practiced in public accounting offices. Public accounting firms can have one or more such offices. This is in contrast to medicine where physicians have offices, but another institution—the hospital—is also an essential element in the practice of medicine.[5] Public accountants often do a substantial amount of work in a client's office. However, the role of the public accountant working in a client's office is vastly different than the role of a physician working in a hospital. For example, in a hospital a physician must observe various hospital regulations and policies. In contrast, when working in a client's office, a public accountant is subject to few constraints.

Hospitals and physicians provide a number of health related services to society. In the process of providing such services, a number of ethical issues and/or dilemmas can arise which in some instances may involve extending or sustaining human life.[6] In recent years, as discussed later in this paper, an increasing number of hospitals have organized ethics committees. Also, some hospitals are using ethics consultants.[7] The ethical issues and/or dilemmas that public accountants and/or public accounting firms face are no less complex but are generally of a different nature than those encountered by hospitals and physicians. Examples of issues and/or dilemmas that public accountants and/or public accounting firms may face include: independence; scope of services; confidentiality; practice development; and differences on accounting issues. These ethical issues and/or dilemmas are discussed in detail later in this paper.

Certified Public Accountants (CPAs) can join the American Institute of Certified Public Accountants and/or the various CPA societies. These organizations usually have an ethics committee and/or staff that can provide advice to public accounting practitioners relating to ethical issues and/or dilemmas. For example, a question that a public accountant might have regarding an issue and/or dilemma that has been addressed previously in the professional literature probably can be adequately answered informally by an appropriate staff member or ethics committee member of one of these organizations. In contrast, a new and/or complex ethical issue and/or dilemma may require a written request to the ethics committee for an opinion, perhaps a meeting or meetings of the ethics committee, and then a formal response from the committee. In such a situation, especially if time is an important factor, requesting an opinion about the issue from a professional association may not always be a feasible alternative.

There are other reasons for not contacting a professional association for an opinion on an ethical issue and/or dilemma. Examples of such reasons include:

- situations that a public accounting firm would consider so sensitive that the partners may not wish to have the

---

[5]One source, Elliot Gene Cohen and David C. Thomasma, "Taking Ethics Seriously," *Healthcare Executive*, July/August, 1987, p. 25, notes that "for more than 80 percent of the American population, death occurs at the hospital...."

[6]See Troyen A. Brennan, "Ethics Committees and Decisions to Limit Care: The Experience at the Massachusetts General Hospital," *The Journal of the American Medical Association*, August 12, 1988, pp. 803-807.

[7]See Joyce Bermel, "Ethics Consultants: A Self-Portrait of Decision Makers," *Hastings Center Report*, December, 1985, p. 2.

issue known to individuals outside the firm. Even though members of a professional association ethics committee are bound by rules of confidentiality, the partners may feel that the situation should not be discussed outside the firm.

• situations in which a public accounting firm may wish to require its professionals to adhere to standards that are even higher than the formal ethical rules and interpretations of a professional association.[8] The firm may feel that the "morally responsible" alternative in a particular situation may call for an action that is at a higher level than such existing rules or interpretations require.[9] Thus, as a matter of policy, a public accounting firm may in particular situations want its personnel to do what they themselves feel is the morally responsible action even though their response may be beyond what would be required by the ethics rules and interpretations of a professional association.

ETHICAL COMPLEXITIES OF PUBLIC ACCOUNTING

The code of ethics of the AICPA has been evolving for a number of years.[10] As the practice of public accounting has expanded into new areas and as business transactions have become increasingly complex, the ethical issues in public accounting also have increased in complexity. An exhaustive listing of all possible ethical issues and/or dilemmas that may affect public accountants and/or public accounting firms would be difficult to complete. New issues and/or dilemmas are constantly arising and some issues and/or dilemmas are closely related and difficult to place in a mutually exclusive category. An example of the latter are the issues of independence and scope of services.

Some of the ethical issues and/or dilemmas that arise in public accounting may be handled routinely by following the policies that a public accounting firm has established

for dealing with such matters. Alternatively, notwithstanding a public accounting firm's existing policies, ethical issues and/or dilemmas may arise in practice that require careful thought and decision making on the part of the affected individuals and/or firm.

Several major ethical issues and/or dilemmas, mentioned earlier in this paper, that individuals and firms in public accounting practice may encounter are discussed next. The issues and/or dilemmas provide examples of the ethical complexities that public accountants and public accounting firms can encounter and for which they may require assistance. They include:

• *Independence* — audit independence is one of the more unique ethical issues facing public accountants. The value of an external auditor's opinion on the financial statements of an entity is to a large measure a function of the auditor's independence. Standards relating to audit independence are constantly evolving.[11] Also, some issues relating to independence are clear while others are somewhat ambiguous.

---

[8]See the discussion in Loeb, "Teaching Students Accounting Ethics: Some Crucial Issues," pp. 318-319.

[9]For discussions of "moral responsibility" see, for example, John Ladd, "Philosophical Remarks On Professional Responsibility in Organizations," *Applied Philosophy*, Fall, 1982, especially pp. 67-68; Albert Blumenthal, *Moral Responsibility: Mankind's Greatest Need, Principles and Practical Applications of Scientific Utilitarian Ethics*, Rayline Press, Santa Ana, California, 1975, especially pp. 40-51; and Stephen E. Loeb and Suzanne N. Cory, "Whistleblowing and Management Accounting: An Approach," *Journal of Business Ethics* (forthcoming).

[10]See, for example, Casler. Also, see Loeb, "Teaching Students Accounting Ethics: Some Crucial Issues," p. 319.

[11]See, for example, R. Glen Berryman, "Auditor Independence: Its Historical Development and Some Proposals for Research," in Howard F. Stettler, editor, *Contemporary Auditing Problems: Proceedings of the 1974 Arthur Andersen/University of Kansas Symposium on Auditing Problems*, 1974, especially pp. 1-10; Casler, pp. 7-26; and Gary John Previts, *The Scope of CPA Services: A Study of the Development of the Concept of Independence and the Profession's Role in Society*, John Wiley & Sons, New York, 1985.

- *Scope of services* — closely associated with the issue of audit independence is the question of what services an external auditor should perform for a client beyond financial auditing. In other words what other services (e.g., consulting, tax return preparation and tax advice, and so on) are compatible with financial auditing. For example, at what point and for which services might a public accounting firm lose its independence by providing non-audit services to an audit client?[12]

- *Confidentiality* — when should an independent auditor remain silent about a matter and when should an independent auditor act as a "public watch dog?"[13] Further, what should an independent auditor do if the interests of two different clients are in direct conflict? For example, what should a public accounting firm do when it finds that the information developed during the audit of one client materially affects its audit of another client.[14]

- *Practice development* — in the late 1970s, following several U.S. Supreme Court decisions and pressure from the United States Department of Justice, the public accounting profession removed many ethical proscriptions relating to advertising and the solicitation of clients.[15] Public accounting firms now have a good deal of latitude as to practice development. However, public accountants still are required to keep their practice development efforts within certain limits (see Rule 502 of the AICPA code of ethics[16]). There are limits to what a public accounting firm can say or claim in an advertisement (an advertisement, for example, should not be untrue[17]). A public accounting firm should have a policy delimiting the nature and extent of its professional development activities.

- *Differences on accounting issues* — a situation can occur in which a difference exists between the manner

in which the management of an entity wishes to account for a transaction and the manner the entity's independent auditor believes the transaction should be handled. Such a situation can be important if the differences in positions of the parties can result in material differences in the financial statements. In such a situation, an entity may threaten to "shop" for another public accounting firm that will agree with management's position on the accounting issue.[18]

ETHICS COMMITTEES AND CONSULTANTS IN MEDICINE

Ethics Committees In Medicine

As noted above, many hospitals faced with complex ethical issues and/or dilemmas have formed ethics committees. An article pub-

---

[12]See, for example, Casler, pp. 23-26; Previts; and Robert Chatov, "The Possible New Shape of Accounting in the United States,"*Journal of Accounting and Public Policy,* Fall 1985, pp. 164-166, 169-170.

[13]United States *v.* Arthur Young & Company et al., 104 S. Ct. 1503 (1984).

[14]See John E. Beach, "Code of Ethics: The Professional Catch 22," *Journal of Accounting and Public Policy,* Winter 1984, pp. 311-323, for a discussion of such conflicts.

[15]Kenneth J. Bialkin, "Government Antitrust Enforcement and the Rules of Conduct," *Journal of Accountancy,* May 1987, pp. 105, 106. Bialkin, p. 106 also notes the existence of a Federal Trade Commission "study of the accounting profession" that included consideration of the "rule against advertising and solicitation." He (p. 106) notes that "while the changes to Rule 502 [relating to advertising and solicitation] were in direct response to specific challenges by the Antitrust Division [of the Department of Justice], the additional concerns expressed by the FTC inquiry should not be entirely discounted."

[16]American Institute of Certified Public Accountants (AICPA), *AICPA Professional Standards,* Volume 2, Continually Updated, ET Section 502.

[17]Ibid.

[18]See, for example, Robert J. Sack,"Commercialism in the Profession: A Threat to be Managed," *Journal of Accountancy,* October 1985, pp. 126, 128, 130; Daniel L. Goelzer, "The Opinion-Shopping Controversy," *Corporate Accounting,* Fall 1986, pp. 9-14; and Grace W. Weinstein, *The Bottom Line: Inside Accounting Today,* New American Library, New York, 1987, pp. 71-73.

lished in 1986 citing "recent surveys" indicates that "may be as high as 60 percent" of U.S. hospitals use ethics committees.[19] A note published in early 1988 indicates the extraordinary growth in hospital ethics committees in the United States from "one percent of ... hospitals" in the U.S. during 1982 to "today" more than "60 percent of hospitals with ... beds" for at least 200 patients.[20]

Reamer notes that "in hospitals ... institutional ethics committees ... have existed for a number of years to provide opportunities for health care professionals to exchange ideas about ethical issues."[21] He also indicates "institutional review boards [that] review ethical issues related to biomedical research and the use of human subjects have existed in hospitals for two decades...."[22] In the remainder of this current paper, institutional ethics committees in hospitals will be referred to as hospital ethics committees.

Reamer points out that hospital ethics committees came into prominence

> in 1976, when the New Jersey Supreme Court ruled that Karen Anne Quinlan's family and physicians should consult an ethics committee in deciding whether to remove her from life-support systems....
>
> ... [In 1983 a presidential] commission suggested that health care institutions experiment with ethics committees in an effort to improve the quality of decision making related to clinical care.... [23]

Rosner indicates that

> ...IRBs [Institutional Review Boards] developed very differently from hospital ethics committees. The role of IRBs was mandated and specified by federal regulations. Institutional review boards are widespread and generally accepted as useful by the biomedical community and the lay public.... [Hospital ethics committees] were motivated in part by a need for legal protection for medical personnel and hospitals, but the reasons for the formulation and goals of the specific committees are diverse and poorly defined.[24]

Hospital ethics committees can have a variety of functions.[25] The following six possible functions that a hospital ethics committee might possibly perform are adapted and/ or quoted from Thomasma and Monagle:[26]

1. Educational — relating to ethical issues,

2. Serving as a forum for the discussion and analysis of ethical issues by individuals from a variety of backgrounds,

3. Suggesting policies, given limited resources, to assist with the maintenance of quality services in the hospital,

4. Assist in development of announced "institutional commitments" (for example, "mission, philosophy"),

5. Assist in the "developing [of positions] regarding ethical" matters,

6. Provide assistance to an individual physician faced with an ethical dilemma.

Thomasma and Monagle assert that "... hospital ethics committees should represent a broad range of value perspectives, professional expertise, and community representation."[27] These authors suggest that such a committee might include in its composition representation from: physicians (from various specialties), nurses, "social services," ethicists, the hospital administration, and "the hospital board."[28]

---

[19]Joan McIver Gibson and Thomasine Kimbrough Kushner, "Will The 'Conscience of an Institution' Become Society's Servant?", *Hastings Center Report*, June, 1986, p. 9.

[20]Cynthia B. Cohen, "Birth Of A Network," *Hastings Center Report*, February/March, 1988, p. 11.

[21]Frederic G. Reamer, "Ethics Committees In Social Work," *Social Work*, May-June, 1987, p. 188.

[22]Ibid.

[23]Ibid.

[24]Fred Rosner, "Hospital Medical Ethics Committees: A Review of Their Development," *Journal of the American Medical Association*, May 10, 1985, p. 2694.

[25]See David C. Thomasma and John F. Monagle, "Hospital Ethics Committees: Roles, Membership, and Structure," pp. 397-403, in John F. Monagle and David C. Thomasma, eds., *Medical Ethics: A Guide for Health Professionals*, Aspen Publishers, Inc., 1988.

[26]Thomasma and Monagle, p. 398. See Thomasma and Monagle, p. 397 for the source of their material.

[27]Thomasma and Monagle, p. 403.

[28]Ibid.

Reamer notes that some social workers serve on hospital ethics committees.[29] Further, he advocates the use of ethics committees in social work noting that "... it is time for the profession to introduce forums that enable social workers to reflect on the [ethical] issues carefully and systematically."[30]

Gibson and Kushner in an article published in 1986 note that "ethics committees today are more solidly established than in the past, and many have achieved the status of permanent standing committee of the medical staff."[31] However, hospital ethics committees are not without problems.[32] In the next section some of these problems are reviewed.

Some Possible Problems With Hospital Ethics Committees

In a recent discussion concerning hospital ethics committees with an attending physician practicing at a community hospital on the east coast of the United States, I was told that this physician's hospital had established an ethics committee. However, after involvement in two cases, the committee had ceased being used because it was considered too complex, too time consuming for a physician, and possibly interfering with the professional judgment of a physician. Some similar sentiments were noted in an article by Dr. Mark Siegler.[33] The latter notes that "such [hospital ethics] committees may expand the number of participants in the decision from those directly involved in the case to an unmanageable collection of noninvolved professional and moral 'experts'...."[34] Further, Siegler expresses concern about the effect of the physician relinquishing some of his or her "medical responsibility" for a patient to a hospital ethics committee.[35] Additionally, Siegler worries that "these committees ... may have serious conflicts of interest between their responsibility to the individual patient and their efforts to minimize hospital risk, to develop sound hospital policies, and perhaps even to allocate economic resources most efficiently."[36] On a different tack, Gibson and Kushner express concern that hospital ethics committees generally are not provided adequate resources.[37]

Ethics Consultants

Recently, some individuals have begun to specialize as ethics consultants to provide advice to health related professionals and institutions. An editorial in *The Lancet* states that "bioethics committees in the USA ... may include ... perhaps a representative of the new profession of ethics consultants."[38] A note published in the December 1985 issue of the *Hastings Center Report*, mentioned some of the findings of a National Institute of Health poll of ethics consultants.[39] Of 38 individuals participating in this study, the largest number had a "philosophy" background and the next largest number reported a "theology/divinity" background.[40] Also, Purtilo describes an example of an ethical dilemma in which a physician or hospital may request the assistance of an ethics consultant.[41] LaPuma et al. discuss an "ethics consultation service"[42] at one particular hospital.[43] Additionally, the legal profession and the process it serves uses

[29]Reamer, p. 189.

[30]Ibid., p. 191.

[31]Gibson and Kushner, p. 10.

[32]The existence of problems is suggested by Gibson and Kushner, p. 10 as well as others such as Mark Siegler, "Ethics Committees: Decisions By Bureaucracy," *Hastings Center Report*, June, 1986.

[33]Mark Siegler, "Ethics Committees: Decisions By Bureaucracy."

[34]Ibid., p. 22.

[35]Ibid.

[36]Ibid.

[37]Gibson and Kushner, p. 10.

[38]Editorial, "Who's For Bioethics Committees?", *The Lancet*, May 3, 1986, p. 1016.

[39]Bormel, p. 2.

[40]Ibid.

[41]Ruth B. Purtilo, "Ethics Consultations In The Hospital," *The New England Journal of Medicine*, October 11, 1984, p. 983.

[42]John LaPuma, Carol B. Stocking, Marc D. Silverstein, Andrea DiMartini, and Mark Siegler, "An Ethical Consultation Service in a Teaching Hospital: Utilization and Evaluation," *The Journal of the American Medical Association*, August 12, 1988, p. 808.

[43]Ibid., pp. 808-811.

ethics consultants (experts).[44] For example, ethics experts have testified in court cases.[45]

ETHICS COMMITTEES AND/OR CONSULTANTS WITHIN PUBLIC ACCOUNTING FIRMS

Public Accounting Firm Ethics Committee

Should public accounting firms have ethics committees? If one responds positively to such a question, a number of other issues then arise. In this section the issue of possible functions of a firm and/or office ethics committee is addressed. This is followed by a discussion of the form an ethics committee might take and the possible composition of the membership of such committees.

Functions of Committee

Earlier in this paper it was noted that independent public accountants practice within an institutional framework of public accounting offices and firms. Public accounting firms may have procedures or policies relating to ethical issues. For example, the AICPA in *Statement on Quality Control Standards No. 1* suggests the establishment of "policies and procedures" relating to "independence."[46] However, I am not aware of existing firm or office ethics committees in public accounting that perform functions parallel to those that hospital ethics committees may perform or that have an interdisciplinary composition.[47]

Functions that a public accounting firm ethics committee might perform include: (1) helping develop and periodically reviewing a formal ethical philosophy for the firm; (2) coordinating ethics education for the firm; (3) proposing firm policies relating to ethics; and (4) responding in a timely manner to ethical issues and/or dilemmas that are brought to the ethics committee by a partner and/or members of the professional staff. These functions are based on and are parallel to some of the functions that were mentioned earlier that a hospital ethics committee might perform.[48]

An ethics committee could help a public accounting firm in developing a formal firm ethical philosophy and then in periodically assessing the firm's progress under such a philosophy. Research relating to professional firms — both in public accounting[49] and law[50]

— has indicated that professional firms can have different "ethical climates." Generally, firm and/or office management will likely set such a climate — probably more reactively than proactively.[51] An ethics committee could

[44] Peter G. McAllen and Richard Delgado, "Moral Experts in the Courtroom," *The Hastings Center Report*, February, 1984, pp. 27-34; John J. Paris, "An Ethicist Takes The Stand," *The Hastings Center Report*, February, 1984, pp. 32-33; and Michael S. Yesley, "The Moral Expert Witness: Function or Footnote?", *The Hastings Center Report*, February, 1984, pp. 28-29.

[45] McAllen and Delgado, pp. 27-34; Paris, pp. 32-33; and Yesley, pp. 28-29.

[46] American Institute of Certified Public Accountants, *Statement on Quality Control Standards No. 1*, "System of Quality Control for a CPA Firm," American Institute of Certified Public Accountants, 1979, para. 7a.

[47] An article published several years ago (The Center for Business Ethics at Bentley College, "Are Corporations Institutionalizing Ethics?", *Journal of Business Ethics*, April 1986) reported the results of a survey of major corporations regarding ethics. That study (The Center for Business Ethics at Bentley College, p. 87) reported that 40 companies had responded that they use ethics committees in some manner (the article mentioned some of the tasks these committees were assigned). Patrick E. Murphy, "Implementing Business Ethics," *Journal of Business Ethics*, December, 1988, in discussing business ethics advocates the use of ethics committees in businesses (p. 909). Murphy, p. 909 mentions one company which he reports has assigned such a committee the tasks of "interpreting, clarifying, communicating and [adjudicating] the company's code [of ethics]."

[48] See footnote 26 for the source of the ideas for these functions. Some of the tasks of an ethics committee in a business mentioned in The Center for Business Ethics at Bentley College (p. 87) are somewhat similar to these suggested functions.

[49] Stephen Edward Loeb, "A Behavioral Study of CPA Ethics," Ph. D. dissertation, University of Wisconsin, 1970, pp. 185-197.

[50] Jerome E. Carlin, *Lawyers' Ethics: A Survey of the New York City Bar*, Russell Sage Foundation, New York, 1966, Chapter 6.

[51] The National Commission on Fraudulent Financial Reporting (p. 32) recognizes the importance of "top management" in setting "tone." In discussing public companies, the National Commission on Fraudulent Financial Reporting states "the tone set by top management — the corporate environment or culture within which financial reporting occurs — is the most important factor contributing to the integrity of the financial reporting process" (p. 32). Later in its report the National Commission on Fraudulent Financial Reporting notes (p. 56) that "the tone that top managements of public accounting firms set is just as important in the firms as that set by top managements in public companies." Also, see the discussion in Murphy, p. 910.

suggest that an office or a firm proactively establish a formal ethical philosophy, and in turn, the ethical climate of the office or firm. If a firm or office were to develop a formal ethical philosophy, an ethics committee might periodically assist in an evaluation as to how the firm or office was progressing under such an ethical philosophy.

In the dynamic environment of current public accounting practice, continuing education is needed, and, in fact, is mandated by the AICPA By-laws, the requirements of the AICPA Division for CPA Firms, and the requirements to practice in many jurisdictions.[52] Ethics education should be an important aspect of a public accountant's professional development. One study, for example, found attentiveness to ethical issues to be an important factor in explaining variation of ethical behavior in public accounting practice.[53] Further, as noted earlier in this paper, the Treadway Commission recommended that ethics be a part of a public accountant's continuing education. Specifically, that commission recommended

As part of their continuing professional education, independent public accountants, ... should study the forces and opportunities that contribute to fraudulent financial reporting, the risk factors that may indicate its occurrence, and the relevant ethical and technical standards.[54] [emphasis in original].

Consequently, a firm ethics committee could serve as a facilitating mechanism within a public accounting firm to coordinate ethics related continuing education and to provide assurance that such continuing education is consistent with the firm's ethical philosophy.

An ethics committee could propose firm policies relating to specific ethical issues and/or dilemmas. As suggested earlier, not all matters relating to ethics that occur in public accounting have clear answers or solutions. Further, a firm or office may wish to set ethical standards that are higher than those required by appropriate authorities[55] (for example, a firm might not wish to advertise or might wish to have independence standards that are higher than those required by a professional association[56] or the Securities and Exchange Commission[57]).

Additionally, an ethics committee could, on a timely basis, assist partner or professional staff in the recognition of and/or solution of ethical issues and/or dilemmas that might arise in practice. An ethics committee could assist in what Callahan refers to as "recognizing ethical issues."[58] In the complexity of the current business environment, a public accountant may benefit from a committee with which he or she can discuss and confirm the ethical nature of an issue and/or dilemma. This may be especially important given the limited training in ethics currently provided by most college or university accounting programs.[59] Further, an ethics com-

---

[52]As to the AICPA By-laws see AICPA, *AICPA Professional Standards*, Volume 2, BL Sections 230 and 230R; as to the AICPA Division for CPA Firms, see, for example, Walter G. Kell, William C. Boynton, and Richard E. Ziegler, *Modern Auditing, Fourth Edition*, John Wiley & Sons, New York, 1989, pp. 18-19; and as to practice requirements, see, for example, Kell, Boynton, and Ziegler, p. 21 and Weinstein, pp. 77-89.

[53]Loeb, "A Behavioral Study of CPA Ethics," pp. 173-176.

[54]National Commission on Fraudulent Financial Reporting, p. 85.

[55]Earlier in this paper it was suggested that a public accounting firm might wish in some situations to have its professionals follow standards that were higher than those required by a professional association.

[56] See, for example, Donald H. Taylor and G. William Glezen, *Auditing: Integrated Concepts and Procedures, Fourth Edition*, John Wiley & Sons, 1988, pp. 84-85 and David Lavin, "Perceptions of the Independence of the Auditor," *The Accounting Review*, January 1976, pp. 41-50 for discussion of different positions the AICPA and the Securities and Exchange Commission (SEC) can have on an ethics issue.

[57]This possibility was confirmed to the author in a conversation with a staff member of the SEC.

[58]Daniel Callahan, "Goals In The Teaching Of Ethics," in Daniel Callahan and Sissela Bok, eds., *Ethics Teaching In Higher Education*, Plenum Press, New York, 1980, p. 65.

[59]See, for example, Loeb, "Teaching Students Accounting Ethics: Some Crucial Issues," pp. 316-317; National Commission on Fraudulent Financial Reporting, p. 82; Jean C. Wyer, Primary Researcher, Abstract of "Fraudulent Financial Reporting: The Potential for Educational Impact" in National Commission on Fraudulent Financial Reporting, *Report of the National Commission on Fraudulent Financial Reporting*, October 1987, p. 108, and Jeffrey R. Cohen and Laurie W. Pant, "Accounting Educators' Perceptions of Ethics in the Curriculum," *Issues in Accounting Education*, Spring 1989.

mittee could suggest alternative solutions that are within the ethical philosophy or ethical policies that the firm or office had set in conjunction with its ethics committee. Thus, an ethics committee could facilitate the solution to an ethical issue and/or dilemma without referring the matter to an individual or group outside the public accounting firm. Additionally, the ethics committee could assist in determining when an issue and/or dilemma should be referred to an individual or group outside the firm.

There is another function an ethics committee could possibly serve — that of ombudsman for a public accounting firm.[60] In such a role an ethics committee could provide a service for the public accounting firm's professional staff, clients, and third-party users of the firm's audit reports. For example, an ethics committee could serve as a mechanism for a professional staff member to appeal a decision of an immediate superior.[61] Thus, the ethics committee could assist an individual staff member solve what that person believes is an ethical dilemma. An ethics committee could also serve as an additional vehicle (beyond, for example, the engagement partner) within a public accounting firm where a client or user of a firm's audit reports could bring a complaint concerning the firm or a firm policy. This would give a public accounting firm an additional opportunity to resolve an issue without the other party taking the issue outside the firm.

Organization of Ethics Committee

The organization of a public accounting firm ethics committee likely would be a function of the size and nature of the public accounting firm's practice. National firms might have a firm-wide committee with possibly committees at regional and/or local office level. In such a situation, local or regional committees might report to the firm-wide committee. Such a decentralized organization structure might provide a more timely response to local office issues. Regional firms with multiple offices might have firm-wide and/or local office ethics committees. Local firms, with one office, could have a firm ethics committee within the office.

To be of value, an ethics committee in a public accounting firm would need access to and the support of the level of management to which it reports. For example, in a national firm, such a firm-wide committee might report to the firm managing partner and/or managing committee. In a local firm an ethics committee might report to the managing partner, a limited number of partners, or all partners. Management support should be such that the committee is able to operate independently within the firm and committee members are comfortable in providing objective opinions and advice.

Composition of Committee

Similar to a hospital ethics committee a public accounting firm ethics committee might be interdisciplinary. Thus, such a committee might, for example, contain some partners of the firm, professional staff, firm in-house legal counsel, external legal counsel, and perhaps, one or more ethicists. As much as possible, the partners and professional staff who serve on such a committee should be representative

---

[60] One source, Bob Quilitch and Kevin Christensen, "Using An Ombudsman And A Rights Committee To Handle Client Complaints," *Hospital & Community Psychiatry*, February 1981, pp. 127-129 describes the use of an ombudsman. Michael Brody, "Listen To Your Whistleblower," *Fortune*, November 24, 1986, pp. 77-78, discusses the use of this concept in U.S. corporations. Jonathan P. West, "The Role of the Ombudsman in Resolving Conflicts," in James S. Bowman and Frederick A. Elliston, eds., *Ethics, Government, and Public Policy: A Reference Guide*, Greenwood Press, New York, 1988, pp. 169-200 discusses the use of the ombudsman concept in government. See also The Center for Business Ethics at Bentley College, p. 87.

[61] American Institute of Certified Public Accountants, *Statement on Auditing Standards [SAS] No. 22*, "Planning and Supervision," American Institute of Certified Public Accountants, 1978, para. 12 seems to suggest that a mechanism should exist for dealing with possible "differences" relating to "accounting and auditing issues" that might arise "among" the members of the professional staff who are performing an independent audit. Paragraph 12 of *SAS No. 22* was "renumbered" paragraph 14 as a result of an amendment to *SAS No. 22* by American Institute of Certified Public Accountants, *Statement on Auditing Standards [SAS] No. 48*, "The Effects of Computer Processing on the Examination of Financial Statements," American Institute of Certified Public Accountants, 1984, para. 1.

of the various services that the public accounting firm provides clients (audit, tax, consulting, and so on) and the various industries, if any, in which the firm specializes. Such an interdisciplinary committee would bring together individuals with a variety of backgrounds and provide the firm with a variety of views on ethical issues.[62] Ethicists, although not trained in accounting, could provide assistance in addressing an ethical issue and/or dilemma. Legal counsel could provide advice on the legal aspects of an ethical issue and/or dilemma. The actual composition would likely depend on the size of the firm, the geographic dispersion of the firm, and the nature of the firm's practice.

Ethics Consultants

Many of the reasons advanced for the use of ethics committees could be cited to support the employment of an ethics consultant or consultants in public accounting firms. Depending on the size of a firm, the geographic dispersion of the firm, and the nature of the firm's practice, the consultants could be used at local, regional, or firm-wide levels. Such consultants could serve on ethics committees and also, on a day-to-day basis, serve as advisors to the partners and professional staff on ethical issues and/or dilemmas that may arise. Firm or office ethics committees would likely meet periodically. Consequently, in the interim, ethical consultants could provide quick responses to ethical issues and/or dilemmas that arise.[63]

CONCLUSIONS

In recent years, the medical profession's development of hospital ethics committees and use of ethics consultants provide interesting concepts that may be useful to the public accounting profession. The concepts of ethics committees and/or ethics consultants in public accounting are likely not without problems. However, there are a number of potentially positive functions that an ethics committee and/or ethics consultants might provide to the public accounting profession.

The use of ethics committees and/or consultants by the public accounting profession might result in more ethics education within public accounting firms as well as more discussion of ethical issues by individuals in public accounting practice. Additionally, public accounting firms that have informal policy statements or an informal ethical philosophy might develop formal policy statements on ethics or a formal ethical philosophy. Firms without either informal or formal policy statements or an ethical philosophy might consider developing one or both. Public accountants would have more assistance in the recognition and solution of ethical issues and/or dilemmas. Care would have to be exercised so that the appropriate public accountants, not ethics committees and/or ethics consultants, actually make decisions and establish policy. Further, care would also need to be taken so that decision-making would not become overly complex or unwieldy.[64] However, the potential benefits from using ethics committees and/or consultants mentioned earlier in this paper suggest that the public accounting profession should consider both concepts.

---

[62] See Thomasma and Monagle, p. 403.

[63] See the discussion in Purtilo, p. 984.

[64] These are the types of potential problems that, as noted earlier, have been raised in relation to hospital ethics committees. Thus, the experiences of the medical profession with hospital ethics committees and/or ethics consultants should be considered if the public accounting firms were to utilize ethics committees and/or consultants.

3

Examples of Ethical Issues and Cases

Chapter 2 examined the general issue of ethics in accounting and some of the potential solutions that could be used to socialize accounting students to a greater standard of ethics. This chapter examines examples of ethical issues confronting the profession that are in urgent need of solutions, and reviews famous cases where the ethical standards were not well respected. The special ethical issue of insider trading is presented in the Appendix to this chapter.

ETHICAL ISSUES

The Dilemma of Peer Review

The question is how to regulate the activities of CPA firms and ensure that the quality of the services offered is adequate, with the ultimate purpose of protecting the public from exploitation and inadequate service by accountants. Regulation may be exercised by the government (government regulation), the private sector (private regulation), or the profession itself (peer regulation).

Government regulation of accounting includes the laws, regulations, licensing requirements, courts, legislatures, commissions, and legal procedures used to protect the public from fraud. It has not been proved to be an effective deterrent of unacceptable behavior. Private regulation includes all of the professional requirements used to meet the profession's standards and to provide quality services as good as those provided by the competition. Private regulation uses the market factor as a guide and a judge for the quality of the services provided by the accounting professional. Finally, peer regulation includes voluntary rules established by the members of the accounting profession to improve the quality of the services rendered. It uses peers as a guide and a judge of the quality of services by the accountants. In short, the quality of the services offered by accounting professionals is either evaluated by the market in the case of private regulation or by peers in the case of peer regulation. It is affected by government regulation only in those cases where the accountants have failed to meet the lowest standards acceptable to the community, are charged with wrongdoing, and are brought to trial. If they are found guilty, government regulations provide for various forms of punishment, including possible loss of the privilege to practice.

Some claim that peer and private regulation are not enough to ensure the quality of services provided by the accounting profession and that government regulation should be used. This threat came in 1978 with the introduction of HR. 13175, the so-called Moss Bill (named after John E. Moss, former chairman of the House Commerce Committee's Subcommittee on Oversight and Investigations), which called mainly for the enactment of the National Organization of Securities and Exchange Commission Accountancy. The bill, officially titled the Public Accountancy Regulatory Act, called for action

to establish a National Organization of Securities and Exchange Commission Accountancy, to require that independent public accounting firms be registered with such an Organization in order to furnish audit reports with respect to financial statements filed with the Securities and Exchange Commission, to authorize disciplinary action against such accounting firms and principals in such firms.

It claimed that the accounting profession has not established and appears unable to establish a self-regulatory environment. It also authorized the proposed Accountancy Commission to regulate the quality of services provided by accounting professionals and to impose various sanctions where necessary. Among its provisions were the following:

1. Only one member of the new agency's five-person board could be from a major accounting firm.
2. The Accountancy Commission would review the work of individual accounting firms every three years, checking for "acts or omissions" by such accounting firms or principals in such firms that are contrary to the interest of the investor public.
3. CPA firms' legal liability would be greatly increased, making them accountable for negligence even without evidence of fraud or intentional conduct.

Fortunately for the accounting profession, the Moss Bill never passed the House. The threat did not, however, go unnoticed. The AICPA decided to act to prove that self-regulation or peer regulation is a viable alternative. It first allowed CPAs, in addition to other individuals, to join the Institute. More specifically, it created two sections: the Private Companies Practice Section (PCPS) for small accounting firms serving mostly private companies, and the SEC Practice Section (SECPS) for those firms serving companies registered with the SEC. It also required that in the future all firms in both sections undergo independent peer review to be conducted every three years. In addition to establishing the system of peer reviews, the AICPA decided that the SECPS would be monitored by the Public Oversight Board (POB), comprised of people including, but not limited to, former public officials, lawyers, bankers, securities industry executives, educators, economists, and business executives.

Central to the AICPA innovation is the peer-review requirement, thus keeping the oversight of professional practice within the profession. The peer review is essentially a form of quality control by peers. In general, a firm is provided the name of available reviewers from a bank of reviewers from which it may select a review team. A firm may also choose a "firm-on-firm" review by selecting another CPA firm to review its quality control. In the latter case, a quality-control review panel, selected by the SEC Practice Section peer-review committee, is appointed to oversee the review.

The review itself is similar to an audit. In general, it consists of the following testing procedures:

1. Reviewing the firm's quality-control documents, manuals, checklists, and so on. In effect, the 1979 AICPA Statement on Quality Control Standards No. 1, "System of Quality Control for a CPA Firm," states that "to provide itself with reasonable assurance of meeting its responsibility to provide professional services that conform with professional standards, a firm shall have a system of quality control" (para. 2).

2. Testing the compliance with the documented policies and procedures by interviewing key and selected staff people; reviewing personnel files, administration files, and other evidential matter; or reviewing engagement work papers and reports.

3. Holding an exit conference with the directors of the firm to discuss their findings and to report (a) any significant deficiencies in the quality-control procedures of the firm, (b) any noncompliance with the documented policies and procedures, and (c) any noncompliance with membership requirements of either SECPS or PCPS.

4. Sending a written report and a letter of comments to the firm's managing partner and to the public file at the Institute. The comments on quality-control system design and compliance that seem to attract the peer reviewers' attention focus on categories such as the following: acceptance and continuance of clients, independence, hiring, advancement, professional development, assignment of personnel, consultation, supervision in engagement planning, supervision in engagement performance, supervision in engagement review, and inspection. In all of these categories the reviewers rely on the profession's standards as a basis for evaluation. As an example, Price Waterhouse's letter to Touche Ross concerning its peer-review findings follows:

October 10, 1979
To the Partners of Touche Ross & Co.

We have reviewed the system of quality control for the accounting and auditing practice of Touche Ross & Co. in effect for the year ended March 31, 1979, and have issued our report dated October 10, 1979. This letter should be read in conjunction with that report.

Our review was for the purpose of reporting upon your system of quality control and your compliance with it and with the membership requirements of the SEC Practice Section of the AICPA Division for CPA Firms (the Section). Our review was performed in accordance with the standards promulgated by the peer review committee of the Section; however, our review would not necessarily disclose all weaknesses in the system or lack of compliance with it or with the membership requirements of the Section because our review was based on selective tests.

There are inherent limitations that should be recognized in considering the potential effectiveness of any system of quality control. In the performance of most control procedures, departures can result from misunderstanding of instructions, mistakes of judgment, carelessness, and other personal factors. Projection of any evaluation of a system of quality control to future periods is subject to the risk that the procedures may become inadequate because of changes in conditions or that the degree of compliance with the procedures may deteriorate.

During the course of our review, we noted the following areas which we believe could be improved to further strengthen your system of quality control:

Improved Documentation of Key Issues Considered and Audit Work Performed.

It is the firm's policy to require for every audit engagement a complete record of audit procedures performed and the facts and rationale for key judgments and conclusions. We believe documentation in the engagement record could be improved in the following areas:

- The facts, discussion of the issues considered, consultations, if any, with designated local office consultants and reviewers, and related reasoning for the conclusions reached on significant accounting, auditing and reporting matters
- Procedures performed when using work of outside specialists and internal auditors
- Effect of EDP control reviews on audit scope
- Procedures followed in limited reviews of interim financial information
- Communications between offices participating in a multi-office engagement

We recommend that the importance of appropriate documentation procedures be reemphasized to the professional staff.

Codify Consultation Policies.

The firm's technical inquiry policy requires consultation with the Executive Office Accounting and Auditing Staff in specific instances, as well as in cases where additional consultation outside the local office consultation process is considered necessary. We believe compliance with the firm's consultation policies could be improved by codifying in one firm publication the instances where additional consulting is appropriate or required.

Improve Compliance with Firm Policies on Use of the Work and Reports of Other Auditors.

The firm's written policies on the use of the work and reports of other auditors are reasonable and consistent with authoritative guidance. Firm policy requires timely approval of the National Director of Accounting and Auditing before accepting certain engagements involving other auditors and approval of the Executive Office Accounting and Auditing Technical Staff for exceptions from performing specified audit procedures concerned with the work of other auditors. Based on our review we recommend that the firm review its compliance with firm policy particularly in the areas of (1) acceptance of principal auditor responsibility, (2) reference in the firm's report to the work of other auditors, (3) the performance of appropriate procedures for supervising the work of other auditors, and (4) documentation of other auditor independence.

Improve Compliance with Firm Policy on Client Representation Letters.

The firm's policy requires that representation letters obtained from clients conform with the model letter supplied as a part of the firm's reference material and that deletions, except in certain cases, from specified standard paragraphs be cleared with the Executive Office Accounting and Auditing Technical Staff.

Emphasize Importance of Timely Preparation of Staff Performance Reports.

Firm policy requires timely preparation of a formal written staff evaluation report for each staff member assigned to an engagement of appropriate length and complexity. We recommend that the firm emphasize to the appropriate responsible personnel the importance to the firm's overall quality procedures of timely evaluation of staff performance on quality engagements.

* * * * *

The foregoing matters were considered in determining our opinion set forth in our report dated October 10, 1979, and this letter does not change that report.

Price Waterhouse & Co.

When the review is not favorable, sanctions from the appropriate section may be imposed. The possible sanctions considered in the 1983 SECPS Manual include:

1. Requiring corrective measures by the firm, including consideration by the firm of appropriate actions with respect to individual-firm personnel
2. Additional requirements for continuing professional education
3. Accelerated or special peer reviews
4. Admonishments, censures, or reprimands
5. Monetary fines
6. Suspension from memberships
7. Expulsion from membership

Whether the outcome is favorable or unfavorable, peer review provides various benefits besides the major benefit of keeping government regulation off the backs of CPA firms. Among the tangible benefits are the improvement of quality control before or after the review itself; the educational process created before, and during, the review; and the improvement in the morale resulting from the discovery and correction of any material failure to perform in compliance with the firm's own quality control document. In addition, the cost of peer review is manageable. The SEC Practice Section's rates range from $35 to $90 an hour, depending on the size of the firm reviewed. The PCPS has set one rate for review captains, $45 an hour, and one rate for reviewers, $35 an hour. For a one-office firm with three partners and five professional staff, the total fee for the review would be roughly $2,400 to $3,300, which amounts to an additional cost to do business of only $800 to $1,100 and a guaranteed improvement in quality control.

Why then is the peer review program being criticized? Some of the arguments follow:

1. Peer review might seem to be something that all public accountants would welcome to avoid the feared alternative of government regulation. However, although the large CPA firms have shown a high degree of acceptance and voluntarism, smaller CPA firms have reacted mostly with either apathy or hostility. Their response is based on the belief that, first, the peer review is going to lead to unnecessary additional expenses and new procedures that are most likely irrelevant to the nature of their practices, and that, second, the peer review is of more value to larger CPA firms. But the small practitioners need the peer review system even more than the larger firms, and in most cases the benefits outweigh the costs.

2. Some small as well as large CPA firms are reluctant to let an outside observer, whether or not it is a competitor, evaluate the adequacy of their quality-control policies. One may wonder whether the threat is not the outside observer but the possibility of a qualified report. But these firms should realize that, with adequate preparation, a peer review is much easier to survive than a loss of clients or, in the worst case, a loss of privilege to practice as a result of an inadequate job. Besides, peer review is bound to inspire investors' confidence in the accountants' high professional standards and competency.

3. To date no official sanctions have been imposed to the AICPA SECPS Executive Committee. The most drastic step taken by the peer review committee is to refuse to accept the review report until an appropriate response or modification has been made. What emerges from this behavior is that the SECPS and the PCPS appear to be avoiding tough actions. The whole peer review exercise could be easily misinterpreted as mutual back scratching.

4. Membership in the SECPS and PCPS was not made mandatory by the AICPA. The argument most often used has been that such requirements should be imposed by the federal government and are not the province of a

self-regulatory profession. Although the arguments may have some conceptual merits, the credibility of the peer review system, the integrity of the profession, and the soundness of the quality control may rest on a mandatory membership. It is, however, appropriate to note that the AICPA is taking steps to ensure compliance with quality control. Although the Statement on Quality Standards No. 1, "System of Quality Control for a CPA Firm," does not specifically refer to documentation of compliance, a proposed interpretation, "Documentation of Compliance with a System of Quality Control," advises CPA firms that documentation would ordinarily be required to demonstrate a firm's compliance with its policies and procedures for quality control. That is a very positive step toward making potential peer reviews more effective.

5. There is finally the issue of confidentiality, given that peer review committees' responses to unfavorable reports have been so far nonpublic. As a consequence, the credibility of the program is tarnished. The reason for confidentiality is generally supported by the complexity of the situation involving private rights, the public interest, the litigious nature of the American society, and the misconceptions about the role, rights, and responsibilities of auditors. Although this reason may be legitimate, there is an urgent need for the profession to find a means of publicizing its sanctions for the sake of the credibility of the peer review program in general and self-regulation in particular.

Professionalism versus Commercialism in Accounting

Professionalism in any field is a voluntary commitment to achieve excellence. The existence of soundly conceived or well-written rules of conduct may act as a check for professionalism in a profession. But it is the commitment more than the adherence to rules that defines professionalism. In accounting, professionalism is a commitment on the part of all accountants, preparers, and auditors to uphold both the technical and ethical standards of conduct characterized by a high degree of objectivity and integrity. The main result of professionalism is credible financial reporting. To ensure the maintenance of professionalism in the conduct of certified public accountants, the AICPA has devised a code of professional ethics that prescribes the desirable attitude and conduct of its members.

Although professionalism is at the core of a credible profession, commercialism may be dictated by the nature and special conditions of the market forces. In effect, the changing environment in accounting has led the CPA firms toward more profitable commercial routes that may jeopardize their professionalism. The specter of commercialism arises because of the following developments:

1. CPA firms are facing a competitive practice environment where the auditing segment of practice is either stabilizing or declining. To offset the de-

clining revenues from the audit function, firms have expanded their areas of activities beyond those considered to be the traditional activities of the profession. By doing so they have risked their identity as professionals. The basic question is whether the CPA firms can offer a financial supermarket of services without sacrificing objectivity, independence, and ultimately their status as professionals.

2. Large CPA firms have begun absorbing smaller firms and expanding by opening operating offices in most U.S. cities and establishing affiliations on a worldwide basis. These firms have resorted to aggressive techniques to draw business in a very competitive environment. As a result, a wider gap has been created between them and the remainder of the profession; competitive rivalry rather than camaraderie has become the rule.

3. With the increase in size and the large scope of services offered, the larger firms do not operate any more as professional partnerships but more as any large, divisionalized corporate enterprise. New characteristics include central management, line divisional officers, a board of directors, and a chief executive. The small firms have remained as true partnerships managed by their partners. As a result of these new organizational and management structures, the large CPA firms have found themselves pursuing a continuous goal of increasing revenues and market share and turning the profession into a true commercial business. The main characteristic of a true profession, which is to put unselfish service to clients and the public ahead of income considerations, does not necessarily apply to large CPA firms.

4. With the increase in size and the larger scope of services offered, the larger firms have found themselves offering services and agreeing to financial arrangements that may violate those permissible under the rules of conduct. As an example, a CPA may be offered compensation in the form of commissions for the sale of products or services of others. As another example, some CPAs found themselves implicated in abuses in the application of accounting principles. The result of these new attitudes and conduct of CPA firms is such an increase in lawsuits with monumental claims for damages that large CPA firms have begun building in-house legal departments to cope with all the litigation. This situation has led in part to an erosion of the confidence that the public places in the independence and objectivity of the profession as a whole.

Given this state of affairs, the accounting profession finds itself grappling with the specter of commercialism and yearning for a return to more professionalism. An ideal first step is a revision of the code of ethics to deal with all of the new issues facing the nature of accounting practice. The new rules of conduct should deal with those situations in which the CPA is performing nonattest, nonindependent financial services. The environment in which these services are performed is sufficiently different to warrant a specifically delineated code of conduct that represents a "professional" approach to performing these services. The revision of the code of ethics may not be enough, because the mere prohibition of practices such as advertising, competitive bidding, and contingent fees does not really establish barriers that will effectively deter CPA firms from competing for clients who need and want financial services in addition to an audit, a review, or a compilation. In fact, the profession understood this when it dropped its bans on advertising and solicitation.

The second step, then, is to ensure that those entering the profession possess high levels of skill and expertise. These new entrants have to be taught that their primary role is to protect the public from anything that may jeopardize credible financial reporting.

The third step is to ask each CPA firm to attest that it is following specific guidelines for matters such as soliciting clients and bidding for audit engagements; ensuring that adequate work is performed regardless of fee; advising management, audit committees, and boards of directors on the most appropriate possibility from among reporting choices; setting growth goals affecting the audit practice; and taking positions on FASB proposals independent of client viewpoints. The viability of the guidelines of each CPA firm will then be tested through the peer review process. This last step was proposed in a 1984 address of voluntary commitment, which is the essence of professionalism.

Specialization in the Profession

Two questions in specialization are of prime importance to the profession: (1) Should the accounting profession follow the trend of medicine, law, and engineering and allow its practicing members to designate their specialties? (2) Should the non-CPA specialists used in the CPA firms be given an associate-membership classification in the AICPA?

The answer to the first question is a resounding yes. There is an information explosion in accounting, and no individual CPA can be fully competent in all areas of the accounting function. Specialization is unavoidable in most disciplines and particularly in accounting. Not only is there an information explosion but also an increase in the variety of services demanded from CPA firms. A de facto specialization is already taking place in most CPA firms. It takes the form of a natural segmentation of the typical large CPA firm into audit, tax, and management-advisory-services departments. In fact, CPAs are specializing in two ways. One specialization is by type of client or industry. The next step is a recognition of specialists by officially accrediting them. On September 25, 1974, the Committee on Scope and Structure of the AICPA listed two important benefits of recognition of specialists.

The provision of such recognition would be an incentive to excellence. . . . [M]eeting a set of standards formulated by one's professional colleagues would be a source of personal satisfaction. . . . [It] would demand a vigorous pursuit of knowledge and that, in turn, should benefit the public by insuring an even higher quality of service.

Such recognition, . . . would underscore the point that the specialized areas are legitimately within the profession's scope of services. It would, in effect, validate what is presently being done in practice; . . . what is being done is what ought to be done if firms are to remain fully capable of meeting society's needs.

So accreditation of specialists seems to be the next logical step in the professional evolution process.

The important question is: What is meant by accreditation? It is the public labeling, by an official body, of the competence to practice in accounting. This type of labeling would be facilitated by the present classification of accounting in accepted separate activities. One proposed classification goes as follows:

Accounting and Auditing

1. Auditing and certifying financial reports for management, stockholders, and creditors
2. SEC registrations and regulatory agency reporting
3. Expert testimony in lawsuits
4. Discussions with creditors
5. Bankruptcies

Taxes

1. Preparation of tax returns
2. Defense of returns before the Treasury
3. Obtaining advance rulings
4. Income tax planning
5. Estate planning with attorneys
6. Allocation of taxes and their effect on profit and loss statements

Management Services

1. Systems and work flow
2. EDP feasibility studies
3. Programming the computer
4. Internal reorganization
5. Analysis of material produced by EDP
6. Budgeting

Although the list is not exhaustive, it suggests the type of specialization that may be given in the accounting profession. In fact, Justin Davidson, CPA and former dean of the Business School at Cornell University, proposed the following form labels to be added to the CPA designation: CPE – Certified Public Examiner, CPTA – Certified Public Tax Adviser, CPC – Certified Public Consultant, and CPG – Certified Public Generalist.

The CPE designation would mean that the CPA has chosen to practice primarily, but not exclusively, in the examination function: accounting, auditing, and attest. The CPTA designation would mean that the CPA is an expert in the tax function. The CPC designation would mean that the CPA has chosen to practice primarily, but not exclusively, in the management-services area. The CPG designation would mean that the CPA is a CPA generalist, the accounting equivalent of the family doctor. He or she has familiarity with and the ability to solve routine problems in all areas of accounting practice.

There are various advantages and disadvantages to specialization in the accounting profession. Among the advantages cited in the literature and in practice are the following:

1. Not accrediting specialists may lead anyone to claim to be a specialist.
2. Accrediting specialists confers status and motivates performance.
3. Accrediting specialists promotes cooperation within the profession.
4. Accrediting specialists protects the public.

Among the disadvantages cited in the literature and in practice are the following:

1. Accrediting specialists promotes narrowness.
2. Accrediting specialists is difficult and costs time and money.
3. Accrediting specialists is not accurate for all time.
4. Accrediting specialists creates many internal (within accounting firms) as well as external problems.
5. Accrediting specialists favors large firms that are in a better position to maintain a group of specialists and may tend to downgrade the small CPA firm.

The trend is for accreditation spurred by the demand of the public for some form of labeling. In fact, the drive toward accreditation has already made some material progress. Various new professional designations have emerged to meet the need for specialization. Examples include (1) the Certificate in Management Accounting (CMA) designation administered by the Institute of Management Accounting of the National Association of Accountants, (2) the Certified Cost Analyst (CCA) designation administered by the Institute of Cost Analysis, (3) the Certified Internal Auditor (CIA) designation administered by the Institute of Internal Auditors, and (4) the Certificate in Data Processing (CDP) designation administered by the Data Processing Management Association.

If the trend is clearly in favor of accredited specialization, why doesn't it exist? The Code of Professional Ethics is the primary obstacle. It includes a no-specialization rule to prevent the untrained practitioner from designating himself with a specialty when no mechanism exists to test and accredit such practitioners. With the cry and the need for some form of specialization, the AICPA proposed in 1981 an interpretation of the ethics rule on specialist and expert designation. The AICPA members would be permitted to refer to themselves as experts or specialists in advertising or other forms of solicitation in a manner that is not false, misleading, or deceptive if the institute would modify an interpretation of a rule in its ethics code. More explicitly, under the proposed modification to Interpretation 502-4, "Self-Designation as Expert or Specialist," an AICPA member must be prepared to substantiate the basis for a specialist designation by presenting evidence of the appropriate mix of education and experience. The proposal did not draw sufficient support within the profession. In addition, legal counsel advised the AICPA that interpretation 502-4 probably violated federal antitrust laws and was therefore unenforceable. Consequently, interpretation 502-4 was withdrawn effective September 1981. The effort was another aborted action for the AICPA. But perhaps the AICPA was lucky; it avoided answering such crucial questions as: "What specialties would be recognized? How will specialists be certified or accredited? Who will certify the specialists? Will firms or individuals or both be certified? How will practitioners respond to the implementation of these programs? What will be the effect on state societies, on the structure of practice units, on the public, and the profession?"[1] On the other side, the AICPA may not be that lucky, because this is going to open the floodgates to all sorts of dubious claims.

Non-CPA Associate Membership

The issue started when, in December 1969, the AICPA Board of Directors received a letter from a member requesting that it consider creating an associate-membership classification for non-CPAs serving on the professional staff of CPA firms. Should these people be given an associate membership and be brought into a professional relationship with the Institute? To the substantive ranks of CPAs practicing in small firms, the answer is no not only to professional specialization but especially to some form of affiliation for non-CPA specialists. To most large CPA firms, eager to meet the increasing demands for new services and the need for non-CPA specialists for these services, the answer may be a definite yes. This is especially important for the large CPA firms, since the Institute of Management Consultants, organized by the non-CPA consulting firms, had started a program to accredit "certified management consultants." This is expected to make it difficult for the CPA firms to attract and retain high-caliber non-CPA specialists unless the AICPA starts some form of accreditation for non-CPA specialists. It would be relatively easy to do so, according to the large CPA firms. The associate member would have to satisfy certain qualifications relating to education and experience and would have to pass an exam. The profession would consist of multiple disciplines, which in turn would affect preentry education and entry examination requirements. A useful proposal goes as follows: "to serve as test for entry into the profession, the CPA examination may have to be broadened to cover additional subjects, and postentry examinations might be necessary for the various specializations."[2]

These proposals are not acceptable to a large proportion of the accounting profession. In addition, the general public is silent on the question. There is practically no public cry for the accreditation of specialists, given that the issue is essentially an internal matter within the profession. What the outcome will be in the future on both professional specialization and non-CPA associate membership is difficult to predict. Both issues are essentially political, affecting the revenues of both large and small CPA firms. The resolution will depend on which of the small or large firms will be dominating the future committees examining the questions.

The Dilemma of Independence

Independence is the cornerstone of the accounting profession. To lend credibility to financial assertions and representations made by management, auditors must not only be impartial but must be perceived to be independent by outside users of financial statements. The accounting profession has long recognized the need for auditor independence, both actual and perceived by third parties. Rule 101 of the AICPA Code of Professional Ethics explicitly states that a member or a firm of which the member is a partner or shareholder shall not express an opinion on the financial statements of an enterprise unless the member and his or her firm are independent in respect to such enterprise. The code even suggests that instances in which the CPA is virtually part of management or an employee under management's control would lead to situations in which actual or perceived independence might be impaired. What are those situations? First, one may argue that possible accounting treatments for the same or similar event had the most serious potential adverse effect on independence. Second, one may also argue that situations in which auditors perform nonaudit services for their audit clients may lead to loss of independence. In fact, various studies indicate that

1. Various users see a negative relationship between nonaudit services and independence.

2. The concern by the same users about the lack of independence decreases when a "separate" staff has the responsibility of performing the nonaudit services.

3. Some people argue that before the external auditor decides how much to rely on the internal audit function, he or she should investigate the degree to which that function is independent of the company management. Therefore, the internal auditor, like the external auditor, should also be independent. Some may wonder whether the internal auditor's objectivity is

adversely affected when he or she recommends standards of control for systems or review procedures before they are implemented.

4. The client-auditor relationship is ill-defined. Some authors have argued that it is one of mutual dependency, and others have contended that it is a power relationship. If it is the latter, the threat to independence is built into the structure of this professional role, and one may argue that pressures on auditors not to perform according to professional standards can resist these pressures.

6. Potential causes of a lack of audit independence cited include inadequate educational preparation, providing to clients services incompatible with the attest function, litigation involving the auditor and the client, and client-related economic disincentives such as the threat of being fired, fee nonpayment, or litigation for nonperformance of an audit contract.

7. There are serious doubts that an auditor can maintain his or her independence when an actuary associated with the CPA firm has provided actuarial advice or calculations that are reflected in the audit client's management decisions. The report of the Subcommittee on Reports, Accounting and Management of the Senate Committee on Governmental Affairs, chaired by the late senator Lee Metcalf, *Improving the Accountability of Publicly Owned Corporations and Their Auditors* (the Metcalf Report), recommended that "nonaccounting" management-advisory services of accounting firms, such as actuarial services, be discontinued. In fact, estimating the costs and liabilities of a pension plan and funding those obligations involve many matters of judgment. They should be made by the client. Most actuaries will contend that clients cannot have judgments as informed as the results produced by their actuaries. They must rely on their actuaries. Any connections between an actuary and an auditor are bound to create a problem of lack of independence.

This evidence about actual or perceived independence was bound to create new interest and cause some concerned debate. Congress got into the act first. Both the Metcalf Senate Hearings in 1977 and the Moss House Hearings in 1978 warned that auditor independence would be ensured by congressional action. In fact, the Metcalf Subcommittee charged explicitly that provision of nonaudit services creates a professional and financial interest by the auditor in the client's affairs that is inconsistent with the auditor's responsibility to remain independent in fact and appearance. Congress, however, left it to its appropriate agency—the SEC—to take action.

Following the congressional interest, the AICPA's Commission on Auditors' Responsibilities (the Cohen Commission) looked into the nonaudit services debate and concluded in its 1978 report that too much fuss was being made and that there is no evidence that provision of services other than auditing has actually impaired the independence of auditors. Following the report of the Cohen Commission, the AICPA appointed in 1979 the Public Oversight Board to consider similar issues. The POB agreed with the Cohen

Commission assertion that concern about potential conflicts between management-advisory services (MAS) and the audit function decreases as user knowledge and sophistication increase. The SEC at the time was not impressed with arguments. It adopted ASR No. 250 and No. 264 to emphasize the importance of auditor independence. But the SEC later rescinded both ASR No. 264 and No. 250 after it considered that the profession had made sufficient progress to regulate itself with the issue of independence.

The question remains to determine exactly what auditor independence is and what happens to it when the auditor performs nonaudit services. The real test of an auditor's independence is the perceived nature and extent of his or her relationship with the audit client. If the auditor is so heavily involved in the client's affairs that an outside observer would perceive that the auditor is almost an insider, independence is impaired. If the auditor is merely performing unrelated and acceptable services to the client, independence is not impaired, given that the auditor's skills are needed not only for audit services but for other essential nonaudit services. As long as these nonaudit services are not performed in a way that would cause the auditor to be, or seem to be, an insider, independence is not impaired. In fact, some argue that management would not permit its decision-making authority to be usurped by anyone, including those CPAs providing advisory services.

What really does happen when the auditor performs nonaudit services remains to be answered. The magnitude of nonaudit services is on the increase. Ernst and Whinney conducted a survey of the ASR No. 250 disclosures in 4,319 proxy statements issued from October 1, 1978, through June 30, 1979. The average percentage of total nonaudit services disclosed in the proxy statements was 23 percent, and the average percentage of MAS fees to total audit fees was 8 percent. What is the effect of these activities on the auditor's independence? Most arguments and official positions taken so far imply that too much fuss is being made and that independence is still "safe."

First, for example, in 1983 the Association of Data Processing Service Organizations (ADAPSO) filed a petition requesting that the SEC propose a rule providing that an accounting firm would not be independent if it supplied computer products or services to its audit clients. The commission rejected ADAPSO's petition, because the area of nonaudit service had already rescinded ASR No. 250 and No. 264 and had left it to the accountants to ensure that their performance of nonaudit services did not adversely affect their independence. It is, however, important to note that the SEC has always maintained its position that performance of write-up and other bookkeeping services would adversely affect accountants' independence.

Second, some would argue that the nonaudit services provide the auditor with better insight to improve the efficiency and effectiveness of the client's operation as well as to comment on its reporting to outsiders. In fact, the 1975 report by the POB, *Scope of Services by the CPA Firms*, noted that for clients the following types of benefits accrue from auditor provision of non-audit services:

1. The extensive knowledge of a client's business gained during the audit can translate into cost savings and quality improvements on the consulting side and vice versa.
2. MAS services will attract better candidates in the profession and make the CPA more responsive to the complex needs of today's organizations.
3. The CPA involvement in internal controls and design of information systems will enhance the quality of the statements and make the audit easier and less costly overall.
4. The firm will benefit from advice on not only the weaknesses and defects observed during the audit but from recommendations on the general management aspects of the organization.

Third, some people argue that an audit is a cooperative venture between management concerned with the economic success of the firm and the auditor concerned with fair reporting. The same people argue that the auditor cannot achieve any of these objectives if he or she is totally independent. In fact, total independence is impossible, given that the auditor depends on management for the fees, the information about the business, and access to the records and personnel.

Finally, some argue that the best guarantee of the auditor's independence is his or her own concern for a good "reputation." Society imposes a heavy cost on the auditor whose reputation is damaged. Not only are the costs of litigation extremely high, but the auditor's ability to practice may be threatened. Furthermore, sanctions by state boards against the practitioner can result in the loss of license or suspension of license, which directly affects one's ability to practice. In short, sanctions and lawsuits against auditors for lack of independence may result in financial losses, loss of license, or damaged reputations.

But the question remains to determine what can be done to deal with possible lack of independence. Potential remedies for enhancing auditor independence, advanced by John K. Hank at the June 1978 Arthur Young & Company Professors' Roundtable, include mandatory audit-firm or audit-personnel rotation, shareholder ratification of the audit firm, mandatory review of audit work papers by a partner unconcerned with the audit, public disclosure of auditing-firm financial statements, and increased federal regulation of accounting and auditing.

The most interesting remedy was proposed by John C. Burton, a former chief accountant in the Securities and Exchange Commission, in the April 1980 *Journal of Accountancy*.[3] He suggested a new device to provide compensation to auditors by outside parties. It would consist of a statutory-mandated fee paid by all public companies to a governmental or an independent agency that has the responsibility for selecting and paying auditors. The debate is wide open.

"Low Balling": Another Dilemma

CPA firms large and small are competing for a finite number of firms to whom they are offering, respectively, the same services. As a result, fee competition is common and increasing. One way of beating the competition is through the practice of "low balling" — setting audit fees below total current costs. Low balling may be taking place on initial audit engagements. It may also be taking place when large firms compete with smaller firms for local engagements. Casual evidence on low balling is on the increase. Few companies reported to the Cohen Commission (the AICPA Commission on Auditors' Responsibilities) that in their recent negotiations, the new auditors indicated willingness to offer competitive prices, to make bids with fees guaranteed for several years, to renegotiate prices after receipt of competitive offers, and to set billing rates at as much as 50 percent below normal. Similarly, a 1979 article in the New Orleans *Times-Picayune* reported on the practice of low balling in conjunction with the audit of the City of Shidell:

Leonard Brooke of Deloitte Haskins and Sells said his firm expected just to break even on the first audit at a charge of $16,000. "I'd be amazed if it can be done for $25,000," said Brooke, who admitted his firm was submitting a low proposal the first year in order to do business with the city in succeeding years.

A fee of $15,000 — lowest of the four — was proposed by Wally Giles and Eugene Fremaux of Price Waterhouse. "In reality, that fee does not constitute what our full rate would be if we didn't absorb the first year's start-up cost," said Giles.

Another example may be used to suggest the possibility of low balling. In 1984 the City of Chicago switched auditors from Peat Marwick Mitchell & Company to Arthur Andersen & Company. In the process it saved $37,500 by switching auditors. Peat Marwick was receiving $375,000 for auditing the city's corporate and special funds. Arthur Andersen is charging $337,500 for the same service. But low balling is also observed in diverse environments such as bidding for franchise contracts, cable-television monopolies, and input contracts. Among CPA firms, however, low balling takes two new dimensions. First, it is anticompetitive and unfair to small firms. Second, and more importantly, low balling is alleged to impair auditor independence by creating a receivable from the client similar to an unpaid audit fee. The Cohen Commission agreed with this last statement (p. 121): "We believe that accepting an audit engagement with the expectation of offsetting early losses or lower revenues with fees to be charged in future audits create the same threat to independence [as an unpaid audit fee]." Therefore, these questions arise: Does low balling by auditors impair their independence? Is low balling a natural way to react to the fierce competition among CPA firms? Should low balling be the subject of regulation? Should it be curtailed?

Bias in the World of Partnerships

The paramount destiny and mission of women are to fulfill the noble and benign offices of wife and mother. This is the Law of the Creator.

Justice Joseph P. Bradley,
U.S. Supreme Court, 1873

The Bradley quotation from a century ago refers to one of the most infamous opinions of the Supreme Court that denied Myra Bradwell, an Illinois woman, entry into the practice of law. Times have changed. In the last decade, women have been moving into most professions, including engineering, medicine, and architecture. Of all people enrolled in law school, 38 percent are women; of those enrolled in accounting classes, 50 percent are women. The most dramatic increase in women members is in the field of accounting. At many academic institutions the accounting student body and the accounting honorary organizations are predominantly female. As a result, the accounting profession is fast becoming a female-oriented profession. An editorial in the April 1984 issue of the *Practical Accountant* predicted that by 1990, with the economy on the upside, there is a distinct possibility that the staffs of accounting firms overall will be predominantly female. The editorial suggested that sabbaticals (such as for maternity and child rearing) and increased costs may follow, presenting a serious challenge to the accounting practice in the 1990s.

Although that is a concern, a more important question is whether the situation will affect the selection of partners in CPA firms with a bias against women. A partner shares directly in the profits of a firm, and the position is not only the richest in terms of income, but it also represents the peak of prestige in the profession. Female lawyers and accountants have long complained that getting those coveted partnerships is stymied by the "old boys' " network, in which male partners pick other males to join their rank at the top. A study by the *National Law Journal* of 151 of the largest law firms shows that only 8.3 percent of the partners are women. Studies of certified public accounting firms show only 37 female partners among the 5,985 partners in the country's Big Eight accounting firms. A priori, one would think that bias applied to partnerships would be difficult to uphold, given that Title VII of the 1964 U.S. Civil Rights Act bans discrimination in hiring and firing or in "terms, conditions or privileges of employment" because of a person's race, sex, religion, or national origin. Besides, past court decisions have made clear that Title VII applies to most hiring, firing, and promotion decisions and to many employee benefits. Law and accounting firms have long disagreed with this rationale. First, they argue that advancement to a partnership is a change of status from employee to employer and, therefore, outside the scope of Title VII. Second, they argue that the selection of partners is a business decision rather than an employer-employee relationship, and as such it is not covered by federal civil rights law. Finally, they argue that a partnership is comparable to marriage and therefore to coerce a mismatched or unwanted partnership too closely resembles a statute for the enforcement of shotgun weddings.

Fortunately, a partnership's decision about whether promoting an employee must comply with the antidiscrimination provisions of federal law came to the Supreme Court in 1984 in *Elizabeth Hishon v. King & Spaulding*. Hishon was facing an "up-or-out" policy that law and accounting firms have, stipulating that if you are not made a partner within a specified time, you must leave the firm. Hishon's suit, brought under Title VII of the Civil Rights Act, had been dismissed by the Eleventh U.S. Circuit Court of Appeals. The law firm had argued that application of the law to the partnership-selection process infringed on constitutional rights of free association and free expression. On May 4, 1984, the Supreme Court rejected the argument and ordered the reinstatement of Hishon's suit. (She still must prove at a trial that she was the victim of discrimination, a charge the law firm denies.) It unanimously declared that law firms may not deny partnerships to women solely on the basis of sex. Basically, the court affirmed that law firms cannot discriminate between males and females in selecting partners, and all such promotions must be done on a sex-blind basis.

The decision exposes a variety of partnerships to job-bias lawsuits for refusing to promote women, or men for that matter, to partner status. Besides affecting law firms, the decision affects the securities, accounting, advertising, consulting, and public relations industries. With regard to the accounting profession, the ruling means that Title VII of the 1964 Civil Rights Act requires that women be considered on an equal basis with men in the selection of accounting partners, a *professional niche traditionally dominated by white males*. In effect, the history of the job-bias law does not contain any evidence that Congress meant to exempt partnership-selection decisions. This may lead to a flood of sex-discrimination cases against accounting firms for refusing to promote women to partnership as long as partnership may be proven in court to be a *term, condition, or privilege of employment*. The fact that the Supreme Court decision was unanimous will give additional weight to such lawsuits, because unanimous decisions by the courts are rare. This partnership decision, which follows an earlier Supreme Court decision in *Gunther v. the State of Washington*, puts employers on notice that they can be sued under Title VII for claims by women of less pay for comparable work, and it legitimizes the concept of pay equity. The two civil rights rulings give women accountants a good opportunity for equal pay and partnerships and may shatter the "up-or-out" policy that most accounting firms have.

Opinions for Sale

Is it true that a firm can get the opinion it wants by changing auditors? Actual cases suggest that it is:

1. Deloitte Haskins qualified the opinion of Wespercorp's results for fiscal 1983, ended June 30, 1983, citing potential claims resulting from adjustments to previously reported quarterly data. One disagreement acknowledged by Wespercorp was Deloitte Haskins' questioning of the practice of recognizing revenue upon shipment of computer systems, which Wespercorp considered to have met the GAAP. In 1984 Wespercorp dismissed Deloitte Haskins and retained Touche Ross & Company. Was the disagreement the deciding factor in the switch?

2. Peat Marwick was appointed by the Byrne administration in 1979 to be auditors of Chicago. During the 1983 primaries, ads appeared in the two major daily newspapers signed by concerned Chicago leaders praising the financial health of the city. Anthony M. Mandolini, the partner at Peat Marwick who handled the city account, was one of the signatories. Arthur Andersen was reported to have refused to sign the ads. Following the election, the new mayor, Harold Washington, appointed a task force that reported a potential budget-deficit problem for 1983. As expected, the City Council Finance Committee, which is given the power by the city code to appoint the city's auditor, in 1984 dumped Peat Marwick as the city's auditors in favor of Arthur Andersen and Coopers & Lybrand. Was politics the deciding factor in the switch?

3. Arthur Andersen was an auditor to both Northwest Industries and Pogo Producing Company. In 1981 Northwest acquired 20 percent of Pogo's stock and used the equity method to show 20 percent of Pogo's earnings on its income statement. Northwest paid some $77 million over the book value for the Pogo holdings. For oil and gas acquisition, the acceptable procedure is to allocate the $77 million to proved and unproved oil and gas properties and then use depreciation changes for the proven properties. Thus the more proved the properties, the better for Northwest. At that time Pogo was resisting a takeover by Northwest. So it claimed that only $10 million of the $77 million were in proved reserves, while Northwest claimed $32 million. Besides, Pogo claimed that Northwest had overstated the value of proved reserves by $38 million and that it should reduce its earnings by $38 million in write-offs. Arthur Andersen was understandably reluctant to take the side of Pogo. So Pogo hired Coopers & Lybrand to take its side in court. Is this another case where the right accounting firm will give you the opinion you want?

4. Broadview Financial Corporation, the Cleveland-based savings and loan association, wanted to take immediate gains in its 1982 annual report from some real estate investments while its auditor, Peat Marwick, preferred that the profits be spread over the life of the project. So Broadview Financial

switched auditors and hired Deloitte Haskins & Sells. It also went ahead with the gain recognition and reported a loss of $16.8 million for 1982. Deloitte, however, took the same stand as Peat Marwick by forcing Broadview to revise its loss to $25.4 million and by including in its opinion an emphasis paragraph about the net-worth problem. The switch of auditors in this case did not work to the firm's advantage.

5. *Public Accounting Report*, an industry newsletter, reported that in 1982 the number of publicly held firms firing their auditors jumped 48 percent to 442 from 298 the year before. It also reported that 92 came directly because auditors qualified the companies' reports, and 122 were the result of "accounting disagreements" or "personality conflicts," which is equivalent to disputes over qualifications. The newsletter failed to report whether the qualified firms that switched auditors tended subsequently to receive more clean opinions or fewer qualified opinions.

Client Chasing

One of the major barriers to competition in the accounting profession is the prohibition against one accountant soliciting another's client without the client's invitation. The definition of direct uninvited solicitation is, however, far from clear. A survey of CPAs showed that the respondents believe that the act of handing a potential client a business card does not constitute direct uninvited solicitation. But the respondents believe that writing letters or placing telephone calls to potential clients definitely constitutes direct uninvited solicitation. The survey found also that there are some ambiguities in CPA thinking about what constitutes direct uninvited solicitation. In spite of the difficulties of definition, there are two divergent arguments about whether or not direct uninvited solicitation should be banned.

Supporters of the ban, consisting mainly of small CPA firms, argue that it protects them from unfair competition from large national firms. They also view acts of direct uninvited solicitation as manifestations of a trend away from professionalism to commercialism. Others argue for the ban, using the support of the theories that the CPAs are not independent of clients obtained by direct uninvited solicitation, or do not maintain their independence in mental attitude toward those clients subjected to direct uninvited solicitation by another CPA. This last theory was advanced in a speech by Philip L. Defliese as follows:

The independent auditor's position is unique in that he has two clients—the company he is auditing and the person relying on his opinion on the financial statement: the prospective investor or general public. Only through an independent approach to his task can the reliability of his opinion be assured. The threat of a loss of an engagement or the need to lower his fee (and possibly impair quality), while he is so engaged may consciously or subconsciously affect his independent attitude toward the management he is auditing. This can insure the public interest.

Opponents of the ban, consisting mainly of large CPA firms, argue that it creates a barrier to free competition, to an efficient market for accounting services, and to "fair" fees. This position is also supported by the Justice Department and the Supreme Court. In 1976 the Supreme Court struck down a National Society of Professional Engineers ban on competitive bidding. The Justice Department does not look favorably on any ban on competitive bidding. This attitude was explicitly expressed in September 1979, when the chief of the antitrust division's special litigation section stated that, in the Justice Department's view, a blanket ban on written and oral solicitation by accountants "substantially impedes the ordinary give and take of the marketplace and under cases like [*Professional Engineers, Texas State Board of Public Accountancy,* and *American Institute of Architects*] would be illegal under the antitrust laws absent the state-action exemption." (The state-action exemption is a doctrine that confers immunity from antitrust law for a restraint of trade that is clearly articulated and affirmatively expressed as state policy and is actively supervised by the state itself.) As a result, the Justice Department tried first to convince accountants' national organizations and most state boards to drop the bans. The results were successful with the AICPA and some of the state boards. On March 31, 1975, the AICPA, following a mail ballot of the membership, changed the wording of Rule 502 as follows:

Previous Version: Advertising and Other Forms of Solicitation. A member shall not seek to obtain clients in a manner that is false, misleading, or deceptive. A direct uninvited solicitation of a specific potential client is prohibited.

New Version: Advertising and Other Forms of Solicitation. A member shall not seek to obtain clients in a manner that is false, misleading, or deceptive.

The AICPA dropped the second sentence of the rule that prohibited direct uninvited solicitation.

In 1981 the AICPA special committee on solicitation concluded in its report that

1. A prohibition against unscrupulous solicitation should be added to the current solicitation rule.
2. The AICPA Board of Directors should issue a policy statement that members who choose to engage in the commercial practices of solicitation and advertising should exercise appropriate restraint.
3. The AICPA should not influence state legislators to adopt more stringent bans than the institute itself can impose.
4. The Institute should not require its members to submit copies of all direct uninvited promotional literature for simultaneous or subsequent review.

At the same time, a member of the AICPA Special Committee on Solicitation, Louis W. Donner, remarked that an adverse court decision on a reimposed ban on direct uninvited solicitation not only would likely result in a loss of the ban but would enjoin the AICPA from having any rule or making any statement that solicitation for services is unethical, unprofessional, or contrary to AICPA policy.

In 1982 the state boards in Kentucky and West Virginia dropped the bans following inquiries and threats of action by the Justice Department. In most other states, however, the bans exist, leading to admonishment or revoking of licenses of those accountants caught soliciting. To resolve this problem, the Justice Department has filed a lawsuit against the Louisiana State Board of Accountancy for prohibiting "direct uninvited solicitation." If the Justice Department wins in Louisiana, the bans will disappear in the other states as well, and an interesting "open warfare-client chasing" situation may result.

To avoid any possible warfare, the Board of Directors of the AICPA adopted in December 1982 a policy statement urging members who engage in advertising and solicitation to avoid excesses that could jeopardize adherence to technical and ethical standards. The statement urged members to exercise "common sense, good taste, moderation and individual responsibility" in advertising and solicitation. This statement is in conformity with Rule 502 of the AICPA Rules of Conduct, which deals with prohibition against false, misleading, or deceptive solicitation.

ETHICAL CASES

The E.S.M. Government Securities Case

The Securities and Exchange Commission charged E.S.M. Government Securities with fraud on March 4, 1985. A few days later, Federal District Judge José A. Gonzales froze the assets of E.S.M. Government Securities after the government securities dealer, based in Fort Lauderdale, Florida, closed, leaving customers exposed to losses of about $250 million. The collapse of E.S.M. created ever-widening ripples throughout the U.S. capital markets. With the collapse of more than ten other institutions, this showed some of the vulnerability of parts of the U.S. financial system to the announcement of any bad news. The losses were harder on local authority treasurers, education boards, and small savings and loan institutions involved in the ever-growing (as the deficit grows) government repo market. Fort Lauderdale, the vacation spot, was not new to the financial fraud game. Two years earlier customers of the International Gold Bullion Exchange were faced with wood bars rather than gold bars in the company's vault, and an estimated $75 million of debt was owed to 13,000 creditors.

E.S.M. Government Securities affected a different type of investor, the institutional investor, composed, in this case, of brokers, savings and loan institutions, and municipalities. These institutional investors were involved in complete financing techniques, known as repos and adverse repos.

Repos, or repurchase agreements, are loans made by investors to E.S.M. collateralized by government securities. E.S.M., as the dealer, agrees to buy back the securities at a fixed price, paying a specified interest rate. Adverse repo, or reverse purchase agreements, are loans made to investors after they put up government securities as collateral. Basically, E.S.M., like most government securities dealers, later was involved in both repos and reverse repos in order to make money on the rate differential between the lending rate and the borrowing rate. As a result, the same securities can be used to support what became known as a "daisy chain" of loans.

No problem arises as long as the collateral is safely kept and the lenders request an increase in its value when the interest decreases. E.S.M. was able to attract a large number of institutional investors by offering a high return. In fact, the only reason the Home State Savings Bank—a Cincinnati institution—engaged in repurchase agreements with the little-known Florida securities firm was to increase its return on older, low-yielding securities.

As a result of the failure of E.S.M., the investors were left empty-handed. Home State Savings Bank, at the urging of its owner, financier Marvin Warner, invested heavily in E.S.M. and collapsed in March 1985 with more than $150 million in loans. That also forced the temporary closing of some 70 other savings and loan associations and wiped out the guaranty fund used by the small investors. Some municipalities were also involved and never took possession of the securities, allowing the market value of the collateral to erode without demanding any additional margin. Some of the cities burned by E.S.M. found their bonds placed on Standard and Poor's Credit Watch List. Examples included Pompano Beach, Florida, standing to lose $15 million, and Toledo, Ohio, standing to lose up to $19 million. The State of Ohio, which bailed out Home State Savings Association, found itself trying to recoup $250 million for itself and other Ohio casualties.

The irony of it all is that E.S.M. gave its word to its clients that the securities were being held at banks. Basically, these "naive" clients relied on the trustworthiness of E.S.M., although it is well established that an interest in collateral is only theoretically perfected when you take possession. It was like buying jewelry from a street vendor and allowing him to keep it.

But what went wrong at E.S.M. besides the pledging of the securities collateral to more than one customer? For one thing, E.S.M. was a company plagued by many problems, including trading losses and money siphoned out from it to support the lavish life-styles of its officers. In addition, the SEC charged that E.S.M. had engaged in a pattern of fraud from its inception in 1976, hiding cumulative losses totalling $196.5 million in an affiliated dummy company while its customers were led to believe that it was healthy because of its audited accounts. The E.S.M. court-appointed receiver, Dr. Thomas Tew, submitted a 100-page report to Federal District

Judge José A. Gonzales depicting the stormy, short life of E.S.M. Its survival over the few years of its existence was depicted as resting on three factors: first, the involvement of customers in reverse purchase agreements, in which the customers borrowed from E.S.M. and put up securities as collateral, providing E.S.M. with more collateral than necessary; second, the failure of customers to demand possession of the collateral after being falsely told by E.S.M. that their collateral was being safely held by the Bradford Trust Company; finally, the fact that E.S.M. borrowed more than it lent.

But where was the auditor all these years? Well, the court-appointed receiver for the failed E.S.M. Government Securities filed suit against the Chicago-based accounting firm, then known as Alexander Grant & Company, charging negligence of an "outrageous character," seeking $300 million plus punitive damages from the nation's 11th largest public accounting firm. The City of Toledo was also suing for $58 million and Home State Savings Bank was suing for an unspecified amount. In addition, Cincinnati financier Marvin Warner filed a $1.15 billion suit charging the accounting firm with fraud and negligence in auditing E.S.M. Government Securities. All this followed from SEC civil action.

The SEC charged that since 1976, E.S.M. was unprofitable but stayed in business because repos exceeded reverse repos, and to conceal its loans and liability, every repo was matched by a fictional reverse repo for the same amount on the books of the parent company and vice versa. Its ability to repay the loans from the adverse repos depended on the parent's ability to repay the loan it had received from E.S.M. In turn, the parent's ability to pay the loan depended on the ability of another subsidiary, E.S.M. Financial Groups, Inc., to repay the loans the parent made to it and carried on its books as an account receivable. Neither one could pay the other in the chain. Naturally, the SEC charged that the statement that everything is fairly presented in accordance with generally accepted principles after an examination made in accordance with generally accepted auditing standards is materially false and misleading. Accordingly, the SEC complaint alleged that Alexander Grant is to blame because:

- it failed to understand the nature of E.S.M's business;
- it failed to adequately train the audit team of the E.S.M. engagement;
- it failed to understand the fictitious nature of the term repo and reverse repo transactions between E.S.M. and the parent group;
- it failed to understand that there was no economic purpose for the existence of the parent and of the subsidiary except to transfer and to receive the government's loans;
- it failed to consider whether the subsidiary, E.S.M. Financial Group, Inc., was a going concern;
- it failed to adequately test E.S.M.'s accounts receivable;

- it failed to perform required procedures concerning its security inventory;
- it failed to perform an adequate review of journal entries;
- it failed to use knowledge gained through its provision of tax services to E.S.M.; and
- it failed to perform its impartial quality control review in accordance with generally accepted auditing standards and quality control standards.

In addition, it charged José L. Gomez, the Grant accountant, with the primary responsibility.

Alexander Grant, in the midst of negotiating a merger with Fox and Company of Denver, had to face first the awkward situation of having approved the financial statements of E.S.M. while it was not profitable since 1977; second, the allegation that its managing partner in Miami, José L. Gomez, took a $125,000 bribe in return for clean, unqualified opinions of the financial statements of E.S.M.; and finally, the embarrassment and shock brought to a now-tarnished accounting industry. This came at a time when the U.S. House Committee on Oversights and Investigations held two hearings on accountants' shortcomings in 1985, and when the industry faced a noticeable increase in SEC actions against auditors and in private suits.

It was a rude shock for Alexander Grant. The total damages sought were more than five times Grant's malpractice insurance average and nearly 50 times the partners' capital. At that time Grant, with headquarters in Chicago, had 77 U.S. offices, 450 U.S. partners, and U.S. revenue of $175 million. Some of its major clients included Sundstrand Corporation, Southmark Corporation, Republic Airlines, Orange and Rockland Utilities.

The situation showed how vulnerable professional partners are to mistakes made by colleagues in their firm. The Grant partners were served with court papers stating that their personal assets could be attached by the court to any settlement of the E.S.M. case. Shifting their assets to their wives or relatives was considered by the partners until the firm told them it was not necessary. There was also the unenviable potential loss of clients, of human resources, and credibility to a firm that used to be known as the "Mr. Clean" of the accounting profession faced with the difficulties of attracting new clients and partners.

The suit was in fact justified, given the blatant fraud in the E.S.M. case. Alexander Grant had prepared federal income tax returns for the E.S.M. Groups, Inc., the parent firm, and its subsidiaries and affiliates from 1977 through 1984 and had served as auditor for two subsidiaries. The suit against Alexander Grant charged flagrant manipulation whereby losses were hidden by passing them around.

An example involved a note receivable of $199.7 million from E.S.M. group in E.S.M.'s 1981 financial statement, which was 14 times the net worth of E.S.M. The 1984 balance sheet of E.S.M. indicated a $36 million net worth at a time when the company had an estimated $200 million to $350 million deficit. The statement was certified by Gomez, who, under pressure, retracted the opinion the next day, claiming in a letter to E.S.M. management that the financial statements "may not be relied upon." The damage was done. The "accounting" guy was caught with his hand in the jar. The fact remains, however, that Gomez and Alexander Grant issued a clean opinion of E.S.M.'s financial health only days before the SEC shut the securities dealer down, and that Gomez received a $125,000 payoff for his involvement. The accounting methods used by E.S.M. allowed it to hide its huge losses and create phony assets. Was Gomez the only one involved in Alexander Grant? The proper hypothesis at this time is that he "manipulated" co-workers. He was then fired and barred from working as an independent accountant and agreed in April 1985 to a SEC injunction to pay an unspecified amount of money to cover any profits from illegal transactions he may have made with the E.S.M. audits. The SEC order concluded that Gomez wasn't "independent" when he conducted the E.S.M. audits from 1981 through 1984 and that he engaged in "unethical and improper professional conduct" resulting from accepting payoffs from E.S.M. principals.

Then in November 1986 a federal jury awarded the trustee of the failed E.S.M. Government Securities $70.9 million from Alexander Grant, which was found liable for making false financial statements. In fact, Alexander Grant was to pay a prejudgment amount of about $36 million. In addition, Grant had paid $72.5 million in E.S.M.-related proceedings, which consisted of $50 million to municipalities and $22.5 million to Miami-based American Savings and Loan Association and $2.5 million in related settlements.

Where did the accounting firm go wrong? Generally accepted auditing standards are not formulated to catch conspiracy by a partner. The question, then, is how could the accounting firm's internal controls have failed? And there the answer is deceivingly simple: The person in charge of catching the irregularities was the main culprit. In general, for an audit the managing partner appoints an "engagement partner" to conduct the process of the audit with the help of a manager and an audit team. Any conflicts between the engagement partner and the manager are appealed to the managing partner. In the E.S.M. case Gomez, the managing partner, was also the engagement partner and the manager. He was basically monitoring two levels of internal review and that spells trouble. The trouble was that Gomez's unqualified opinions in E.S.M.'s financial statements were at the heart of the fraud behind E.S.M.'s failure.

There is, however, more to the case than the role played by Gomez. There are the loan auditing standards for transactions widely used by government securities dealers. The collateral in the repurchase agreements may not exist or may have been pledged to more than one customer, as in the case of E.S.M. In addition, the auditor's municipalities may have relied on second-party confirmations, such as the word of the dealer or its auditor, about the existence, status, and location of the collateral. What is needed is a tightening of auditing standards for government securities transactions. For example, a requirement may be the physical delivery of collateral to customers in cases in which the size of the transaction is much larger than the financial strength of the parties involved. It is, however, too late for those cities and individuals burned by this flagrant fraud case.

That is when standard-setting bodies, concerned institutions, and regulators decide to act — when it is too late and the losses to the general public exceed $250 million. Here are some of those appearing on the scene after the frauds. First, the Governmental Accounting Standards Board (GASB), a standard setter for governmental accounting, initiated a study of the accounting and reporting standards for repurchase and reverse repurchase agreements. One wonders if GASB will remember to specifically require disclosures of the collateralization of the investment regarding the nature, value, and holder of the collateral.

Second, at the SEC in the Reagan era, supposedly a guardian of the public interest, the concern was on whether the cost of regulation in the highly liquid government securities market might outweigh the benefits. Would delivery of all the securities cause too much burden on the system? One solution would be an expansion of an industry group overseen by the SEC — the Municipal Securities Rulemaking Board's authority to include oversight of government securities. That would be ideal to those favoring self-regulation rather than an increase in SEC oversight of the securities firm.

Third, Congress appeared on the scene with the usual scenarios: House subcommittee hearings on the role of auditors in the collapse of E.S.M. That gave a chance to the members of the committee to air their "low" opinion of the accounting profession in general and self-regulation in particular and also a chance to members of the accounting industry to draw the usual distinctions between auditor responsibilities and those of management: Management is charged with using and safeguarding assets, establishing the accounting system, with adequate internal controls, and preparing the financial statements that portray the results of their operating decisions. The accountant's role is to maintain independence from clients and to turn out accurate annual audits. Their explanations were naturally far from satisfying, leading Representative Ron Wyden (D-Ore.) to state it simply: "What we have on the table is very obvious and that is a massive failure of the independent auditing system in this country."

Fourth, the AICPA, which since the inception of the FASB and GASB, is merely a union of professionals, set up the usual task force to study the adequacy of existing guidance dealing with audits of repo and reverse repo security transactions. This was done to assure an Arthur Andersen request that the SEC practice session of the AICPA division for certified public accounting firms reconsider extending the section's membership requirements pertaining to SEC clients and nonclients, such as government securities dealers, given that they can equally influence the public securities market.

At the same time, the AICPA maintained its position of self-regulation, despite the uproar generated by E.S.M. That prompted Representative John Dingell (D-Mich.) to comment "Accountants essentially regulate themselves in curious ways with what appears to be a minimum level of discipline. This is conducted in the same manner as necromancy and sorcery in the dark ages — in the dark of the moon with very few attendees." In fact, sorcery characterizes much of what transpired in the E.S.M. case.

The Drysdale Affair

This affair all started with bond prices sliding when Drysdale Government Securities, Inc. disclosed in the month of May 1982 that it wasn't able to pay about $160 million in interest as a result of its huge debts to various banks, including Chase Manhattan Bank, Inc., and about 30 securities firms. That prompted the Federal Reserve System to inject reserves in the banking system to allay the fear created in the market, and to assist the 30 securities firms. Basically, Wall Street failed to follow its own adage, which is to "know your customer." In this case, Drysdale Government Securities was able to fool bankers like Chase in the repurchase agreements arena. It worked like this: An investment banker agrees to sell government securities to a bank with the agreement that he or she will buy it back later on, getting thereby the equivalent of a loan from a bank. The bank, in this case Chase, pays for the security in cash and can use the security to enter into a repurchase agreement, this time with Drysdale. At the end of the agreement the investment banker buys back the security at the arranged price and is entitled to the interest on the security. In this case, Drysdale Government Securities was not able to make these interest payments because it lost too much money selling short the same securities it had bought. Drysdale Government Securities could not pass on $160 million of interest that was due on a large amount of securities that it had temporarily bought.

The problem, in fact, started with Drysdale's aggressive trading, which led to large losses. One strategy used by Drysdale was to sell short government securities with substantial accrued interest built into their prices and buy other securities with little accrued interest, which involved borrowing securities with the hope of replacing them later at lower prices. The mechanics of the strategy went as follows: Drysdale bought security prices whose value was to increase as the interest payment dates approached and sold short those with bloated prices owing to the forthcoming interest payments. This implied that Drysdale was able to go to the market and replace the securities it sold short by buying them at the depressed prices after interest payments.

The whole strategy failed, however, when the market unexpectedly rallied, raising the prices of those bonds that were to be bought to replace those sold short.

Another strategy supposed to have generated heavy losses for Drysdale Government Securities, called "bear spread," involved buying government bonds and bond futures while selling treasury bills.

Who is responsible for the payment of interest? Chase or Drysdale? In any case, Chase decided after all to take over Drysdale's Government securities positions to be liquidated in an orderly manner and also to pay Drysdale debts of more than $160 million.

Drysdale's default showed one more time the dangers of intricate financing agreements and put more pressure for a regulation of government securities trading. In fact, the Manhattan district attorney's office launched a criminal investigation of Drysdale Government Securities' collapse, followed by another investigation by the Securities and Exchange Commission, which has only civil jurisdiction.

In addition, Chase Manhattan Bank and Manufacturers Hanover Trust Company sued the principals, accountants, and agents of Drysdale Government Securities. Arthur Andersen, as the accounting firm, was accused by the clients of Drysdale of being negligent in its review of the firm's financial statements, with Chase claiming $285 million in damages and Manufacturers the sum of $21 million of losses. Chase mentioned specifically the fact that Drysdale Government Securities was insolvent of $135 million in February 1982, falsely stated its subordinated debt and equity amount at $20.8 million, and that Arthur Andersen was fully liable for the amount.

A few weeks later a county grand jury in New York indicted two officers of Drysdale Government Securities on charges of stealing more than $270 million from Chase and more than $20 million from Manufacturers. In addition, it indicted a former partner of Arthur Andersen on charges of issuing false financial statements. Basically it alleged that the day Drysdale Government Securities opened for business in February 1981, its liabilities exceeded its assets by $150 million. Naturally, as in all fraud cases, the accountant was accused of having done the magic trick, certifying that the false information about the Drysdale financial affair conformed with GAAP. In addition, the unqualified opinion given on February 22, 1981, was made without a second Arthur Andersen partner check of the final report, as the accounting firm's procedures required.

The two officers of Drysdale agreed to the court orders that required their compliance with federal securities laws to settle SEC charges of security fraud. The accounting partner from Arthur Andersen was, however, acquitted by a state court of charges that he issued false statements for the now-defunct Drysdale Government Securities. The SEC also settled the civil charges against the partner from Arthur Andersen when he consented to be enjoined from any future violations of the antifraud provisions of the federal securities laws.

A federal jury, however, issued a $17 million judgment against Arthur Andersen in the civil suit brought by Manufacturers. The judgment was upheld by a federal appeals court, contending that Arthur Andersen violated securities laws and committed fraud and negligence in certifying financial statements for Drysdale and its Drysdale Government Securities suit. It was in line with the accountants' liability for violations of federal securities laws, particularly section 10(b) and rule 10(b)-5 concerning fraud in connection with the purchase or sale of securities.

Arthur Andersen appealed to a higher court. The Supreme Court refused to free the company from paying the $17 million, and it was ordered to pay the money to Manufacturers Hanover Trust Company.

All these events underscored one more time the need for the U.S. government securities industry to reexamine many of its informal practices and the need for more federal regulation of the market. It may have been too late, but the Public Securities Association released in October 1988 a nine-page report outlining "business practice guidelines" for participants in the repurchase-agreement market. Specifically it recommended the use of formal written repurchase agreements with extensive details on terms and conditions and the adoption by each security firm of specific formal credit analysis procedures to examine the credit standing of customers and other dealers.

Equity Funding Case

This case started in March 1973 when Equity Funding Corporation of America's stock fell among rumors about the operations of Equity Funding Life Insurance Company, a subsidiary chartered in Illinois and headquartered in Los Angeles. The rumors focused on the accuracy of the subsidiary's reported statements of new policies written and total insurance in force. In response to the rumors, Equity Funding of America did the obvious thing by ordering its independent auditors, Seidman & Seidman, to perform an expanded audit of the subsidiary.

The Securities and Exchange Commission then halted trading in Equity Funding as it began a full-scale investigation. What followed was one of the biggest scandals in the history of the insurance industry. A sizable chunk of the insurance did not exist; it was bogus business, created for the books and sold back to reinsurers. Policy files requested by auditors were forged and employees posed as policyholders when the auditors tried to discover the fraud. Forged death claims for nonexistent policyholders were sent to the trusting reinsurers holding the policy, who would then forward the money to Equity Funding Life. Naturally the latter kept it. In addition, subsidiaries were pressed to illegally transfer their assets to the parent company. All this was discovered after a surprise audit by the Illinois Insurance Department. The same action was taken by their California counterpart.

At Equity they called the whole bogus operation the "y" business. The executors even discussed this with considerable levity. It consisted of the creation of bogus policies for sale to coinsurers. With no commission to pay to agents, the company kept even more money.

In addition to these bogus schemes, the parent put pressure on the subsidiary to generate more earnings. The parent company would declare a target for each quarter. The unaudited quarterly earnings were inflated. Equity Funding Life Insurance would answer the worries of the subsidiaries about the inflated earnings by claiming that its hard-charging sales staff would write a flood of new business that would get the performance up to the target earnings without the use of any creative accounting. But the sales force wasn't delivering and the bogus scheme was. To keep the auditor from discovering the scheme, Equity Funding Life Insurance created the right institution—the forgery party. Scores of employees worked at creating any files requested by auditors, fooling some of the best firms in the business, including Deloitte Haskins & Sells, Peat Marwick & Main, and Seidman & Seidman. But the "y" business had its own drawback because the coinsurer gets almost all the premium paid by the policyholder, and because there are no policyholders, Equity Funding had to pay the premium. The only way to do it is to create more bogus business and more fictitious policies on the books. It became a pyramid scheme bound to be discovered.

In April 1973 the SEC finally filed a suit against Equity Funding Life Insurance Co., charging the company with fraud and other violation of federal security laws. In its suit, the SEC charged that the company was in a massive and prolonged effort to alter its books and records, principally those of Equity Funding Life Insurance, to show the sale of insurance policies, the receipt of premium payments, the creation of assets, and the establishment of reserves, when in fact the insurance policies had not been sold, the premium payments had not been received, the assets did not exist, and the reserves had not been established. At the same time, a federal judge ordered the scandal-ridden company to file protection under Chapter 10 of the Federal Bankruptcy Act. In addition, Touche Ross was appointed by the court to do the formal "fraud audit." What showed up is that more than $2 billion in life insurance was bogus.

The question of crucial importance in this case relates to the failure of auditors to detect the massive fraud. What went wrong with the firms involved? These firms were the national accounting firm of Seidman & Seidman and Wolfson, Weiner, Ratoff, & Lapin, a small accounting firm with offices in Beverly Hills and New York that merged with Seidman & Seidman on February 1, 1972.

Equity Funding was first audited by the Wolfson firm. The man in charge was Solomon Block. While auditing Equity Funding, Block not only was not a certified public accountant but had flunked parts of the CPA examination in 1961, again in 1969, and passed only on April 27, 1973. Ironically, this was the same date the California State Board of Accountancy asked its staff to collect all the information it could about the licensed accountants involved in the Equity Funding scandal. How could a non-CPA be allowed to supervise the audit of a firm the size of Equity Funding? The question boggles the mind. The answer, however, is easy. The head of Wolfson & Weiner was credited with the creation of the basic equity funding concept, whereby customers bought mutual fund shares and used them as collateral to borrow money from Equity Funding to buy Equity Funding life insurance. It was a comfortable relationship, especially since 60 percent of the billings of the small firm were accounted for by Equity Funding. Although independence is not in question here, the relationship was too close to allow the unmasking of the huge fraud. Even after the merger with Seidman & Seidman, Wolfson & Weiner were considered as inside rather than outside auditors. Being so close made them too manageable. Final proofs of Equity Funding's 1972 annual report, which was never printed, show on page 8 a "clean" opinion by Seidman & Seidman giving unqualified certification to the figures. One naturally wonders how a national accounting firm could miss $120 million in nonexistent assets, up to $2 billion in phony insurance policies, and $15 million in bonds supposedly held for equity funding by American National Bank & Trust Company, in Chicago.

It is not necessarily the fault of Seidman & Seidman. But one could use this case to caution national firms from erring by "buying growth" through mergers with local accounting firms rather than building and staffing offices from scratch. It is known that Seidman & Seidman merged with Wolfson, Weiner, Ratoff, & Lapin to get the Equity account. What it also got is a major scandal on its hands. It was even accused later of keeping the lid on the evidence on the Equity Funding case. And in 1975 three former Equity Funding auditors were convicted of fraud and filing false data. The Equity Funding trustee, besides citing the lies, audacity, and luck of the perpetrators in the scandal, also laid responsibility for failure to detect the scandal squarely on the independent accountants.

What about the SEC? Where were they before they were tipped off about the fraud by analyst Raymond L. Dirkes, the man who first uncovered the scandal? What did they do after they were tipped off? Why didn't the SEC launch an investigation immediately? Was the information received very sketchy, as was claimed—not the kind of information that would ring the fire alarm? The agency got firmer information on March 26 but suspended trading only on March 27. But it got "less fine" information on March 9, almost three weeks before it halted trading the company's stock. Was it because it was mere rumor? How about the later revelation that an SEC staff member came close to exposing the bogus scheme? One wonders if the SEC is capable of following leads long before scandals erupt.

What about the performance of generally accepted auditing standards? Could they have detected all the facets of the fraud? Are they to blame for the failure of outside auditors to detect and disclose the massive fraud at Equity Funding Corporation of America? Weren't there any methods to discover the two separate phases of the scheme: first, the exaggeration of earnings for almost a decade by inflating the funded loan receivable and, later, the concocting of phony insurance policies, which were sold to other insurance companies?

On May 5, 1973, the Board of Directors of the AICPA decided to look into the issues and appointed a special committee to study whether auditing standards applicable to the examination of financial statements should be changed in light of Equity Funding. A 46-page report released in 1975 concluded that generally accepted accounting standards weren't to blame, and if properly applied, they would have reasonably assured detection of the fraud.

But the fraud did take place despite the standard audit tests. This only means that the audit standards may fall for certain types of frauds. Examples include forgery, collusion, and unrecorded transactions. Equity Funding comprised a combination of these and more. One should, therefore, possibly expect similar scandals in the future.

The Wedtech Case

Wedtech Corporation, a Bronx-based defense contractor, collapsed in December 1987 amid a scandal involving political payoffs and the use of accounting gimmickry.

With regard to the political scandal, it seemed that Wedtech was receiving favorable treatment as a government contractor, after it committed itself to hiring untrained and seemingly unemployable workers in the South Bronx, prompting President Reagan to call the founder, John Mariotta, a former tool and die maker, "a hero for the 80s." There was more truth in the characterization as the $100 million-a-year military contractor was now listed in the New York Stock Exchange. Then the company was charged with and admitted forging more than $6 million in invoices submitted to the federal government. What emerged was a network of political payoffs used by the company to buy influence by paying off and/or hiring politically connected consultants, relatives of politicians, and former government officials. It had allowed itself to become one of the largest participants in a no-bid defense contract program of the Small Business Administration agency.

With regard to the accounting fraud, the question was how did Wedtech's book manage to receive clean bills of health from the time the company went public in 1983, in light of the scheme that inflated the company's earnings through false invoices and flagrant accounting gimmicks? The answer is simple in all the cases examined in this book. As usual we can find the accountant and/or auditor behind the fraud. It seems in this case that Wedtech got a lot of help in normalizing its situation. In 1983 Main Hurdman, a former member of its previous outside auditor firm, KMG, became Wedtech's president. Before leaving KMG Hurdman allegedly agreed to receive

$1.5 million in Wedtech's stock and a $900,000 loan from Wedtech, which casts a cloud on his independence while auditing the books of Wedtech. Added to that, it seems that Wedtech relied on "percentage of completion" accounting to boost its earnings. Basically, under the percentage of completion method, revenue is recognized on the basis of its current costs, the estimated costs of completing a project, and the certainty of receiving the entire contract price. For example, say Wedtech has a contract with the Defense Department at a cost of $200 million in material and labor and charges $220 million for the job, making $20 million or an 18 percent profit. If it incurred a $40 million cost the first year, it recognizes a $4 million profit, 10 percent of its costs. Up to now everything conforms to generally accepted accounting principles. However, it seems that Wedtech overstated the amount of work done based on the spending already incurred. Wedtech was able to appear profitable and sell more bonds and stocks to the naive public. Where were Wedtech's auditors, KMG, in the face of these overstatements? KMG claimed that it informed the company and its outside attorneys of the fraud and was satisfied that any irregularities had been stopped. Either KMG failed to accomplish its job, or Wedtech's management did a good job to disguise the fraud. The second version is more plausible, as Touche Ross, replacing KMG, gave a clean opinion to Wedtech in 1985, nine months before it filed for Chapter 11, failing to catch the pervasive management fraud still going on in Wedtech.

The accounting firms did not carry the blame alone, as two major Wall Street brokerage firms were sued by Wedtech holders over underwritings. The suit charged that Bear, Stearns & Company and Moseley Securities Corporation failed to exercise "due diligence" in issuing the securities containing false and misleading data about Wedtech's sales, earnings, and receivables.

The case includes a successful disguise of fraud by management, a failure of two major accounting firms to detect and report the fraud, and a naive client—the government of the United States. Wedtech was well connected to two agents of society: political and accounting agents. Did both of them show enough greed and naivete to allow management to carry out its immense and pervasive fraud? How could false data be certified clean by two major accounting firms? Were these firms victimized or plainly ineffective? Why didn't either of the two auditors insist on the use of the completed contract method, rather than the percentage of completion method? Wedtech was not certain it would get the entire amount of the government contracts. If it was urged to use the completed contract method, it wouldn't have been able to record any profit until the completion of the contract.

The Penn Square Case

When federal regulators closed Penn Square, the once-small Oklahoma bank had caused losses for depositors and for five big banks that had bought about $2 billion in loans. How can a small bank fool the big banks, including Continental Illinois National Bank and Trust Company for $1 billion, Chase Manhattan for $200-$300 million, Seafirst Corporation for $400 million, Michigan National Corporation for $200 million, and Northern Trust Corporation for $125 million? The reasons quickly emerging from the scandal included the "gold rush" euphoria about the energy business by banks at the time and their sudden rush to lend money, the less-than-adequate loan review procedures, and the aggressive salesmanship of Penn Square officers aggravated by an inbred relationship with other banks. Penn Square churned out billions of dollars to small oil and gas producers in risky loans made worse by being under collateralized and overvalued.

Where were the auditors? Several months before its collapse, Penn Square got a qualified opinion of its 1980 financial statements by Arthur Young & Company because of the lack of adequacy of reserves for possible loan losses. What else was there for Penn Square to do but fire the auditor who had questioned its lending practices and find another firm, in this case Peat, Marwick, Mitchell & Company, who gave it a clean bill of health. The same judgment that found the adequacy of the reserve for possible loan losses unacceptable because of the lack of supporting documentation of collateral values of certain loans was altered later by Peat Marwick, arguing that the judgment by management that the allowance is adequate at both December 31, 1981 and 1980, and removing the qualification in the 1981 financial statements.

What happened may again be in the realm of creative accounting. It seems that management altered the bank's financial position, leading both Peat Marwick and the U.S. comptroller of the currency to note favorably Penn Square's efforts. The irony is that Peat Marwick's report on March 19 preceded the bank's collapse by only three and a half months. Could anything drastic have happened in seven months to justify the removal of the qualifications? The answer lies again with Peat Marwick. In fact, Peat Marwick knew about problems at the bank and warned directors in May that the bank's problems were on the rise. These problems included inadequate asset and liability management, poor liquidity, a large number of loan-documentation deficiencies, widening loan losses, several lending limit violations, and insufficient capital. But the irony again is that such damaging internal reports are not included with the audited financial statements because of the risk to depositor confidence. Should Peat Marwick have made public those reports to the U.S. comptroller of the currency, to the investors, to the depositors, or to the public? That would have stopped some depositors at least from continuing to place millions of dollars of uninsured money with the bank, buoyed by the unqualified auditor's report. However, Peat Marwick was prohibited by the accounting profession's standard of confidentiality from saying anything to other banks or to the public. The secrecy of the auditor as well as of the regulators allowed Penn Square to continue with its scheme of attracting deposits and loaning to borrowers already crippled by the energy slump.

Who would blame, for example, Professional Asset Management, a California-based broker, for filing a suit alleging that Penn Square's outside auditor, Peat Marwick, and two of the auditor's accountants were negligent in issuing a clean opinion of the bank's 1981 financial statements, and that their behavior in light of their knowledge of Penn Square's problems amounted to fraud? Was Peat Marwick's conclusion of an unqualified report when it knew about serious problems at the bank equivalent to fraud? Instead of sending a private letter to Penn Square's board recommending ways to correct 14 problem areas, should they have qualified the 1981 statements? That makes Peat Marwick liable to third parties for fraudulent information in audit reports.

What really went wrong with Peat Marwick's audit? Well, in 1984 the Federal Deposit Insurance Corp. (FDIC), when suing Peat Marwick for the improper audit of Penn Square, added charges that the partners in Peat Marwick's Oklahoma City office compromised the firm's independence by accepting more than $1 million of loans, directly or indirectly, from Penn Square. This second allegation pointed to a fact that in 1981 all 12 partners in Peat Marwick were members of an Oklahoma general partnership called Doral Associates, which borrowed $566,501 from Penn Square and guaranteed a Penn Square loan of $1,650,000 to a Doral joint venture. It seems that Peat Marwick was aware of these loans and even advised Penn Square to sell those loans to other banks. One more case of the accountant caught with his hands in the cookie jars of the bank.

The case did not stop there for Peat Marwick. In January 1985 a judgment required it to disclose completely an internal study of its 1981 audit of Penn Square. The case was a first test that will open all accounting firms to "self-incrimination" in cases in which firms have been sued for failing to spot financial troubles at client companies. The plaintiff suing Peat Marwick for its audit failure of Penn Square had access to material that incriminated the accounting firm. In effect, the types of reviews a firm performs after an audit is over are candid and sometimes speculative. Can the accounting firms claim privilege for this type of material that should be protected as the work product of the accounting firm's attorney? By saying no the judge created a scary environment.

Peat Marwick's problems were not over, as the Justice Department followed the example of the FDIC by suing the firm and the implicated partners, alleging fraud and conflict of interest in their auditing of Penn Square Bank before it failed. In July 1986 Peat Marwick agreed to a settlement with the FDIC.

CONCLUSIONS

Joseph McGuire observes that:

There are, unquestionably, evil men in business. There are, undoubtedly, evil men in most occupations. There are, furthermore, individuals in business who do not seem to care about right and wrong. Such apparently conscienceless deviants are probably found elsewhere, too. More common in business — as well as in other activities — would appear to be those persons who are so engrossed in the pursuit of their material self-interest that the constraints imposed by ethical standards are not sufficiently strong to deter them from wrong-doing as they race toward their goal.[4]

These evil persons seem to find a home in the accounting profession. Fraud mentality may have crept in the accounting ethos that had seriously adulterated the view of independence and conscience. There is the danger of a mass of accountants becoming Neanderthals in Brooks Brothers suits.

The roots of the dilemma in accounting can be traced to the following conditions:

1. Our profession's focus is on specific rules rather than clearly stated objectives of what we are trying to accomplish. Professional judgments give way to rule and vote, and increasingly, the spirit plays fiddle to the letter.
2. The specter of litigation is pervasive. It causes us to seek protection in detailed rules and to shun judgment which can be second-guessed with hindsight. It has caused us to abandon constraints on competitive practices we used to consider unprofessional. It inhibits disciplinary proceedings.
3. Competition for clients is intense. Isn't it ironic that one branch of our federal government has pressured us to abandon traditional ethical constraints as anticompetitive, while another branch of the same government tells us that competitive excesses cause loss of objectivity and independence, the hallmarks of our profession?
4. We lack meaningful and consistent leadership, example, training or discipline in standards of professional conduct.[5]

NOTES

1. G. Siegel, "Specialization and Segmentation in the Accounting Profession," *Journal of Accountancy* (November 1977), p. 75.

2. W. E. Ohlson, "Specialization: Search for a Solution," *Journal of Accountancy* (September 1982), p. 78.

3. John C. Burton, "A Critical Look at Professionalism and Scope of Services," *Journal of Accountancy* (April 1980).

4. Joseph W. McGuire, "Business, Economics and Ethics: A Research and Action Agenda for the Future," *Review of Social Economy* (December 1982), p. 455.

5. Ralph E. Walters, "Our Slip is Showing," *Outlook* (Winter 1985), p. 68.

Appendix: Accountants and "Insider Trading"

Harold Buchanan II and Bruce R. Gaumnitz

Harold Buchanan is on the staff of the Houston office of Arthur Andersen & Co. Bruce R. Gaumnitz, CPA, Ph.D., is an Assistant Professor, Faculty of Accounting and Management Information Systems, The Ohio State University.

The abuse of "inside" information violates federal law and has received considerable media attention as the result of recent scandals involving such prominent firms as E. F. Hutton, Shearson Lehman, Lazard Frères, Drexel Burnham Lambert, and Watchtell Lipton Rosen & Katz.[1] These alleged violations have seriously hurt the careers of the participants and have tarnished the reputations of their employers. Since accountants routinely have access to nonpublic information and rely upon their reputations for the credibility of their opinions, they are particularly vulnerable to charges of improprieties. As a result, actions constituting the abuse of "inside" information must be clearly understood to prevent devastation of a professional practice.

The purpose of this paper is: (1) to examine the information control problems inherent in the audit process and their relationships to the "insider" trading provisions of the Securities Exchange Act of 1934, Rule 10b-5, and the Insider Trading Sanctions Act of 1984; and (2) to reinforce the need for caution and continuing vigilance with respect to the use of nonpublic information. The paper is organized in four sections. In the first section, the term "insider" is explored and the actions prohibited by the 1934 and 1984 Acts are briefly summarized. These concepts are applied to accountants in the second section where the possibility of information leakage and abuse is considered in an audit setting. The third section evaluates the impact of efficient market research on accountants' liability and the need for insider trading laws. It is followed by a conclusion.

"INSIDERS" AND INFORMATION ABUSE

The Securities Exchange Act of 1934 identifies three groups, directors, officers, and principal stockholders, that are subject to the special trading restrictions and filing requirements imposed by federal law. These individuals are commonly referred to as "insiders" and are identified as:

> Every person who is directly or indirectly the beneficial owner of more than 10 per centum of any class of any equity security (other than an exempted security) which is registered pursuant to section 78l of this title, or who is a director or an officer of the issuer of such security, shall file... [15 USC § 78p(a)]

Although the term "insider" is not actually used in the Act, the three groups that it identifies have been termed "insiders" by the courts.[2] Over time, however, the courts have interpreted the law and expanded their definition of "insider" to include not only these three groups, but others as well. For example, in Securities and Exchange Commission v. Texas Gulf Sulphur Co., the Court of Appeals held that:

For their helpful comments on this paper, we are indebted to Andrew D. Bailey, Jr., Thomas J. Burns, and Daniel L. Jensen.

---

[1] See "Why Wasn't $1 Million a Year Enough? A Lot more than Greed Led to the Insider Trading Scandal" in *Business Week*, August 25, 1986, for a summary of some of these events.

[2] Blau v. Lamb, 163 F.Sup. 528 provides an illustration.

Source: Harold Buchanan II and Bruce R. Gaumnitz, "Accountants and 'Insider Trading,' " *Accounting Horizons* (December 1987): 7–11. Reprinted with permission.

...not only are directors or management officers of corporations "insiders" within meaning of rule of Securities and Exchange Commission, ...but rule is also applicable to one possessing information, though they may not be strictly termed an "insider" within meaning of Securities Exchange Act, and thus *anyone in possession of material inside information is an "insider"*...[401 F.2d 833] (emphasis added)

This extension of the concept of "insider" to include those who know facts of special significance about a security or its issuer that are not generally available is well established and has become part of the American Law Institute's Federal Securities Code.[3] For accountants, the important characteristic of this expanded definition is that it is no longer necessary to be an officer, director, or major shareholder to be convicted of insider trading. In other words, the distinction between trading by "insiders" and trading on the basis of "inside information" has broken down and anyone acting upon material nonpublic information may violate federal securities law.

Prohibited Actions

Three complimentary rules are widely applied to the regulation of insider trading. These are (1) Rule 10b-5,[4] (2) the short-swing trading rules of the Securities Exchange Act of 1934,[5] and (3) the Insider Trading Sanctions Act of 1984. Perhaps the rule of broadest scope is Rule 10b-5. This rule, familiar to many accountants as a result of Ultramares v. Touche[6] and Ernst & Ernst v. Hochfelder[7] provides that it is unlawful for any person to employ manipulative or deceptive devices in connection with the purchase or sale of securities [17 CFR § 240.10b-5]. Since the withholding of material nonpublic information in connection with a security transaction can be viewed as a deception, Rule 10b-5 effectively proscribes insider trading activity.[8] A more specific rule, providing for the disposition of profits on short-term trades by insiders is found in the Securities Exchange Act of 1934.[9]

Once again, however, it is recent extensions of these rules that are of greatest potential concern to accountants. While Rule 10b-5 and the Securities Exchange Act address trading for the insider's account, they do little to address the communication or sharing of inside information. This is done by the Insider Trading Sanctions Act of 1984 which states:[10]

Whenever it shall appear to the Commission that any person has violated any provision of

this title or the rules or regulations thereunder by purchasing or selling a security while in possession of material nonpublic information ...the Commission may bring an action in a United States district court to seek, and the court shall have jurisdiction to impose, a civil penalty to be paid by such person, *or any person aiding and abetting the violation of such person.* (emphasis added)

While there are exception provisions in this statute to eliminate liability for innocent parties (*e.g.*, the stockbroker who unknowingly executed an improper transaction), these exceptions are limited to those aiding and abetting in a manner other than by communicating inside information.

The possible consequences of this statute to the accountant should be clear. Not only is it unlawful to trade for one's own account on the basis of nonpublic information, but the giving of "tips" to others who act upon them is a federal violation as well. Hence, liability now extends not only to those benefiting from trades based upon inside information, but also to their information sources and providers as well.

INSIDE INFORMATION IN THE AUDIT SETTING

As part of the ordinary course of the audit process, independent external auditors routinely examine records and have access to material information that is not available to the general public. For example, auditors review earnings per share disclosures before financial

---

[3] See ALI Federal Securities Code § 1603(b).

[4] Rule 10b-5 is one of the general rules and regulations enforced by the Securities and Exchange Commission under amendments to the Securities Exchange Act of 1934. The rule was enacted by Congress on December 22, 1948 and modified August 11, 1951 [see 13 FR 8183 and 16 FR 7928, respectively]. It is found in the Code of Federal Regulations 17 CFR § 240.10b-5.

[5] 15 U.S.C. § 78p(b).

[6] Ultramares v. Touche, 255 N.Y. 170.

[7] Ernst & Ernst v. Hochfelder, 425 U.S. 190.

[8] Rule 10b-5 states that "It shall be unlawful...to omit to state a material fact necessary in order to make the statements made, in light of the circumstances under which they were made, not misleading, or (c) to engage in any act, practice, or course of business which operates or would operate as a fraud or deceit upon any person, in connection with the purchase or sale of any security."

[9] 15 U.S.C. § 78p(b).

[10] See 98 Stat. 1264 or 15 U.S.C. § 78u(2)(A).

statements are issued. This gives them information that could be advantageous in anticipating stock price movements when earnings data are released. Alternatively, an auditor may uncover fraud, have knowledge of adjustments required for fair presentation of financial statements, or know that a qualified opinion will be expressed even before this is known by officers, directors, or major shareholders.

The point of this discussion is that auditors will typically possess material inside information about their clients. As a result, they are "insiders" as this term has been interpreted by the courts and, as a result, are subject to trading restrictions on client securities imposed by the Securities Act. While this does not suggest that the accountant will make improper use of this information, it does indicate that abuse is possible.

Fortunately, accountants have long had rules prohibiting trading in client securities. Although these rules stem primarily from the need for auditor independence,[11] they nonetheless forbid financial ties to client companies. This includes both direct ownership of and trading in client securities. Thus, the accountants' deep concern for independence has led to employer monitoring of security holdings, has prohibited trading activity, and so has helped prevent violations of section 78p(b) of the United States Code (personal trading by insiders).

This concern for independence, however, does little to limit the release of nonpublic information in violation of the Insider Trading Sanctions Act. Our ethics rules, to be sure, state that confidential client information shall not be disclosed,[12] but these rules are only binding upon members of the American Institute of Certified Public Accountants—and not all audit team members necessarily qualify. While this is mitigated to some extent by employers' codes of ethics, once information is in an employee's hands very little can be done to control or restrict its use.

Without question, two factors contributing to this security problem are the desire to do quality work and competitive pressures. Since the audit process involves sampling from masses of data and an examination of their interrelationships to determine if financial statements are fairly presented, it is natural to give audit team members considerable freedom to ask questions, review client documents, and examine working papers. In addition to contributing to the learning process for junior employees,

this freedom improves the quality of the audit by providing more cross-checks on the work of others, and by allowing team members to test the reasonableness of numbers by comparing them with other relevant data.

Competitive pressures dictate that quality audits be performed as efficiently as possible. High security and efficiency, however, are conflicting objectives since security measures result not only in initial direct costs (*e.g.*, costs for vaults, locking devices, and file encryption software) but in the continuing costs these measures impose through clumsy availability of information. This slows the progress of an audit and so produces lower short-run profits.

On the other hand, long-run profits could be substantially improved if security measures were imposed to restrict information usage provided that these measures prevented wrongful information disclosures. This could prevent charges of insider trading, the resulting legal defense fees, possible civil penalties, and damage to the firm's reputation regardless of the outcome of the suit. The essence of these arguments is (1) that the more people there are who have material inside information, no matter how carefully they may be screened, the greater the risk to the firm, and (2) that (costly) security precautions can be taken to reduce this risk.

Since it is unrealistic to try to control the dissemination of information, control must be achieved through employee training and by limiting freedom to examine client documents and audit working papers. In other words, security can be maintained only if employees are carefully screened and data are released to them only on a "need to know" basis. A heavy dose of ethical indoctrination that is regularly reinforced and scrupulously observed by senior role models can help ethical behavior become a way of life for new employees. On the chance that this is insufficient, clear explanations of the potential legal consequences of releasing inside information and the fact that this can be a federal offense should also be provided.

More severe measures might include attempts to confine the assignment of new employees to clients without publicly traded securities, or the banning of direct financial interests in publicly held companies by all

---

[11] AICPA AU § 220 provides a discussion of the requirement for auditor independence.

[12] AICPA ET § 301.02.

employees.[13] Both of these approaches serve to eliminate the incentive for reciprocal information transfers with friends (*i.e.*, an employee at X & Co. invests in securities of Z & Co.'s audit clients based upon tips supplied by a friend working at Z, and provides similar information about X's clients to this friend in exchange). Thus, by not having valuable information to exchange, or by being unable to invest on the basis of tips supplied by a confederate, the temptation to engage in unethical acts can be reduced. In any case, trust must ultimately be placed in some small number of very carefully screened and upright individuals. The extent of security precautions that should be adopted is a matter of prudence, professional judgment, risk preferences, and cost/benefit analysis.

The frequently adopted "It can't happen here" attitude seems fine until lightning strikes. After such an event there is only regret. Thus far, accountants apparently have trained their employees well and have avoided accusations of insider trading, for the most part. One careless, greedy, or malicious employee, however, is all that is needed to do serious damage to a firm. It is now readily apparent that such prominent companies as E. F. Hutton, Shearson Lehman, Lazard Frères, Drexel Burnham Lambert, and Wachtell Lipton Rosen & Katz should have been more careful.

Moreover, unlike the E.S.M. Government Securities case at Alexander Grant & Co. (now Grant Thornton) which implicated a partner, information leakage is possible from lower level employees with relatively limited responsibility. All that is needed is the opportunity to discover information of value and the willingness to participate in illegal transactions for financial gain. Given the large numbers of employees who might divulge inside information, the accountants' window of vulnerability is large. In view of this, the cost of reinforcing employee familiarity with the rules of ethics is low in comparison with the potential benefits.

THE IMPACT OF EFFICIENT MARKET RESEARCH

Anderson[14] predicted that knowledge of market efficiency would affect accountants' "privity" defense established by Ultramares v. Touche by (1) broadening the classes of individuals to which auditors are liable through foreseeable usage and (2) decreasing the number of shareowners presumed to have actually suffered damages due to the speed with which the market impounds public information. The foreseeability rule suggests that if the market is widely known to rapidly reflect information in security prices, all securities traders are parties who can reasonably be foreseen to suffer injury as a result of auditor negligence or the misuse of information. The relationship of the speed of market price adjustment to "insider" trading liability is a function of the degree of efficiency present in securities markets. While Anderson implicitly assumed semi-strong efficiency in his analysis (*i.e.*, that security prices quickly adjust to reflect all public information), no unfair trading advantage would exist for "insiders" if the market were strong-form efficient (*i.e.*, instantaneously reflected all information, both public and private). In a strong-form efficient market, private information would have no value, would produce no trading advantage, and so its use would not hurt those without access to it. Hence, a convincing showing that securities markets are strong-form efficient could provide a defense against charges of unfair trading activity and might eliminate the need to regulate security trading by insiders.

Strong-form efficiency, however, is not supported by the literature. Dyckman and Morse, for example, citing studies of insiders by Lorie and Niederhoffer,[15] Jaffe,[16] and Finnerty,[17] among others, conclude that "Insiders appear to have information that is not fully reflected in prices."[18] This conclusion is corroborated by

---

[13] Exceptions might be made for holdings of mutual funds, closed-end investment companies, home mortgages, savings accounts, and money market funds. Purchases of United States government securities could be unrestricted. Ownership might also be allowed to permit interests in companies where the CPA serves as an officer or director or is otherwise already an "insider" on other grounds *e.g.*, professional corporation shareholder).

[14] James A. Anderson, "The Potential Impact of Knowledge of Market Efficiency on the Legal Liability of Auditors," *The Accounting Review* (April 1977), pp. 417-426.

[15] James Lorie and Victor Niederhoffer, "Predictive and Statistical Properties of Insider Trading," *Journal of Law and Economics* (April 1968), pp. 35-53.

[16] Jeffrey Jaffe, "Special Information and Insider Trading," *The Journal of Business* (July 1974), pp. 410-428.

[17] Joseph E. Finnerty, "Insiders and Market Efficiency," *The Journal of Finance* (September 1976), pp. 1141-1148.

[18] Thomas Dyckman and Dale Morse, *Efficient Capital Markets and Accounting: A Critical Analysis*, 2nd ed. (Englewood Cliffs, New Jersey: Prentice-Hall, 1986), p. 47.

Larker, Reder, and Simon[19] who studied insider trading activity around the time of mandated accounting changes and is consistent with Ronen[20] who argued that regulation of insider trading slows information dissemination and so results in valuable private information. Quasi-insiders, such as the specialists making markets in securities, have also been found to possess valuable non-public information [Niederhoffer and Osborne[21]].

In a more general context, Fama[22] found little support for the strong form of the efficient market hypothesis, although he did find that market prices do rapidly reflect publicly available information. This conclusion was stated concisely by Lorie and Hamilton, "There is no evidence, however, that groups other than specialists or corporate insiders can use special information to earn above normal profits,"[23] and was recently reaffirmed by Sharpe as follows: "The strong form is, as the term suggests, strong and...markets are not generally efficient in this sense."[24]

Hence, it appears that existence of the strong form of the efficient market hypothesis is unlikely, and that it is possible to earn abnormal profits based upon inside information. As a result, if one believes that this potential trading advantage of insiders should be curbed, a legislated attempt to discourage abuse by imposing sanctions (*e.g.*, through the Securities Exchange Act) is appropriate.[25]

SUMMARY

The courts have held that anyone in possession of material nonpublic information is an "insider" and so is subject to restrictions on security trading. These restrictions include not only a prohibition of trading for one's own account but also proscribe the distribution of "inside" information to others. This ban on the sharing of nonpublic information is formalized in the Insider Trading Sanctions Act of 1984.

Accountants' need for independence led. to standards of conduct that were sufficient to provide protection against the personal trading restrictions of the Securities Exchange Act of 1934. Additional measures, however, are needed to ensure compliance with the 1984 act. Rule 301 of the AICPA Code of Professional Ethics is consistent with this law but is limited in scope. Ethical training for all employees, familiarity with the law, rudimentary security measures, and simple prudence can substantially reduce the likelihood of both improper disclosures of confidential client information and violations of federal security regulations. These precautions may prevent disciplinary actions, save the careers of employees, and prevent irreparable damage to a firm's reputation. Caution with respect to inside information is necessary for accountants.

---

[19] David F. Larker, Renee E. Reder, and Daniel T. Simon, "Trades by Insiders and Mandated Accounting Standards," *The Accounting Review* (July 1983), pp. 606-620.

[20] Joshua Ronen, "The Effect of Insider Trading Rules on Information Generation and Disclosures by Corporations," *The Accounting Review* (April 1977), pp. 438-449.

[21] Victor Niederhoffer and M. Osborne, "Market Making and Reversal on the Stock Exchange," *Journal of the American Statistical Association* (December 1966), pp. 897-916.

[22] Eugene F. Fama, "Efficient Capital Markets: A Review of Theory and Empirical Work," *The Journal of Finance* (May 1970), pp. 383-417.

[23] James Lorie and Mary Hamilton, *The Stock Market: Theories and Evidence* (Homewood, Illinois: Richard D. Irwin, 1973), p. 96.

[24] William F. Sharpe, *Investments*, 3rd ed. (Englewood Cliffs, New Jersey: Prentice-Hall, 1985), p. 68.

[25] Even though legislation may be appropriate, the effectiveness of this act which was in force during the time periods covered by the studies quoted above is open to question.

4

Honesty in the Accounting Environment

Honesty is essential to the conduct of accounting to maintain the trust put by the general public in the profession of accounting as a guarantor of truth. The absence of honesty in accounting is generally caused by the phenomenon of fraud. Unfortunately, fraud in the accounting environment is on the increase, causing enormous losses to firms, individuals, and society and creating a morale problem in the workplace. It takes place as corporate fraud, fraudulent financial reporting, white-collar crime, or audit failures. This chapter explicates the lack of honesty in the accounting environment, provides some theoretical explanations from the field of criminology, and explores some outcome situations arising from corporate fraud.[1]

NATURE OF FRAUD IN THE ACCOUNTING ENVIRONMENT

Fraud has many definitions. It is a crime. The Michigan Criminal law states:

Fraud is a generic term, and embraces all the multifarious means which human ingenuity can devise, which are resorted to by one individual to get advantage over another by false representations. No definite and invariable rule can be laid down as a general proposition in defining fraud, as it includes surprise, trick, cunning and unfair ways by which another is cheated. The only boundaries defining it are those that limit human knavery. It is the intentional deception of another person, by lying and cheating for the purpose of deriving an unjust, personal, social, political or economic advantage over another person.[2]

It is definitely immoral.

Within a business organization fraud can be perpetrated for or against the firm. It is then a corporate fraud. It can be perpetrated by management or a person in a position of trust. It is then a management or white-collar crime. It may involve the use of an accounting system to portray a false image of the firm. It is then a form of fraudulent financial reporting. It may also involve a failure of the auditor to detect errors or misstatements. It is then an audit failure. In all these cases, the accountant as preparer, auditor, or user stands to suffer heavy losses.

Corporate Fraud

Corporate frauds or economic crimes are perpetrated generally by officers, executives, and/or profit center managers of public companies to satisfy their short-term economic needs. In fact, it may be the short-term-oriented management style that creates the need for corporate fraud given the pressure to increase current profitability in the face of few opportunities and the need to take unwise risks with the firm's resources. As confirmed by Jack Bologna,

rarely is compensation based on the longer term growth and development of the firm. As a consequence of this myopic view of performance criteria, the executives and officers of many public companies have a built-in incentive or motivation to play fast and loose with their firm's assets and financial data.[3]

In fact, more than the pressure for short-term profitability it is the economic greed and avarice that blot social values and lead to corporate fraud. Evidence from the Federal Bureau of Investigation shows that arrests from two categories of corporate fraud have climbed: fraud jumped 75 percent between 1976 and 1986, and embezzlement rose 26 percent.[4] In fact, corporate fraud goes beyond mere fraud and embezzlement. It points to a myriad of activities that may result in corporate fraud. The increase in corporate fraud in the United States and elsewhere is the result of the evasion in business ethics.

Fraudulent Financial Reporting

Fraudulent financial reporting is so rampant that a special commission was created to investigate it: the National Commission on Fraudulent Financial Reporting. The Commission defined fraudulent financial reporting as "intentional or reckless conduct, whether act or omission, that results in materially misleading financial statements."[5] It undermines the integrity of financial information and can affect a range of victims: shareholders, creditors, employees, auditors, and even competitors. It is used by firms that are facing economic crises as well as by those motivated by a misguided opportunism. Examples of common types of fraudulent practices include: manipulating, falsifying or altering records or documents; suppressing or omitting the effects of completed transactions from records of documents; recording transactions without substance; misapplying accounting policies; and failing to disclose significant information.[6] It shows a deliberate strategy to deceive by distorting the information and the information records. It results from a number of documented dysfunctional behaviors: smoothing, biasing, focusing, gaming, filtering, and illegal acts. These generally occur when managers have a low belief in the analyzability of information and a low belief in the measurability and verifiability of data.[7] Of all these documented dysfunctional behaviors the one most likely to result in fraudulent financial reporting is the occurrence of illegal acts by violation of a private or public law through frauds. It does not always start with an illegal act. Managers are known to choose accounting methods in terms of their economic consequences. Various studies have argued that managerial preferences for accounting methods and procedures may vary, depending on the expected economic consequences of those methods and procedures. It has been well-established that the manager's choice of accounting methods may depend on the effect on reported income, the degree of owner versus manager control of the company,[8] and methods of determining managerial bonuses.[9] This effort to use accounting methods to show a good picture of the company becomes more pressing on managers facing some form of financial distress, and in need of showing the economic events in the best optimistic way. This may lead to suppressing or delaying the dissemination of negative information.[10,11] The next natural step for these managers is to use fraudulent financial reporting. To hide difficulties and to deceive investors, declining and failing companies have resorted to the following fraudulent reporting practices:

(a) prematurely recognizing income, (b) improperly treated operating leases as sales, (c) inflated inventory by improper application of the LIFO inventory method, (d) included fictitious amounts in inventories, (e) failed to recognize losses through write-offs and allowances, (f) improperly capitalized or deferred costs and expenses, (g) included unusual gains in operating income, (h) overvalued marketable securities, (i) created "sham" year-end transactions to boost reported earnings, and (j) charged their accounting practices to increase earnings without disclosing the changes.[12]

In fact, one factor in the increase of fraudulent financial reporting that has escaped scrutiny is the failure of accounting education institutions to teach the ways of detecting fraud and the importance of its detection to the entire financial reporting system. The emphasis in the university and the CPA exam for that matter is with financial auditing rather than with forensic, fraud or investigative reporting. J. C. Threadway, Jr., the chairman of the National Commission on Fraudulent Financial Reporting saw it the following way:

If you go back to the accounting literature of the 1920s or earlier, you'll find the detection of fraud mentioned as the objective of an audit much more prominently. Our work to date in looking at the way accounting and auditing are taught today in colleges and business schools indicates that fraud detection is largely ignored. In fact, there are texts currently in use that do not even talk about the detection of fraud.[13]

Because the SEC is dedicated to the protection of the interests of investors and the integrity of capital markets, it is concerned that the adequate disclosures are provided for the public to allow a better judgment of the situation. One financial disclosure fraud enforcement program called for disclosures in four areas:

1. Liquidity problems, such as (a) decreased inflow of collections from sales to customers, (b) the lack of availability of credit from suppliers, bankers, and others, and (c) the inability to meet maturing obligations when they fall due.
2. Operating trends and factors affecting profits and losses, such as (a) curtailment of operations, (b) decline of orders, (c) increased competition, or (d) cost overruns on major contracts.
3. Material increases in problem loans must be reported by financial institutions.
4. Corporations cannot avoid their disclosure obligations when they approach business decline or failure.[14]

Obviously there is a need for corporations to adopt measures to reduce exposure on causes of fraudulent and questionable financial reporting practices.

White-Collar Crime

White-collar crime was a concern for Emile Durkheim, who was convinced that the "anomie state" of "occupational ethics" was the cause "of the incessant recurrent conflicts, and the multifarious disorders of which the economic world exhibits so sad a spectacle."[15] At the same time, E. A. Ross noticed the rise in vulnerability created by the increasing complicated forms of interdependence in society and the exploitations of these vulnerabilities by a new class he called "criminaloid."[16] He argued that a new criminal was at large, one "who picks pockets with a railway rebate, murders with an adulterant instead of a bludgeon, burglarizes with a 'rake-off' instead of a jimmy, cheats with a company prospectus instead of a deck of cards, or scuttles his town instead of his ship."[17] The phrase "white-collar crime" was in fact originated in Edwin Sutherland's presidential address to the American Sociological Society in December 1939.[18] He defined it as "a crime committed by a person of respectability and high social status in the course of his occupation."[19] A debate followed with M. B. Clinard defining white-collar crime as restricted only to "illegal activities among business and professional men,"[20] and F. E. Harting defining it as "a violation of law regulating business, which is committed for a firm by the firm or its agents in the conduct of its business."[21] Basically, one view of white-collar crime focused on occupation and the other focused on the organization. But in fact, it is the world of both occupation and organization that is the world of white-collar crime and that constitutes what the knife and gun are to street crime.[22] White-collar crimes have not been condemned as vehemently as other common crimes. One reason is that their crime is not to cause physical injury but to further organizational goals. But in fact, individuals were found not only to consider organizational crimes in the physical impact to be far more serious than those with physical impact, but they also rate physical organizational crimes as equal in seriousness to a range of common crimes.[23] Another reason for the indifference to white-collar crime may be the possibility that members of the general public are themselves committing white-collar crimes on a smaller scale.[24] In addition, the white-collar criminal generally finds support for his behavior in group norms that place him in a different position from the common criminal. As V. Aubert explains:

> But what distinguishes the white-collar criminal in this aspect is that his group often has an elaborate and widely accepted ideological rationalization for the offenses, and is a group of great social significance outside the sphere of criminal activity — usually a group with considerable economic and political power.[25]

The white-collar criminal is motivated by social norms, accepted and enforced by groups that indirectly give support to the illegal activity. In a lot of cases the organization itself is committing the white-collar crime, sometimes because it may be the only response to economic demands.

White-collar crime may be characterized by five principal components: intent to commit the crime, disguise of purpose, reliance on the naivete of the victim(s), voluntary victim action to assist the offender, and concealment of the violation.[26] Unlike traditional crime, its objective is to steal kingly sums rather than small sums of money and its modus operandi is to use technology and mass communication rather than brute force and crude tools. In addition, white-collar crime relies on the ignorance and greed of its victims.[27] It inflicts economic harm, physical harm, and damage to the social fabric.

White-collar crime can be occupational or organizational. Occupational crime arises from violations committed by individuals or small groups in connection with their occupations.[28] Examples include the following:

> Tax evasion; embezzlement; illegal manipulations in the retail sale of used cars and other products; fraudulent repairs of automobiles, television sets, and appliances; check-kiting; and violations in the sale of securities. Some government employees and politicians commit a number of occupational offenses such as the direct misappropriation of public funds through padded payrolls, the illegal placement of rela-

tives on their payrolls, or the acceptance of monetary payments from appointees. They may also gain financially by giving favors to business firms. . . . Physicians may prescribe narcotics illegally, perform illegal abortions, make fraudulent reports or give false testimony in accidental cases, or they may split the fees. Illegal activities among lawyers include the misappropriation of funds in receiverships, abetting perjury testimony from witnesses, and various forms of "ambulance chasing."[29]

Organizational crimes are crimes committed as part of working on behalf of an organization. In constructing a model for organizational crime, H. C. Finney and H. R. Lesieur concluded that the "essential components in its development were a recognition that organizations as well as individuals commit crimes to achieve their objectives and solve their problems and that commitment to deviant courses of action involves normal processes of decision making under conditions of limited rationality."[30]

The organizational crimes are characteristic of deviant organizations. As explained by L. W. Sherman,

industrial air pollution, discriminatory employment practices, price fixing, and fraudulent corporate financial reporting are examples of crimes that only formal organizations are capable of committing. The decisions to commit these criminal acts are made by individuals in control of those organizations. If these crimes are defined as organizational actions, then the organizations committing them can be defined as deviant organizations.[31]

Deviance committed by an organization is collective rule-breaking action that helps achieve organizational goals. Deviance committed in an organization is individual or collective rule-breaking action that does not help to achieve organizational goals, or that is harmful to those goals."[32]

The sources of organizational deviance are either the existence of deviant goals, or deviant means, both deviant from societal norms or laws.[33]

Audit Failure

Auditors are expected to detect and correct or reveal any material omissions or misstatements of financial information. When auditors fail to meet these expectations an audit failure is the inevitable result. It is then the level of audit quality that can avoid the incurrence of audit failures. Audit quality has been defined as the probability that financial statements contain no material omission or misstatements.[34] It has also been defined in terms of audit risk, with high-quality services reflecting lower audit risk.[35] Audit risk was defined as the risk that "the auditor may unknowingly fail to appropriately modify his opinion on financial statements that are materially misstated."[36]

Audit failures do, however, occur and as a consequence bring audit firms face to face with costly litigation, loss of reputation, not to mention court-imposed judgments and out-of-court settlements. It is the client's or the users' losses that lead to the litigation situation and the potential of payments to the plaintiffs. Litigation can be used as an indirect measure of audit quality using an inverse relation—auditors with relatively low (high) litigation offer higher (lower) quality suppliers. This relationship was in fact verified in a study indicating as expected that non-Big Eight firms as a group had higher litigation occurrence rates than the Big Eight, and supporting the Big Eight as quality differentiated auditors.[37]

But not all litigations follow directly from audit failures. In a study describing the role of business failures and management fraud in both legal actions brought against auditors and the settlement of such actions, Zoe-Vonna Palmrose found that nearly half of the cases alleging audit failures involved business failures or clients with severe financial difficulties, and a majority of lawsuits involving bankrupt clients also involved management fraud.[38] This points to the fact that business failures and management fraud play a great role in the occurrence of audit failures, which calls for the auditor to take a responsible attitude in the detection of fraud as it may affect the audit quality, the audit risk, and the potential costly litigations. As stated by J. E. Connor,

establishing the requirement to identify the conditions underlying fraudulent reporting as an independent objective of the audit process would help to clarify auditor responsibility and increase auditor awareness of this responsibility. Performance of the recommended procedures of management control review and evaluation and fraud risk evaluation would improve the probability of detecting conditions leading to misstated financial statements. The required focus on financial condition would help to identify more effectively those entities that would qualify as business failure candidates in the near term.[39]

While management fraud and business failure may play a great role in audit failures, there are other reasons for such failures. For example, K. St. Pierre and J. Anderson's extended analysis of documented audit failures identified three other reasons, namely error centering on auditors' interpretation of generally accepted accounting principles, error centering on auditor's interpretation of generally accepted auditing standards or the implementation of generally accepted auditing standards, and error centering on fraud of the auditor.[40]

FRAMEWORK FOR FRAUD IN THE ACCOUNTING ENVIRONMENT

We have established that fraud is rampant in the accounting environment, taking the shape of corporate fraud, fraudulent financial reporting, white-collar crime, and audit failures. The main issue that arises is to determine the causes and above all an explanation for the situation. Descriptive characteristics of the person or the situation that may lead to fraud in the accounting environment abound. For example, there is a need to watch for "red flags" that do not necessarily prove management fraud, but when enough of them exist, there is the potential for corporate fraud. Examples of the red-flag characteristics to be wary of in the course of an audit include the following:

- A person who is a wheeler dealer
- A person without a well-defined code of ethics
- A person who is neurotic, manic-depressive, or emotionally unstable
- A person who is arrogant or egocentric
- A person with a psychopathic personality[41]

In examining the corporate structures and practices that create opportunities for key individuals in a company to commit fraud for corporate benefit, Albert et al. suggest a consideration of the following 17 specific red flags:

1. Related-party transactions
2. The use of several different audit firms, or the frequent changing of auditors
3. Reluctance to give auditors needed data
4. The use of several different legal firms or the frequent changing of legal counsels
5. The use of unusually large number of banks, none of which can see the entire picture
6. Continuous problems with various regulatory agencies
7. A complex business structure
8. No effective internal auditing staff
9. High degree of computerization in the firm
10. Inadequate internal control system, or failure to enforce existing internal controls
11. Rapid turnover of key employees
12. Involvement in atypical or "hot" industries
13. Large year-end and/or unusual transactions
14. Unduly liberal accounting practices
15. Poor accounting records
16. Inadequately staffed accounting department
17. Inadequate disclosure of questionable or unusual accounting practices. [42]

K. A. Merchant cites as causes of financial reporting organizational factors and personal circumstances. "By providing incentives for deception, by failing to persuade managers and employees that chances of detection are higher and penalties severe, and by failing to provide adequate moral guidance and leadership, corporations increase the use of illegal and unethical practices."[43]

While these descriptive characteristics may be useful for a detection of the potential of fraud in the corporate environment, they do not provide an adequate normative explanation of why fraud happens. The field of criminology, however, offers various models and theories that are very much applicable to fraud in the accounting environment and may offer alternative explanations for the phenomenon.

The Conflict Approach

The consensus approach and the conflict approach are two major views that hypothesize about law and society.[44] Influenced by anthropological and sociological studies of primitive law, the consensus approach sees the law developing out of public opinion as a reflection of popular will. The conflict approach sees laws as originating in a political context where influential interest groups pass laws that are beneficial to them. A third view argues for an integrated approach, which focuses on the different functions of the consensus and the conflict approaches, with the conflict approach ideal to explain the creation of criminal law and the consensus perspective the operation of the law.

In the case of the accountant and fraud, it can be argued using the conflict approach that accounting interest groups presented a favorable picture of their problematic situation by insisting that they could control for fraud and worked to get their view of the situation more widely recognized. The process led to less stringent regulation enacted for fraudulent reporting cases and white-collar crime. Basically, it fits with the notion that the criminal law that emerges after the creation of the state is designed to protect the interests of those who control the machinery of the state and that includes the accounting profession.

The consensus approach refers instead to the widespread consensus about the community's reaction to accounting fraud and to the legislation enacted. The consensus approach to accounting fraud may have resulted from either the ignorance or the indifference of the general public to the situation. Another explanation is the idea of differential consensus related to the support of criminal laws.[45] While serious crimes receive strong support for vigorous actions, crimes relating to the conduct of business and professional activities generate an apathetic response.

If one adopts a conflict model of crime, then the origin of the fraudulent practices in accounting may be linked to a society's political and economic development. As society's political and economic development reach higher stages, institutions are created to accommodate new needs and to check aggressive impulses. In the process these restraining institutions create a system of inequality and spur the aggressive and acquisitive impulses that the consensus model of crime mistakes for part of human nature. It is the powerful elites rather than the general will that arise to label the fraudulent practices in accounting as criminal because these crimes affect these elites as they are related to property and its possession and control. At the same time, members of that same elite constitute a major component of those participating in the fraudulent practices in accounting. What causes these people to engage in the practices remains the question. The conflict model of crime would attribute the practices to a system of inequality that values certain kinds of aggressive behavior rather than strain, social disorganization, or inadequate socialization as in the consensus model. Basically, those engaging in fraudulent practices in accounting are reacting to the life conditions of their own social class: acquisitive behavior of the powerful on one hand and the high-risk property crimes of the powerless on the other. One would conclude that the focus of the attack on the fraudulent practices should be toward the societal institutions that led to the isolation of the individuals. It implies a reorganization of these institutions to eliminate the illegal possession of rights, privileges, and position.

The Ecological Theory

An examination of some of the notorious accounting frauds, white-collar crimes, and/or audit failures may suggest that some criminal types are attracted to business in general and to accounting in particular. Therefore, the criminal cases are not indicative of a general phenomena in the field but the result of the criminal actions of the minority of criminal types that have been attracted to the discipline of accounting. This approach is known as the "Lombrosian" view of criminology.

The central tenet of Lombroso's early explanations of crime is that criminals represent a particular physical type, distinctively different from noncriminals. In general terms, he claimed that criminals represent a form of degeneracy which was manifested in physical characteristics reflective of earlier forms of evolution. He described criminals as atavistic, a throwback to an earlier form of evolutionary life. For instance, he thought ears of unusual size, sloping foreheads, excessive long arms, receding chins, and twisted noses were indicative of physical characteristics found among criminals.[46]

But with the Lombrosian theory of a physical "criminal type" losing its appeal, the ecological theory appears as a viable and better alternative to an explanation of the fraud phenomenon in accounting. It adopts as a basis of explanation of corporate fraud the concept of social disorganization, which is generally defined as the decrease of influence of existing rules of behavior on individual members of the group. Criminal behavior in the accounting field is to be taken as an indicator of a basic social disorganization. First, weak social organization of the discipline of accounting leads to criminal behavior. Second, with the social control of the discipline waning because of the general public indifference, some accountants are freed from moral sensitivities and are predisposed to corporate fraud, white-collar crime, and/or audit failure. It is then the general public's failure to function effectively as an agency of social control that is the immediate cause of corporate fraud, white-collar crime, fraudulent financial reporting, and/or audit failure. Basically, some accountants are freed from moral sensitivities when social control breaks down or fails to function properly.

The Cultural Transmission Theory

Unlike the ecological theory that assumes that criminal behavior is a product of common values incapable of realization because of social disorganization, the cultural transmission theory attempted to identify the mechanisms relating social structure to criminal behavior. One mechanism is the concept of differential association, which maintains that a person commits a crime because he or she perceives more favorable than unfavorable definitions of law violation. A person learns to become a criminal. As explained by Sutherland,

As part of the process of learning practical business, a young man with idealism and thoughtfulness for others is inducted into white-collar crime. In many cases he is ordered by a manager to do things which he regards as unethical or illegal, while in other cases he learns from those who have the same rank as his own how they make a success. He learns specific techniques for violating the law, together with definitions of situations in which those techniques may be used. Also he develops a general ideology.[47]

The cultural transmission theory assumes then that delinquents have different values than nondelinquents. Criminal behavior is the result of values condoning crime. The criminals have been socialized into the values condoning crime. They were transmitted into a culture of crime. Their criminal behavior is an expression of specific values.[48] The following nine propositions constitute an articulation of Sutherland's theory of differential association for the explanation of crime.

1. Criminal behavior is learned.
2. Criminal behavior is learned in interaction with other persons in a process of communication.
3. The principal part of the learning of criminal behavior occurs within intimate personal groups.
4. When criminal behavior is learned, the learning includes (a) techniques of committing the crime, which are sometimes very simple; (b) the specific direction of motives, drives, rationalizations, and attitudes.

5. The specific direction of motives and drives is learned from definitions of legal codes as favorable and unfavorable.

6. A person becomes delinquent because of an excess of definitions favorable to violation of law over definitions unfavorable to violation of law. This is the principle of differential association.

7. Differential associations may vary in frequency, duration, priority, and intensity.

8. The process of learning criminal behavior by association with criminal and anticriminal patterns involves all the mechanisms that are involved in any other learning.

9. While criminal behavior is an expression of general needs and values, it is not explained by those general needs and values since noncriminal behavior is an expression of the same needs and values.[49]

Basically, what is implied is that fraudulent behavior in accounting is learned; it is learned indirectly or by indirect association with those who practice the illegal behavior. An accountant engages in fraud because of the intimacy of his or her contact with fraudulent behavior. This has been called the process of "differential association." Sutherland explains as follows:

It is a genetic explanation of both white-collar criminals and lower-class criminality. Those who become white-collar criminals generally start their careers in good neighborhoods and good homes, graduate from colleges with some idealism, and with little selection on their part, get into particular business situations in which criminality is practically a folk way. The lower-class criminals generally start their careers in deteriorated neighborhoods and families, find delinquents at hand from whom they acquire the attitudes toward, and the techniques of, crime through association with delinquents and through partial segregation from law-abiding people. The essentials of the process are the same for the two classes of criminals.[50]

Anomie Theories

Anomie as introduced by Durkheim is a state of normlessness or lack of regulation, a disordered relationship between the individual and the social order, which can explain various forms of deviant behavior.[51] Robert Merton's formulation of anomie does not focus on the discontinuity between the life experiences of an individual, but between the lack of fit between values and norms that confuse the individual.[52] As an example in achieving the American dream, individuals may find themselves in dilemmas between cultural goals and the means specified to achieve them, leading to seek ways to adopt. These ways include conformity, innovation, ritualism, retreatism, and rebellion.[53]

Conformity to the norms and use of legitimate means to attain success does not lead to deviance. Innovation refers to the use of illicit means to attain success and may explain white-collar crime in general and fraudulent accounting and auditing practices in particular. Merton alludes as follows: "On the top economic level, the pressures toward innovation not infrequently erase the distinction between business-like stirrings this side of the mores and sharp practices beyond the mores."[54] Ritualism refers to an abandoning of the success goal. "Though one draws in one's horizons, one continues to abide almost compulsively by institutional norms."[55] Retreatism is basically a tacit withdrawal from the race, a way of escaping from it all. Finally, rebellion is a revolutionary rejection of the goals of success and the means of reaching it.

Those adaptations are a result of the emphasis in our society on economic success and on the difficulty of achieving it.

It is only when a system of cultural values extols, virtually above all else, certain *common* success-goals for the population at large while the social structure rigorously restricts or completely closes access to approved modes of reaching these goals *for a considerable part of the same population,* that deviant behavior ensues on a large scale.[56]

Interestingly enough, Merton goes as far as suggesting that deviance develops among scientists because of the emphasis on originality. Given limited opportunity and short supply, scientists would resort to devices such as reporting only data that support one's hypothesis, secrecy, stealing ideas, and fabricating data.[57]

Unlike Durkheim, Merton believed that anomie is a permanent feature of all modern industrial societies. Their emphasis on achievement and the pressures that result lead to deviance. The anomie thesis was further explored in the work of Albert Cohen[58] and Richard Cloward and Lloyd Ohlin.[59] Cohen attributes the origins of criminal behavior to the impact of ambition across those social positions where the possibilities of achievement are limited. What results is a nonutilitarian delinquent subculture.[60] Individuals placed in low social positions accept societal values of ambition but are unable to realize them because of lack of legitimate opportunities to do so. Cloward and Ohlin suggest that the resulting delinquent behavior is, however, conditioned by the presence or absence of appropriate illegitimate means.[61]

Corporate fraud, fraudulent reporting practices, white-collar crime, and/ or audit failures are a result of anomie in modern societies. Basically, delinquent accountants emerge among those whose status, power, and security of income are relatively low but whose level of aspiration is high, so that they strive to emerge from the bottom even using illegal ways. Fraudulent behavior among accountants is then the solution to status anxiety. It results from the discrepancy between the generally accepted values of ambition and achievement and the inability to realize them, and the availability of appropriate illegitimate means.

A Framework for Fraud in Accounting

The various theories from the field of criminology offer alternative explanations for the phenomena of corporate fraud, white-collar crime, fraudulent financial reporting, and audit failures. They can be integrated in a framework to be used for identifying the situations most conducive to those phenomena (see Exhibit 4.1). Basically, the frameworks will postulate that corporate fraud, white-collar crime, fraudulent financial reporting, and audit failures will occur most often in:

1. *Situations where accounting and business groups have presented a favorable picture of their problematic situation by insisting that they can control for fraud and have worked to get their view of the situation more widely recognized.* What may exist is a situation where the accountants and/or businesspeople have stated that they are taking private actions to avoid pub-

Exhibit 4.1
A Framework for Fraud in Accounting

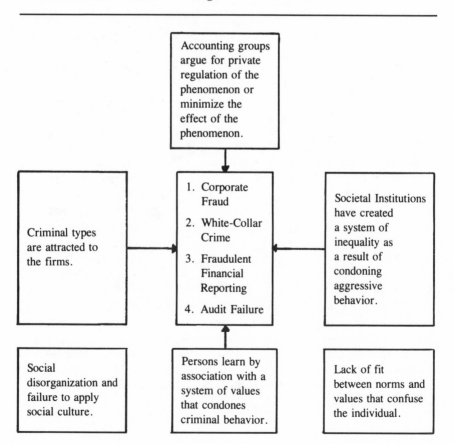

lic regulation of the phenomena, where in fact their actions were mere cosmetic changes and/or camouflage of serious problems in the profession. There have been ample examples of situations where the accounting profession has argued for private regulation of various problems affecting the profession, the discipline, and/or standard setting, and has thwarted the actions of legislators trying to put a stop to the abuses. One only has to recall the failure of various congressional committees investigating the profession to enact any fundamental regulations to change the nature, character, structure, and behaviors of the profession to illustrate the point. From a conflict approach, part of this view is clearly a situation where the interests of those who control the machinery of the state, and that includes the power of the accounting profession, are protected from stringent regulation.

2. *Situations where societal institutions have accumulated power, privileges, and position creating a perception of inequality from those who are not members of these institutions.* Basically, the situation may lead to an isolation of individuals where the acquisitive behavior of the powerful is evident in their daily life. The lower level accountant may react to this situation of powerlessness, inferiority, and exclusion by resorting to the various types of illegal activities covered in this chapter. It would be a mere reaction to a system of inequality that values aggressive behavior as explained by the conflict model.

3. *Situations where firms in general have attracted some criminal types.* This Lombrosian view of the phenomena has been found to apply to various accounting frauds. Examples of characteristics to be examined in order to assess the probability of fraud include:

1. A person with low moral character
2. A person who rationalizes contradictory behavior
3. A person with a strong code of personal ethics
4. A person who is a "wheeler-dealer"
5. A person lacking stability
6. A person with a strong desire to beat the system
7. A person who has a criminal or questionable background
8. A person with a poor credit rating and/or financial status.[62]

4. *Situations where social disorganization in general and failure to apply social control exists.* Basically, weak social organization of the discipline and failure of the general public to be concerned creates a climate conducive to fraud.

5. *Situations where persons are placed in a system of values that condones corporate fraud, white-collar crime, fraudulent financial reporting, and audit failures.*

6. *Situations where there is a lack of fit between values and norms that compose the individual.*

OUTCOME SITUATIONS ARISING FROM CORPORATE FRAUD

Away from RICO to ADR

There is definitely a dramatic increase in the number of claims against CPAs and the amounts sought by claimants as a result of the expanding scope of accountants' liability and RICO (Racketeer Influenced and Corrupt Organizations Act) liability. RICO, originally used by persons victimized by a "pattern of racketeering activity" to sue for treble damages and attorney fees, has been used more and more in commercial litigation growing out of fraudulent securities offerings, corporate failures, and investment disappointments. An account alleging that codefendant auditors (sometimes in alleged conspiracy with their client and its management) had violated the federal mail and securities fraud statutes by improperly auditing and issuing audit opinions on their client's financial statements on two or more specified occasions, and by employing in the operations of their firms (in or affecting interstate commerce) the fees received for those audits, by reason of which plaintiffs were injured in their business or property, is claimed to allege a violation of statutory provisions of the RICO Act.[63] Efforts were made in 1987 to reform the civil provisions of RICO. In fact, a Senate bill introduced by Howard Metzenbaum continues to permit plaintiffs to seek multiple damages in cases otherwise punishable under the securities laws if the plaintiffs are small investors.[64] The definition of small investor will include more than 50 percent of the over 45 million investors in securities in the United States. That spells bad news for the accounting profession. Witness the following statement made by B. Z. Lee, the AICPA's choice for testifying to the need to reform RICO: "Of greatest concern to the accounting profession . . . is the fact that RICO continues to be used to evade the standards of the securities laws and to raise the stakes in ordinary litigation arising from securities transactions."[65]

For now, fraudulent cases involving auditors will continue to be prosecuted with RICO liability in mind. In these fraudulent cases accountants have found themselves named as codefendants. The rationale behind the courts' proneness to hold auditors liable for losses associated with business failures results from the belief that auditors "(1) can best prevent the losses associated with business failures and (2) are able to spread their liability through insurance."[66] What auditors face is a dangerous gamble, which is trial by jury, especially with the risk of RICO-treble damage judgments. Not only may the average juror not understand the complexities of the cases, but the CPA may face the situation of claims without merit because their factual and legal positions may be misunderstood or rejected by the same jurors. The trial by jury may also be an expensive alternative even if the CPA's position prevailed. Witness the following assessment of the situation:

Even if the accountant ultimately prevails at trial, the costs of protracted litigation, including attorneys' fees and deposition costs, can be prohibitively high. Thus, even a win before a jury often translates into great pecuniary loss. Litigation costs and exposure aside, an additional substantial burden is placed on an accountant defendant who is called away from practice — losing both time and fees — and required to produce and review records, study claimants' documents and testimony, appear as a witness on deposition, attend depositions of others and be in attendance at trial.[67]

The trial by jury can also be detrimental to accountants because of the several often-repeated arguments that are increasingly persuasive in courts. These arguments include the perceptions that auditors are equipped to prevent the losses associated with business failures, accountants are deep pockets that can use their insurance to spread the losses, and equity calls for placing losses resulting from business failures on auditors.[68] What appear to be more beneficial options for resolving claims against CPAs are the ADR (Alternative Dispute Resolution) methods, namely arbitration, court-assessed arbitration, mediation, or mistrial.

In fact, the AICPA Special Committee on Accountants' legal liability prepared in 1987 a paper on ADR as a flexible approach to resolving litigation with a client by transforming the typical confrontational position into one of cooperation to reach a mutually advantageous solution.[69] One suggestion made is for the accountant and his client to agree on some element of an engagement letter or on a separate agreement that any disputes between them will be determined by ADR procedures. The following two model paragraphs are offered for an engagement letter, one specifically for arbitration and the other for general procedure:

Model Arbitration Paragraph

Any controversy or claim arising out of or relating to our engagement to [describe service, e.g., audit the company's financial statements] shall be resolved by arbitration in accordance with the Commercial Arbitration Rules of the American Arbitration Association, and judgment on the award rendered by the Arbitrator(s) may be rendered in any Court having proper jurisdiction.

Model General ADR Paragraph

In the event of any dispute between us relating to our engagement to [describe engagement, e.g., audit the company's financial statements; prepare the company's tax returns], we mutually agree to try in good faith to resolve the dispute through negotiation or alternative dispute resolution techniques before pursuing full-scale litigation.[70]

Arbitration is now appearing as the more viable option. The pros for arbitration include its informal nature, the choice of knowledgeable professionals as arbitrators, its low cost, its avoidance of the wrong judgments by an unsophisticated jury, the neutralizing of the hostility factor to professionals and sympathy factor to alleged victims prevalent in a jury trial, and the elimination of the risk of a runaway jury's returning a verdict that far exceeds actual losses. These features are summed up as follows:

In arbitration, extensive and time consuming discovery, which has become standard practice in litigation, is generally not permitted. During the preparatory stages of arbitration, lengthy depositions usually aren't allowed and limited documentation is exchanged on an informal basis. At arbitration hearings, the rules of evidence are more relaxed. Because of the expertise of the members of the panel, the need for experts to make detailed explanations to unsophisticated jurors is substantially reduced. Fewer witnesses need to be called to testify, fewer technical requirements need be met and fewer technical evidentiary objections and arguments need be made.[71]

Naturally there are limitations to arbitration, the major ones being the absence of judicial review and the loss of the court's requirement that evidence be legally admissible and weighed in accordance with legal principles. Other limitations are expressed as follows:

While the American Institute of CPAs legal liability special committee has submitted proposed alternative dispute resolution and arbitration clauses, the inclusion of these clauses in the initial engagement letter may subject a member to a coverage defense in any subsequent litigation. . . . Arbitration includes numerous negative points such as limited discovery, limited appeal and a difficulty in confining the arbitrators' decision to case and statutory law. This is particularly true when a defense may involve a question of privity. These negative points severely affect the insurer's ability to defend an insured in a malpractice claim. It seems to me that a CPA may subject himself to an insurance coverage dispute by including an arbitration clause in the initial engagement letter, since the clause binds the CPA and his insurer to submit to future arbitration.[72]

The Liability Exposure Expands

With the number of lawsuits filed in 1987 reaching one private lawsuit for every 15 Americans, the accountants were not immune to the epidemic of lawsuits. The consequences include escalating judgments and legal costs and astronomic increases in the premiums for professional liability. Even the AICPA professional liability insurance plan increased the premium to 200 percent by the end of 1985 along with a coupling of deductibles and reduction in the maximum coverage available from $20 million in 1984 to $5 million in 1985. The situation is explained as follows: "As a result of the premium increase, some medium-sized firms previously paying about $3,400 for $5 million in coverage saw their bills jump to $10,250. In addition, the deductible per claim doubled from $3,500 to $7,000."[73]

To make things worse than they are, megasuits are now being filed against the eight largest accounting firms. Examples include the $260 million damage suit filed in 1985 by the British government for alleged negligence against the auditors of the Delorean Motor Company in Northern Ireland, and the $100 million judgment brought against an Australian accounting partnership in *Cambridge Credit Corporation Ltd. v. Hutcheson.*[74]

The nature of the accounting liability has changed since the first English lawsuit against an auditor in 1887.[75] Two major suits had a profound effect — Judge (later Justice) Benjamin N. Cardozo's opinion in *Ultramares Corp. v. Touche* in 1931[76] and the McKesson & Robbins business fraud and settlement with accountants in 1938.[77] The *Ultramares v. Touche* decision was that accountants are liable for negligence to their clients and to those they know will be using their work product. More precisely, Judge Cardozo held that accountants could not be held liable to third parties because it might "expose accountants to a liability in an indeterminate amount for an indeterminate time to an indeterminate class. The hazards of business conducted on these terms are so extreme as to enkindle doubt whether a flaw may not exist in the implication of a duty that exposes to these consequences."[78]

The doctrine known as the "privity defense" has been recently eroded with a dramatic expansion in the scope of an auditor's availability for negligence. As Newton Minow states: "The new theory seems to be that the accountant should be held responsible for a business that doesn't function properly."[79] The new *doctrine of indeterminate liability* extends the accountants' liability to any investor or creditor who can convince the court or a jury that the accountant, in hindsight, could have prevented a business failure or fraud by disclosing it. Another new doctrine known as *fraud-on-the-market theory* allows investors to recover from defendants for alleged misrepresentations of which the investors were completely unaware as long as reliance on the statements by the market affected the price of the security bought or sold by the plaintiff. An example of the new doctrines came in 1983 when the New Jersey Supreme Court, in *H. Rosenblaum, Inc. v. Adler,* held that the accountants can be held of negligence to any reasonable "third parties" relying on that information, especially that the accountants are able to use and misuse:

Independent auditors have apparently been able to obtain liability insurance covering these risks or otherwise to satisfy their financial obligation. We have no reason to believe they may not purchase malpractice insurance policies that cover their negligence leading to misstatements relied upon by persons who received the audit from the company pursuant to a proper business purpose. Much of the additional costs incurred either because of more thorough auditing review or increased insurance premiums would be borne by the business entity and its stockholders or its customers.[80]

There is definitely a misperception of the accounting profession and its work product. Victor Earle, general counsel of Peat, Marwick, Mitchell & Company stated this misperception with prescience two decades ago as follows:

The misconceptions in the public mind are at least fivefold: first, as to *scope*—that auditors make a 100 percent examination of the company's records, which can be depended upon to recover all errors or misconduct; second, as to *evaluation*—that auditors pass the wisdom and legality of a company's multitudinous business decisions; third, as to *precision*—that the numbers set forth in a company's audited financial statements are immutable absolutes; fourth, as to *reducibility*—that the audited results of a company's operations for a year can be synthesized into a single number; and fifth, as to *approval*—that by expressing an option on a company's financial statement, the auditors "certify" its health and attractiveness for investment purposes."[81]

The liability exposure of U.S. accounting firms doing audits of overseas subsidiaries of American companies also increased tremendously in March 1988 when a federal judge ruled that U.S.-based accounting firms can be sued in U.S. courts for allegedly shoddy audits in other nations. The decision came after the court denied a motion by Arthur Anderson & Company to throw out a $260 million suit against it by the British government for allegedly negligent audits after the collapse of Delorean Motor Company's Irish unit. That the U.S. courts will have jurisdiction in such cases spells more trouble for American accounting firms as U.S. courts are known to be far tougher on accountants than English and European courts.[82]

In March 1988 the liability exposure took a different dimension when the Supreme Court made it easier for shareholders to file class-action lawsuits against companies that issue misleading information. In its ruling, the Supreme Court endorsed the efficient market hypothesis, which maintains that all publicly available information is reflected in the market price. Therefore, shareholders alleging misleading information and security fraud don't have to prove that they have relied on the misleading information. Basically, nobody can hide anymore behind a white collar.[83]

Those developments put the accounting profession in a dangerous situation as all business failures could be blamed on them and as the normal risks of investment may be shifted from the investor to the accountant. Frivolous litigation may arise, leading the accounting profession to avoid serving riskier industries, and to avoid innovations in their own practice. A case in point is the review of earnings forecasts. Minow explains as follows: "accountants would be discouraged from innovations within their own practice, such as review of earnings forecasts, which, though potentially highly useful to the investing public, are necessarily speculative and, in the current climate, pose obvious litigation risks to accountants."[84]

Fraud Engagement: The Issues

Fraud as the intentional deception, misappropriation of resources, or the distortion of data to the advantage of the perpetrator may involve either a manager or an employee. Management fraud is the most difficult to detect and can cause irreparable damage. The conduct of an audit in accordance with generally accepted accounting principles does not anticipate deceit and may fail to detect fraud. The key to fraud prevention could be effective and functioning internal controls. However, some fraud schemes may be effectively designed to work within the framework of an effective internal control system. The level of assurance of these controls becomes the key. Fraud is most associated with a problem of integrity and therefore not easily quantifiable. What may be needed besides the audit is a fraud engagement. It is different from a generally accepted auditing standard-based audit in the following way:

In short, the fraud engagement requires a specialized program that is singularly designed for discovery. It is ideally concerned with what lies behind transactions, with regard to materiality, and is not concerned with the application of generally accepted accounting principles unless misapplication has led to fraudulent statements. In its purest form, therefore, it is a hybrid of auditing and management advisory services. And the individual searching for fraud must have a detection mentality that is tempered with a high level of innovation and skepticism.[85]

Fraud engagement should be looking for specifically recurring fraud schemes and watch for specific indicia of fraud. Recurring fraudulent schemes include petty cash embezzlement, generally camouflaged by false or inadequate documentation; accounts payable fraud, involving the formation of a dummy corporation to invoice the payer and receive the funds; cash inventory schemes, where inventory is purchased with cash or its equivalent, rather than by check, and is not placed on the books; false-payroll schemes, involving the creation of a fictitious employee, with management cashing his or her spurious payroll checks; lapping schemes where employees steal from one customer's account and attempt to cover the theft by applying to that account later collections from another customer; and kickback schemes.[86] All these schemes involve some diversion of assets or information followed by the prevention or deferral of the activities' disclosure. They can be detected if certain indicators are watched carefully, especially those that are present time and again when fraud occurs. The following types of indicia are an example of the type of irregularity that deserve closer scrutiny:

1. High rates of employee turnover, particularly in the accounting or bookkeeping departments.
2. Refusal to use serially numbered documents or the undocumented destruction of missing numbers.
3. Excessive and unjustified cash transactions.
4. Excessive and unjustified use of exchange items, such as cashiers' checks, travelers' checks and money orders.
5. Failure to reconcile checking accounts.

6. Excessive number of checking accounts with a true business purpose.

7. The existence of liens and other financial encumbrances before a bankruptcy, which may indicate that the bankruptcy was planned.

8. Photocopies of invoices in files.

9. A manager or employee who falls in debt.

10. Excessive number of unexplained corporate checks bearing second endorsements.

11. Excessive or material changes in bad-debt write-off.

12. Inappropriate freight expenses in relation to historical sales or industry norms.

13. Inappropriate ratio of inventory components.

14. Business dealings with no apparent economic purpose.

15. Assets apparently sold but possession maintained.

16. Assets sold for much less than they are worth.

17. Continuous rollover of loans to management or loans to employees not normally included in the loans accounts.

18. Questionable changes in financial ratios, such as net income and inventory.

19. Questionable leave practices, such as the failure or refusal of an employee to take leave.[87]

It follows that auditors have to expand their role to that of police officers and engage in detecting and reporting fraud and financial weaknesses in the firms they audit. The three-year examination of the auditing profession ending in 1988 by the House Subcommittee on Oversight and Investigations had a nonnegotiable item for the profession, which is to be the voluntary protector of the investor or face a legislation that will make it mandatory.[88] For that Congress will use the Treadway findings as a basis for the legislation and increase the SEC power to impose sanctions and push for criminal prosecution. One would not blame Congress as the typical situation now shows a failure of auditing standards when they allow auditors to wait until a company has failed before notifying the SEC of possible fraud. A case in point is the ZZZZ Best One Company, where Ernst and Whinney had good reason long before ZZZZ Best collapsed that much of the statements of the carpet cleaning company were fraudulent. It was over and of no use to anyone when Ernst and Whinney decided to make its knowledge of fraud public. It was only after the bankruptcy that Ernst and Whinney filed documents with the SEC indicating that it had been tipped off that ZZZZ Best really was little more than a giant Ponzi scheme, costing investors more than $70 million.

Fraud auditing is then one solution to the problem of fraudulent financial reporting and fraud in general. It was referred to as the creation of an environment that encourages the detection and prevention of frauds in commercial transactions.[89] The advent of federal, criminal, and regulatory statutes involving business calls for some form of fraud auditing. When fraud auditing fails to connect the problems and frauds do happen, is there a role for forensic and investigative accounting? Forensic auditing deals with the relation and application of financial facts to legal problems.[90] What is then the difference between forensic accounting, fraud auditing, investigative auditing, and financial auditing? The answer to a survey among the staff members of Peat Marwick Lindquist Holmes, a Toronto-based firm of chartered accountants, is very illustrative of the difference:

Forensic accounting is a general term used to describe any investigation of a financial nature that can result in some matter that has legal consequence.

Fraud auditing is a specialized discipline within forensic accounting, which involves the investigation of a particular criminal activity, namely fraud.

Investigative auditing involves the review of financial documentation for a specific purpose, which could relate to litigation support and insurance claims as well as criminal matters.[91]

Forensic accounting goes beyond routine auditing. It specializes in uncovering fraud in the ledger of business contracts and bank statements. Forensic auditors will prepare a written profile of every key person involved with the company, including corporate officers, employees, and vendors. Keeping track of everything is the objective. The following comment by Douglas Carmichael illustrates the extent of the investigation under forensic auditing: "When the death of a company (occurs) under mysterious circumstances, forensic accountants are essential. . . . Other accountants may look at the charts. But forensic accountants actually dig into the body."[92]

CONCLUSIONS

There is definitely an emerging problem for the accounting profession arising from the increase of fraud in the accounting environment. The credibility of the profession and the field as a guarantor of the integrity of financial recording systems will suffer more unless drastic measures are taken to make the accountant and the auditor face the fraud problem as a major concern. The immorality of the phenomenon should be accentuated in special courses in the ethical problems of the profession. The education community should take the lead in sensitizing the students to the existence, the gravity, the immorality, and the consequences of the problem. The short-term-oriented management style that may account for a large proportion of corporate fraud needs to be deemphasized because of its myopic view of the environment.

NOTES

1. Ahmed Belkaoui, *The Coming Crisis in Accounting* (Westport, Conn.: Quorum Books, 1990), pp. 61–94.

2. *Michigan Law Review,* ch. 66, sect. 1529.

3. Jack Bologna, *Corporate Fraud: The Basics of Prevention and Detection* (Boston: Butterworths, 1984), p. 10.

4. "Ethics 101," *U.S. News and World Report,* March 14, 1988, p. 76.

5. National Commission on Fraudulent Financial Reporting, *Report of the National Commission on Fraudulent Financial Reporting* (Washington, D.C., April 1987), p. 2.

6. K. A. Merchant, *Fraudulent and Questionable Financial Reporting: A Corporate Perspective* (Morristown, N.J.: Financial Executives Research Foundation, 1987), p. 5.

7. J. G. Birnberg, L. Turopolec, and S. M. Young, "The Organizational Context of Accounting," *Accounting, Organizations and Society* (July 1983), p. 2.

8. D. S. Dhaliwal, G. L. Salamon, and E. D. Smith, "The Effect of Owner Versus Management Control on the Choice of Accounting Methods," *Journal of Accounting and Economics,* 1 (1982), pp. 41–53.

9. P. M. Healy, "The Effects of Bonus Schemes on Accounting Decisions," *Journal of Accounting and Economics,* 1–3 (1985), pp. 85–107.

10. K. B. Schwartz, "Accounting Changes by Corporations Facing Possible Insolvency," *Journal of Accounting, Auditing and Finance,* (Fall 1982), pp. 32–43.

11. K. B. Schwartz and K. Menon, "Auditor Switches by Failing Firms," *The Accounting Review* (April 1985), pp. 248–261.

12. John M. Fedders and L. Glenn Perry, "Policing Financial Disclosure Fraud: The SEC's Top Priority," *Journal of Accountancy* (July 1984), p. 59.

13. Bill Lietbag, "Profile: James C. Treadway, Jr.," *Journal of Accountancy* (September 1986), p. 80.

14. Fedders and Perry, "Policing Financial Disclosure Fraud," p. 59.

15. Emile Durkheim, *The Division of Labor of Society,* trans. George Simpson (New York: Free Press, 1964), p. 2.

16. E. A. Ross, *Sins and Society* (Boston: Houghton Mifflin, 1907).

17. Ibid., p. 7.

18. Edwin Sutherland, "White Collar Criminality, *American Sociological Review* 5 (February 1940), pp. 110–123.

19. Edwin Sutherland, *White Collar Crime* (New York: Dryden Press, 1949), p. 9.

20. M. B. Clinard and R. F. Reier, *Sociology of Deviant Behavior* (New York: Holt, Rinehart and Winston, 1979), p. viii.

21. F. E. Hartung, "White Collar Offenses in the Wholesale Meat Industry in Detroit," *American Journal of Sociology,* 56 (1950), p. 25.

22. S. Wheeler and M. L. Rothman, "The Organization as Weapon in White-Collar Crime," *Michigan Law Review* (June 1982), pp. 1403–1476.

23. L. S. Shrager and O. F. Short, Jr., "How Serious a Crime? Perceptions of Organizational and Common Crimes," in G. Geis and E. Stotland (eds.), *White-Collar Crimes: Theory and Research* (London: Sage, 1980), p. 26.

24. V. Aubert, "White-Collar Crime and Social Structure," *American Journal of Sociology* (November 1952), p. 265.

25. Ibid., p. 266.

26. H. Edelhertz, E. Stotland, M. Walsh, and J. Weimberg, *The Investigation of White Collar Crime: A Manual for Law Enforcement Agencies,* U.S. Department of Justice, LEAA (Washington, D.C.: U.S. Government Printing Office, 1970).

27. August Bequai, *White-Collar Crime: A 20th Century Crisis* (Lexington, Mass.: Lexington Books, 1978), p. 13.

28. M. B. Clinard and R. Quinney, *Criminal Behavior Systems: A Typology* (New York: Holt, Rinehart and Winston, 1973), pp. 187–205.

29. M. B. Clinard, *Corporate Ethics and Crime: The Role of Middle Management* (Beverly Hills, Calif.: Sage, 1983), p. 13.

30. H. C. Finney and H. R. Lesieur, "A Contingency Theory of Organizational Crime," in S. B. Bacharach (ed.), *Research in the Sociology of Organizations: A Research Annual* (Greenwich, Conn.: JAI Press, 1982), p. 289.

31. L. W. Sherman, "Deviant Organizations," in M. D. Ermann and R. J. Lundman (eds.), *Corporate and Governmental Deviance: Problems of Organizational Behavior in Contemporary Society* (Oxford: Oxford University Press, 1982), p. 63.

32. Ibid, p. 64.

33. Ibid, p. 66.

34. Zoe-Vonna Palmrose, "An Analysis of Auditor Litigation and Audit Service Quality," *The Accounting Review* (January 1988), p. 56.

35. Linda E. DeAngelo, "Auditor Size and Audit Quality," *Journal of Accounting and Economics* (December 1981), pp. 183–199.

36. American Institute of Certified Public Accountants, *Professional Standards,* Vol. 1 (New York: AICPA, 1985), SAS no. 47.

37. Palmrose, "An Analysis of Auditor Litigation," p. 72.

38. Zoe-Vonna Palmrose, "Litigation and Independent Auditors: The Role of Business Failures and Management Fraud," *Auditing: A Journal of Practice and Theory* (Spring 1987), pp. 90–103.

39. J. E. Connor, "Enhancing Public Confidence in the Accounting Profession," *Journal of Accountancy* (July 1986), p. 83.

40. K. St. Pierre and J. Anderson, "An Analysis of Audit Failures Based on Documented Legal Cases," *Journal of Accounting Auditing and Finance* (Fall 1984), pp. 229–247.

41. J. Bologna, *Corporate Fraud,* p. 39.

42. W. Steve Albert et al., *How to Detect and Prevent Business Fraud* (Englewood Cliffs, N.J.: Prentice-Hall, 1987, p. 66.

43. Merchant, *Fraudulent and Questionable Financial Reporting,* p. 12.

44. James T. Carey, *Introduction to Criminology* (Englewood Cliffs, N.J.: Prentice Hall, 1978), p. 8.

45. Don L. Gibbons, "Crime and Punishment: A Study in Social Attitudes," *Social Forces* (June 1969), pp. 391–397.

46. J. Robert Lilly, Francis T. Cullen, and R. A. Ball, *Criminology Theory: Context and Consequences* (Newbury Park, Calif.: Sage, 1989), p. 28.

47. Sutherland, *White Collar Crime,* p. 240.

48. Walter B. Miller, "Lower Class Culture as a Generating Milieu of Gang Delinquency," *Journal of Social Issues,* 14, no. 3 (1958), pp. 5–19.

49. E. H. Sutherland and Donald R. Cressy, *Criminology,* 18th ed. (Philadelphia: Lippincott, 1970), pp. 25–26.

50. Sutherland, "White Collar Criminality," p. 12.

51. Durkheim, *The Division of Labor in Society.*

52. Robert K. Merton, "Social Structure and Anomie," *American Sociological Review* (October 1938), pp. 672–682.

53. Robert K. Merton, *Social Theory and Social Structure* (New York Free Press, 1957), pp. 131–160.

54. Ibid, p. 144.

55. Ibid., p. 150.

56. Ibid., p. 146.

57. Robert K. Merton, "Priorities in Scientific Discovery: A Chapter in the Sociology of Science," *American Sociological Review* (December 1957), pp. 635–659.

58. Albert K. Cohen, *Delinquent Boys: The Culture of the Gang* (New York: Free Press, 1955).

59. Richard A. Cloward and Lloyd E. Ohlin, *Delinquency and Opportunity* (New York: Free Press, 1960).

60. Albert K. Cohen, "The Study of Social Disorganization and Deviant Behavior," in Robert K. Merton, Leonard Boorm, and Leonard S. Cottrell, Jr. (eds.), *Sociology Today: Problems and Prospects* (New York: Harper and Row, 1959).

61. Cloward and Ohlin, *Delinquency and Opportunity.*

62. Albert et al., *How to Detect and Prevent Business Fraud,* p. 84.

63. R. James Gomley, "RICO and the Professional Accountant," *Journal of Accounting, Auditing and Finance* (Fall 1983), pp. 51–60.

64. Ibid.

65. "AICPA Testifies at RICO Hearings: Support Boucher Proposal," *Journal of Accountancy* (January 1988), p. 82.

66. Richard S. Banick and Douglas C. Broeker, "Arbitration: An Option for Resolving Claims Against CPAs," *Journal of Accountancy* (October 1987), p. 124.

67. Ibid., p. 126.

68. Stevens H. Collins, "Professional Liability: The Situation Worsens," *Journal of Accountancy* (November 1985), p. 66.

69. American Institute of Certified Public Accountants, Special Committee on Accountants' Legal Liability, *Alternative Dispute Resolution* (New York: AICPA, 1987).

70. Ibid., pp. 2 and 8.

71. Ibid., p. 126.

72. Joseph D. Steward, "Arbitration," *Journal of Accountancy* (February 1988), pp. 12–13.

73. Collins, "Professional Liability," p. 57.

74. Ibid., p. 57.

75. *Leeds Estate, Building & Investment Co. v. Shepherd,* 36, Ch. D. 787 (1887).

76. *Ultramares Corp. v. Touche,* 225 N.Y.170, 174 N.E. 441 (1931).

77. See Denzil Y. Causey Jr., *Duties and Liabilities of Public Accountants* (Homewood, Ill.: Dow-Jones-Irwin, 1982), pp. 16–17.

78. *Ultramares Corp. v. Touche.*

79. Newton N. Minow, "Accountants' Liability and the Litigation Explosion," *Journal of Accountancy* (September 1984), p. 72.

80. *Rosenblaum Inc. v. Adler,* Slip Op. A-39/85 New Jersey: June 9, 1983, p. 21.

81. Victor Earle, "Accountants on Trial in a Theater of the Absurd," *Fortune* (May 1972), p. 227.

82. Lee Berton, "Accounting Firms Can Be Sued in U.S. Over Audits Done Abroad, Judge Rules," *Wall Street Journal* (March 10, 1988), p. 2.

83. Lawrence J. Tell, "Giliam's Legacy: Nobody Can Hide Behind a White Collar," *Business Week* (February 8, 1988), p. 69.

84. Minow, "Accountants' Liability and the Litigation Explosion," p. 80.

85. Marvin M. Levy, "Financial Fraud: Schemes and Indicia," *Journal of Accountancy* (August 1985), p. 79.

86. Ibid., pp. 79–86.

87. Ibid., pp. 86–87.

88. Sallie Gaines, "From Balance Sheet to Fraud Beat," *Chicago Tribune* (February 28, 1988), Sec. 7, p. 5.

89. Jack G. Bologna and Robert J. Lindquist, *Fraud Auditing and Forensic Accounting* (New York: John Wiley, 1987), p. 22.

90. Ibid., p. 85.

91. Ibid., p. 91.

92. D. Akst and L. Berton, "Accountants Who Specialize in Detecting Fraud Find Themselves in Great Demand," *Wall Street Journal* (February 26, 1988), Sec. 2, p. 17.

BIBLIOGRAPHY

American Institute of Certified Public Accountants, Special Committee on Accountants' Legal Liability. *Alternative Dispute Resolution.* New York: AICPA, 1987.

———. *Professional Standards,* Vol. 1. New York: AICPA, 1985, SAS No. 47.

Aubert, V., "White-Collar Crime and Social Structure." *American Journal of Sociology* (November 1952), p. 265.

Banick, Richard S. and Douglas C. Broeker. "Arbitration: An Option for Resolving Claims Against CPAs." *Journal of Accountancy* (October 1987), p. 124.

Bequai, A., *White-Collar Crime: A 20th Century Crisis.* Lexington, MA: Lexington Books, 1978, p. 13.

Berton, L. "Accounting Firms Can Be Sued in U.S. Over Audits Done Abroad, Judge Rules." *Wall Street Journal* (March 10, 1988), p. 2.

Birnberg, J. G., L. Turopolec, and S. M. Young. "The Organizational Context of Accounting." *Accounting, Organizations and Society* (July 1983), pp. 111–130.

Bologna, J. *Corporate Fraud: The Basics of Prevention and Detection* Boston: Butterworths, 1984, p. 39.

——— and R. J. Lindquist. *Fraud Auditing and Forensic Accounting* New York: John Wiley, 1987, pp. 22, 85, 91.

Carey, J. T. *Introduction to Criminology.* Englewood Cliffs, N.J.: Prentice Hall, 1978.

Causey, D. Y., Jr. *Duties and Liabilities of Public Accountants.* Homewood, Ill.: Dow-Jones-Irwin, 1982, pp. 16–17.

Cloward, R. A. and L. E. Ohlin. *Delinquency and Opportunity.* New York: Free Press, 1960.

Cohen, Albert K. *Delinquent Boys: The Culture of the Gang.* New York: Free Press, 1955.

———. "The Study of Social Disorganization and Deviant Behavior." In Robert K. Merton, Leonard Boorm and Leonard S. Cottrell, Jr. (eds.), *Sociology Today: Problems and Prospects.* New York: Harper and Row, 1959.

Collins, Steven H. "Professional Liability: The Situation Worsens." *Journal of Accountancy* (November 1985), pp. 57 and 66.

Connor, J. E. "Enhancing Public Confidence in the Accounting Profession." *Journal of Accountancy* (July 1986), p. 83.

DeAngelo, Linda E. "Auditor Size and Audit Quality." *Journal of Accounting and Economics* (December 1981), pp. 183–199.

Dhaliwal, D. S., G. L. Salamon, and E. D. Smith, "The Effect of Owner Versus Management Control on the Choice of Accounting Methods." *Journal of Accounting and Economics* 1 (1982), pp. 41–53.

Durkheim, Emile. *The Division of Labor of Society,* trans. George Simpson. New York: Free Press, 1964, p. 2.

Earle, V. "Accountants on Trial in a Theater of the Absurd." *Fortune* (May 1972), p. 227.

Edelhertz, H., E. Stotland, M. Walsh, and J. Weimberg. *The Investigation of White Collar Crime: A Manual for Law Enforcement Agencies.* U.S. Department of Justice, LEAA. Washington, D.C.: U.S. Government Printing Office, 1970.

"Ethics 101." *U.S. News and World Report,* March 14, 1988, p. 76.

Fedders, John M. and L. Glenn Perry. "Policing Financial Disclosure Fraud: The SEC's Top Priority." *Journal of Accountancy* (July 1984), p. 59.

Gaines, Sallie. "From Balance Sheet to Fraud Beat." *Chicago Tribune* (February 28, 1988), Sec. 7, p. 5.

Gibbons, D. L. "Crime and Punishment: A Study in Social Attitudes." *Social Forces* (June 1969), pp. 391–397.

Gomley, R. J. "RICO and the Professional Accountant." *Journal of Accounting, Auditing and Finance* (Fall 1983), pp. 51–60.

Hartung, F. E. "White Collar Offenses in the Wholesale Meat Industry in Detroit." *American Journal of Sociology,* 56 (1950), p. 25.

Healy, P. M. "The Effect of Bonus Schemes on Accounting Decisions." *Journal of Accounting and Economics,* 1–3 (1985), pp. 85–107.

Leeds Estate, Building & Investment Co. v. Shepherd, 36, Ch. D. 787 (1887).

Levy, Marvin M. "Financial Fraud: Schemes and Indicia." *Journal of Accountancy* (August 1985), p. 79.

Lietbag, Bill. "Profile: James C. Treadway, Jr." *Journal of Accountancy* (September 1986), p. 80.

Lilien, S. and V. Pastena. "Intermethod Comparability: The Case of the Oil and Gas Industry." *The Accounting Review* (July 1981), pp. 690–703.

Merchant, K. A. *Fraudulent and Questionable Financial Reporting: A Corporate Perspective.* Morristown, N.J.: Financial Executives Research Foundation, 1987.

Merton, R. K. "Social Structure and Anomie." *American Sociological Review* (October 1938), pp. 672–682.

————. "Priorities in Scientific Discovery: A Chapter in the Sociology of Science." *American Sociological Review* (December 1957), pp. 635–659.

————. *Social Theory and Social Structure.* New York: Free Press, 1957, pp. 131–160.

Michigan Law Review, ch. 66, sec. 1529.

Miller, Walter B. "Lower Class Culture as a Generating Milieu of Gang Delinquency." *Journal of Social Issues,* 14, no. 3 (1958), pp. 5–19.

Minow, Newton N. "Accountants' Liability and the Litigation Explosion." *Journal of Accountancy* (September 1984), pp. 72, 80.

National Commission on Fraudulent Financial Reporting. *Report of the National Commission on Fraudulent Financial Reporting.* Washington, D.C., April 1987, p. 2.

Palmrose, Zoe-Vonna. "An Analysis of Auditor Litigation and Audit Service Quality." *The Accounting Review* (January 1988), pp. 56, 72.

———. "Litigation and Independent Auditors: The Role of Business Failures and Management Fraud." *Auditing: A Journal of Practice and Theory* (Spring 1987), pp. 90–103.

Rosenblaum v. Adler, Slip Op. A-39/85 New Jersey, June 9, 1983, p. 21.

Ross, E. A. *Sins and Society.* Boston: Houghton Mifflin, 1907.

Russell, H. F. *Foozles and Fraud.* Altamonte Springs, Fla.: The Institute of Internal Auditors, 1977.

Schwartz, K. B. "Accounting Changes by Corporations Facing Possible Insolvency." *Journal of Accounting, Auditing and Finance* (Fall 1982), pp. 32–43.

——— and K. Menon. "Auditor Switches by Failing Firms." *The Accounting Review* (April 1985), pp. 248–261.

Shrager, L. S. and O. F. Short, Jr. "How Serious a Crime? Perceptions of Organizational and Common Crimes." In G. Geis and E. Stotland (eds.), *White-Collar Crime: Theory and Research.* London: Sage, 1980, p. 26.

Steward, Joseph D. "Arbitration." *Journal of Accountancy* (February 1988), pp. 12–13.

St. Pierre, K. and J. Anderson. "An Analysis of Audit Failures Based on Documated Legal Cases." *Journal of Accounting Auditing and Finance* (Fall 1984), pp. 229–247.

Sutherland, E. *White Collar Crime.* New York: Dryden Press, 1949, p. 9.

———. "White-Collar Criminality." *American Sociological Review,* 5 (February 1940).

Tell, Lawrence J. "Giliam's Legacy: Nobody Can Hide Behind a White Collar." *Business Week* (February 8, 1988), p. 69.

Uecker, W. C., A. P. Brief, and W. R. Kinney, Jr. "Perception of the Internal and External Auditor as a Deterrent to Corporate Irregularities." *The Accounting Review* (July 1981), pp. 465–478.

Ultramares Corp. v. Touche, 225 N.Y. 170, 179–180, 174 N.E. 441, 444 (1931).

Wheeler, S. and M. L. Rothman. "The Organization as Weapon in White-Collar Crime." *Michigan Law Review* (June 1982), pp. 1403–1476.

5

Accounting and Social Responsibility

Following World War II, most of the economies of the Western countries, some of the socialist countries, and even some of the Third World countries have experienced constant growth and increasing strength and have produced new arrays of goods and services intended to meet people's high expectations and living standards. What was asked from the economy was an improvement in the quality of life. To most people this concept meant more than the provision of goods and services. It is rather a state of the world depending on a satisfactory resolution of all social issues: ecology, technology, pollution, urban blight, education, housing, crime, energy, urban congestion, poverty, population growth, monopoly power, consumer problems, discrimination, high national debt, and so forth. All the sectors of the economy moved at one point or another to tackle these issues and improve the quality of life. *The result has been far from perfect.* A. W. Clausen ventures the following explanation: "I submit that a major reason for our inadequate response is that we find the quality of life issue confusing—and that the prime cause of that confusion is a lack of even the crudest form of measurements of 'quality.' "[1]

It is easy to concur with the above statement and suggest that the confusion may be cleared with the development of an "arithmetic of quality" leading to an eventual "social report."[2] Such a social report would identify, evaluate, and measure those aspects essential to maintain an adequate quality of life for all the members of a nation as defined by social goals. Daniel Bell rightfully argues that these social goals should deal with the "ability of an individual citizen to establish a career commensurate with his abilities and live a full and healthy life equal to his biological potential, and include a definition of the levels of an adequate standard of living and the elements of a decent physical and social environment."[3] The arithmetic of quality and the eventual production of social reports in conformity with social goals at both the firm and national levels is the purpose of socioeconomic accounting. *Socioeconomic accounting is a call for the measurement of the total performance of economic and government units and their contribution to the quality of life of all the members of a nation.* Most people would enthusiastically espouse this goal. There are, however, various individuals who might object to this concern with the quality of the environment. The most disturbing example of this type of individual is reported by Clausen as follows:

Some quite literally don't give a damn about the quality of the environment. In a recent speech before Bank of America managers, Louis Banks, Editorial Director of Time Inc., described a vivid recollection of lunching in an elegant Manhattan apartment, surrounded by priceless impressionist paintings, and hearing one of Wall Street's venerable geniuses remark: "I think the city is past saving, and I think my responsibility is to sit back and figure how I can profit from its decline and fall." Mr. Banks went on to say he regretted to report that particular Nero is still fiddling — and still prospering.[4]

Luckily, this particular Nero is among a minority with the wrong vision of truth. He failed to understand that the quality of life around him is heavily dependent on the quality of life of all the individuals in the nation. Prosperous individuals, firms, or nations in a troubled and spoiled environment may be able to shelter themselves in a ghetto of economic well-being but may not be able to secure the best quality of life given the interrelated social issues that define the quality of life. That is why a measurement of the total performance of economic and governmental units and their contribution to the quality of life of all the members of a nation is an important task; that is why we should be interested in the prolegomenon to accounting and social responsibility.

CORPORATE SOCIAL INVOLVEMENT IN THREE ENTERPRISE MODELS

None of our institutions exists by itself and is an end in itself. Every one is an organ of our society and exists for the sake of society. Business is no exception. Free enterprise cannot be justified as being good for business. It can be justified only as being good for society.[5]

This is the attitude that is beginning to dominate the public view of business organization: first, business is a corporate citizen; and second, it should be a good corporate citizen. This attitude arose from the need to control the overwhelming effects of large corporate entities on society and to involve businessmen in correcting some of society's ills. This point of view, however, is not accepted by everyone concerned with corporate society relationships. Sometimes labeled as strict constructionists, they criticize the social responsibility advocates and argue mainly that profit maximization is the only acceptable objective of business corporations. The debate has generated a huge literature arguing both viewpoints. They are presented next.

The Classical View

The classical view of firm behavior as formulated in the nineteenth century argued for perfect competition where the economic behavior is separate and distinct from other types of behavior, the objective function is to maximize profits, and the criterion of business performance is economic efficiency and progress. So motivated by these principles, the business firm was considered to have discharged its responsibilities to society if it efficiently met the market demands for its product. This view evolved to become known as the fundamentalist position. Fundamentalism rests on the market contract model for a description and a prescription of corporate-society relationships. As Lee Preston and James Post describe the situation, "according to the market contract model, each unit (firm or individual) in society makes an implicit market contract model with other members of society, providing them with goods and services they desire on terms more favorable than they can obtain elsewhere and obtaining its own requirements and rewards from them in return."[6]

This description implies that the responsibility of individuals and firms is to identify and respond to market stimuli and to make profits for the shareholders. Any corporate action on social issues is considered to violate management's responsibility to shareholders. As the most outspoken supporter of the fundamentalist position, Milton Friedman refutes the notion that the responsibility of corporate officials goes beyond serving the interests of their stockholders or their members. In a free economy, Friedman maintains that "there is one and only one social responsibility of business—to use its resources and engage its activities designed to increase its profits so long as it stays within the rules of the game, which is to say, engages in open and free competition, without deception and fraud."[7]

Friedman's view derives first from a general view holding that an individual should be allowed to pursue his or her own interest. Because, to quote Adam Smith, "by pursuing his own interest, he frequently promotes that of the society more effectually than when he really intends to promote it."[8] It derives also from a question of knowledge and propriety. Corporate officials may not know what the social interest is and are not appointed to serve the social interest. The corporation is a creation of the stockholders, who own it and decide on its conduct. Friedman asks a relevant question: "Is it tolerable that these public functions of taxation, expenditure, and control be exercised by the people who happen at the time to be in charge of particular enterprises, chosen for those posts by strictly private groups?"[9]

This view is reflected in most textbooks in the field of corporate finance and accounting, where authors operate on the assumption that management's primary goal is to maximize the wealth of its stockholders, and it is generally referred to as the shareholder wealth maximization (SWM) model. The firm accepts all projects yielding more than the cost of capital, and in equity financing prefers retaining earnings to issuing new stocks. Management is assumed to use decision rules and techniques that are in the best interests of the stockholders in terms of maximizing their wealth.

The classical, fundamentalist, or SWM view is generally defended on two grounds, one positive and one legal.[10] The positive case argues that role specialization and the market contract define the nature of corporate society relationships and allow the achievement of a social optimum. Therefore management cannot expand its role without affecting the performance of those tasks defined by the market contract, possibly leading to decreased efficiency and misallocation of resources. The legal case argues that the corporate character acts as a limitation on the nature and scope of business activities and on the legal responsibilities of managers. Basically, it limits their authority to consider or modify the nonmarket aspects of their activities.

The Managerial View

The managerial view arose in the 1930s as a result of the gap existing between the classical view and the new nature of corporation business. Adolf Berle and Gardiner Means were the first to point to the effects of the widespread separation of ownership from the management of the large business corporations and the greater decision-making powers held by these managers.[11] From these criticisms emerged a managerial view focusing on the central role of professional managers. The corporation is viewed now as a permanent *institution* with a life and purpose of its own. The managers/trustees run these corporations in the interests not only of shareholders but also of the employees, customers, suppliers, and other parties having rights in the organization that are not merely contractual claims.[12] According to an accepted manifesto of the managerial view, the modern professional manager also regards himself, not as an owner disposing of personal property as he sees fit, but as a trustee balancing the interests of many diverse participants and constituents in the enterprise, whose interests sometimes conflict with those of others.[13]

What all this implies is that the managers have enough discretionary control of corporate resources to consider adding social responsibility considerations in setting the objectives of the corporation. The extent of the involvement in social responsibility is defined mainly by the humanitarian predispositions of its management and is controlled by fears of stockholder dissatisfaction, of losing competitive power, and of adverse effects on earnings. The managerial view is not, however, indifferent to profit maximization. It merely adds an additional consideration in the resource allocation procedure, which is to recognize responsibility for other things besides profit maximization.[14]

The Social Environment View

The social environment model views the large corporation as a repository of huge economic and political power with concomitantly important social responsibilities. The large corporation is believed to have a keen interest in the total societal environment and not merely its markets. It recognizes explicitly the impact not only of economic forces but also of political and social forces. Consequently it responds to social demands for active participation in correcting some of society's ills, such as "inadequate educational systems, hard-core unemployment, hazardous pollution of natural resources, antiquated transportation, shameful housing, insufficient and ineffective public facilities, lack of equal opportunity for all, and a highly dangerous failure of communication between young and old, black and white."[15]

In adopting this more socially responsible attitude and responding to the pressures of new dimensions — social, human, and environmental — business organizations may have to alter their main objective, whether stockholder wealth maximization or management welfare maximization, to include as an additional constraint the welfare of society at large. This view is referred to as the "social welfare maximization model."[16] Under this model, the firm undertakes all projects that, in addition to the usual profitability objective, minimize the social costs and maximize the social benefits created by the productive operations of the firm. Consider, for example, the following assertions:

Business decision-making today is a mixture of altruism, self-interest, and good citizenship. Managers do take actions which are in the social interest even though there is a cost involved and the connection with long range profits is quite remote. . . .

The kind of managers we are discussing can be called social responsive managers. In their decision making they give substantial weight to social inputs along with economic and technical inputs, and they seek to provide social outputs for a wide variety of claimants. The change toward this type of role would take years, but the trend is clear. . . .

In order to perform their new socio-economic role effectively, business leaders need to develop value systems that recognize responsibilities to claimants other than stockholders. There is a strong evidence that managers already have this kind of value system.[17]

PARADIGMATIC THOUGHTS FAVORABLE TO
SOCIOECONOMIC ACCOUNTING

The literature in the social sciences in general and in sociology and social work in particular is witnessing a resurgence of new paradigms challenging the early focus on individual welfare and encouraging a more general focus on social welfare, the environment, and a total ecosystem perspective. These paradigms may be used as a justification for the expansion of the scope of conventional accounting to include the social measurement, reporting, and verification aspects of social accounting. These paradigms include a *commitment to social welfare paradigm, a new environment paradigm, an ecosystem perspective, and a sociologizing mode of management.* In what follows, each of these paradigms is examined.

Toward a Commitment to Social Welfare

An examination of the history of mankind shows that human survival has been possible only through cooperation. Consider for example the following insight by Stewart C. Easton, a historian:

It used to be thought that man in a state of nature was forced to compete with all other human beings for his very subsistence, or, in the famous words of Thomas Hobbes, that his life was "solitary, poor, nasty, brutish and short." We have no record of such a way of life, either in early times, or among present-day "primitive" men. And it no longer seems as probable to us as it did in the nineteenth century, under the influence of the biological ideas of Darwin, that human survival was a matter of success in the constant struggle for existence, if this struggle is conceived of as a struggle between human beings. It now seems much more probable that survival has always been due to successful cooperation between human beings to resist the always dangerous forces of nature.[18]

More recently, with the concern for ecological preservation and the protection and promotion of human life, the cooperation has taken the form of social welfare programs and services as important answers to the various personal and social perils threatening human life. A good definition of social welfare is provided by Walter Friedlander and Robert Apte's statement: "Social welfare is a system of laws, programs, and benefits which strengthen or assure provisions for meeting social needs recognized as basic for the welfare of the population and the functioning of social order."[19] Thus, social welfare includes all programs for meeting the basic social needs; it has its roots in religion, humanitarianism, and compassion. It calls for the creation of social structures or social agencies that have been appropriately described as the institutionalization of the philanthropic impulse and love of mankind.

The rationale for social welfare depends on two views — whether social welfare is needed for emergency situations or as a permanently needed function of society. Harold Wilensky and Charles Lebeaux put it this way:

Two conceptions of social welfare seem to be dominant in the United States today; the *residual* and the *institutional*. The first holds that social welfare institutions should come into play only when the normal structures of supply, the family, and the market, break down. The second, in contrast, sees the welfare services as normal, "first-line" functions of modern industrial society.[20]

It is rather evident that both views constitute an acceptable rationale for social welfare, although the institutional approach is the one that will eventually prevail in the future as a way of *continuously* answering the various personal and social perils that threaten the delicate balance of human life and the fragility of human security.

The Human Exceptionalism Paradigm Versus the New Environment Paradigm

For a long time the human exceptionalism paradigm (HEP) dominated the environmental discipline in sociology before the emergence of the new environment paradigm (NEP). The HEP views humans as unique among earth's creatures with a culture that can change infinitely and more rapidly than biological traits, with human traits and human differences as the result of acculturation, not biology. The NEP views humans as but one among many species interrelated by cause-and-effect linkages and bounded by a world with finite limits on economic, social, and political growth. The NEP is a result of the interest in societal changes not explainable by traditional sociological theories. It in turn has led to the emergence of environmental sociology.

The numerous competing theoretical perspectives in sociology—e.g., functionalism, symbolic interactionism, ethnomethodology, conflict theory, Marxism—all focus on men's relations with themselves rather than with the environment. This *anthropocentric* view represents the HEP. William R. Catton, Jr. and Riley E. Dunlap presented the following assumptions underlying HEP:

1. Humans are unique among earth's creatures, for they have culture.
2. Culture can vary almost infinitely and can change much more rapidly than biological traits.
3. Thus, many human differences are socially induced rather than inborn, they can be socially altered, and inconvenient differences can be eliminated.
4. Thus, also, cultural accumulation means that progress can continue without limit, making all social problems ultimately soluble.[21]

As a result of this position the ecosystem dependence of human systems was for a long time neglected in the sociological literature on economic development. The belief was that there were no limits to technological improvement, growth, and abundance.

The NEP emerged as a result of a new literature highlighting the problems for human society that may arise from the limitations of the ecological world. This literature included the works of Rachel Carson, Barry Commoner, Paul Ehrlich, and Garrett Hardin.[22] The NEP led to the acceptance of environmental variables as a legitimate area of inquiry for sociologists and the emergence of a new set of assumptions different from those of HEP. They include the following:

1. Human beings are but one species among the many that are interdependently involved in the biotic communities that shape our social life.
2. Intricate linkages of cause and effect and feedback in the web of nature produce many unintended consequences from purposive human action.
3. The world is finite, so there are potent physical and biological limits constraining economic growth, social progress, and other societal phenomena.[23]

These assumptions point clearly to the importance of environmental facts to understanding and explaining social facts. It is evident that human beings, as truly as other species of the organism, cannot ignore ecology or leave the ecology scene and are therefore engaged in what mathematical biologists can describe as the game of "existential Gambler's Ruin," wherein the optimal strategy in human encounters with environmental selection pressures is to minimize the stakes.[24] The environment is to be perceived as a factor that may influence and in turn be influenced by human behavior.

One tangible outcome of NEP is the emergence of *social impact statements,* which consider the total impact of a project on the environment.

The Ecosystem Perspective

Everyone is being exposed to speeches, literature, and other media on ecology and the "environmental crisis." Both topics are presented either as matters of fact or as the beginning of the imminent extinction of life on earth. In either case the global ecosystem is threatened, and the source of the problems remains to be clearly identified. Is the crisis due to the failure to limit growth as dictated by market-oriented policies? If it is, then the ecological crisis is nothing but a crisis in the economic organization of the global ecosystem as much as a new social and political crisis. Natural environment is then not the problem, it is the economic organization dictating its use that is the problem.[25] The damage is further aggravated by the nature of some of the relationships in the ecosystem:

1. The ecosystem processes are interlinked, and small changes in one process may produce large and unexpected effects and disturbances in other processes.
2. Most of the ecological changes are irreversible.
3. There is no complete scientific theory to deal with the complexity of ecosystemic processes and relations. Ecological systems are open systems while all theories and analysis deal with closed systems. Anthony Wilden warns as a consequence that the "inability of present theory to deal properly with these and other much more complex interactions means that *every ecological statement we read about is inherently and necessarily much more conservative in its estimates and predictions than the probable future state of the reality it is describing.*"[26]

Given these problems, a kind of ecosystem understanding and perspective is needed to protect human future.

To adopt this ecosystem perspective, a position has to be taken concerning the ideology of growth. More explicitly, are there limits to growth and hence a solution to the ecological crisis? The publication of the Club of Rome's *The Limits to Growth* provides one possible answer to the question.[27] *The Limits to Growth* is based on a cybernetic and systemic world model as a basis for computer simulations of the future development of the global socioeconomic system and as such includes in the simulation various factors and combinations of factors such as population growth, capital growth, available land for agriculture, pollution, and renewable resources. The results of the simulation point to a definite exhaustion of the world's natural resources over the next hundred years. The authors conclude by identifying an "ideal" program for a stable world system with the following policies to be introduced beginning in 1975:

1. The stabilization of population by equalizing the birth and death rate;
2. The stabilization of industrial capital by equalizing the depreciation and the investment rate, beginning in 1990;
3. The reduction of the consumption of natural resources to one-fourth of the 1970 level per unit of industrial output;
4. The shifting of economic preferences in society away from material goods toward services, such as education;
5. The reduction of pollution per unit of industrial output to one-fourth of its 1970 level;
6. The diversion of capital to food production with the goal of providing food for all people and overcoming traditional inequalities in distribution;
7. The diversion of a part of agricultural capital toward soil enrichment and preservation to avoid soil erosion and depletion;
8. An increase in the lifetime of industrial capital to counteract the low final level of capital stock resulting from the first seven policies.

The Limits to Growth is a call to some international intervention to ensure human future. It is also an ideological statement for checking and limiting growth – in brief, it is an ecosystem perspective.

The necessity for an ecosystem perspective is more evident when uncontrolled population growth and the environmental problems are analyzed in terms of the "tragedy of the commons."[28] Men attempt to maximize their gain. In the absence of controls, Hardin argues, they are driven by rational calculations of self-interest to overexploit or abuse the commons, whether it is a pasture shared by herdsmen or the earth's atmosphere. "Freedom in a commons brings ruin to all."[29] Given the absence of technical solutions to the problem, Hardin suggests the use of stringent controls ("mutual coercion, mutually agreed upon") to escape the "remorseless working of things" that characterizes the logic of a free commons.[30]

The Economizing Versus the Sociologizing Mode

The economizing mode and the sociologizing mode are two extreme perspectives suggested within which the actions of the corporation can be estimated and judged.[31]

Economizing results from the collaboration of the engineer and the economist to determine the best allocation of scarce resources among competing ends. Economizing is basically concerned with reaching a level of efficiency in the use of resources. It relies on engineering for designing the machines and determining the optimal way to use these machines in order to produce a maximum output within a given physical layout. It relies on economics to find the optimal mix of men and machines in the organization of production.

With economics, comes a rational division of labor, specialization of function, complementarity of relations, the uses of production functions (the best mix of capital and labor at relative prices), programming (the best ordering of scheduling of mixed batches in production, or in transportation), etc. The words we associate with economizing are "maximization," "optimization," "least cost," in short, the components of a conception of rationality.[32]

Economizing relies naturally on the market system and the resulting price system to evaluate the firm's allocation of resources. And more importantly, the economizing mode focuses on individual satisfaction as the unit for which costs and benefits are recognized and measured.

Unlike the economizing mode, the sociologizing mode focuses on the society's need in a coordinated fashion and taking into account a notion of the public interest. The sociologizing mode addresses two fundamental issues: the conscious establishment of social justice by the inclusion of all persons into the society; and the relative size of the public and the private sector.

Which of the two modes is more appropriate for the business corporation of today? The trend is clearly toward the sociologizing mode, mainly as a reaction to the increasing criticism toward the corporation reinforced by the feeling that corporate performance has caused the quality of life in society to deteriorate. Daniel Bell illustrates the new situation when he states that the "sense of identity between the self-interest of the corporation and the public interest has been replaced by a sense of incongruence."[33] The best evidence of the shift toward sociologizing is the increase in corporate participation in providing social benefits to their employees.[34]

THE CORPORATE SOCIAL PERFORMANCE MODEL

The focus in social responsibility started as early as 1953 when H. R. Bowen argued that managers should strive to "pursue those policies, to make those decisions, or to follow those lines of action which are desirable in terms of the objectives and values of our society."[35] The two fundamental premises of the social contract and moral agency are at the core of this concept of social responsibility. First, the social contract imposes on the firm a set of rights and obligations, as a condition of legitimacy.[36] Second, as a moral agent within society, firms have "the capacity to use moral rules in decision making" and "the capacity to control not only overt corporate acts, but also the structure of politics and rules."[37]

Efforts were made to model the concept of social responsibility of firms. They are explained next.

Wartick and Cochran's Model

A. B. Carroll presented a corporate social performance model as a three-dimensional integration of corporate social responsibility, corporate social responsiveness, and social issues.[38] Building on Carroll's work, S. L. Wartick and P. L. Cochran presented a corporate social performance model that reflects an underlying interaction among the principles of social responsibility, the process of social responsiveness, and the policies developed to address social issues.[39] The model is shown in Exhibit 5.1.

Social responsibility, the first dimension of the model, includes an economic responsibility to maximize profits within the rules of the game,[40] contrasted with a public responsibility to act along "widely shared and generally acknowledged principles directing and controlling actions that have broad implications for society at large or major portions thereof."[41] Social contract and moral agency institute the fundamental premises of social responsibility and define the main social obligations of the firm: economic, legal, ethical, and discretionary.

Social responsiveness, the second dimension of the model, focuses on the social response processes. Social responsiveness has been adequately defined as:

Exhibit 5.1
The Corporate Social Performance Model

Principles	Processes	Policies
Corporate Social Responsibilities	*Corporate Social Responsiveness*	*Social Issues Management*
1. Economic	1. Reactive	1. Issues Identification
2. Legal	2. Defensive	2. Issues Analysis
3. Ethical	3. Accommodative	3. Response Development
4. Discretionary	4. Proactive	
Directed at	*Directed at*	*Directed at*
1. The Social Contract of Business	1. The Capacity to Respond to Changing Societal Conditions	1. Minimizing "Surprises"
2. Business as a Moral Agent	2. Managerial Approaches to Developing Responses	2. Determining Effective Corporate Social Policies
Philosophical Orientation	*Institutional Orientation*	*Organizational Orientation*

Source: S. L. Wartick and P. L. Cochran, "The Evolution of the Corporate Social Performance Model," *Academy of Management Review*, 10, no. 4 (1985), p. 767. Reprinted with permission.

corporate social responsiveness, which has been discussed by some as an alternate to social responsibility is, rather, the action phase of management responding in the social sphere. In a sense, being responsive enables organizations to act on their social responsibilities without getting bogged down in the quagmire of definitional problems that can so easily occur if organizations try to get a precise fix on what their true responsibilities are before acting.[42]

It shows social responsiveness as a reactive, defensive, accommodative, and proactive process aimed at providing the means for meeting the social obligations set by the first dimension.

Social issues management, the third dimension of the model, focuses on the operationalization of social responsiveness. The issue management process is shown to consist of identification, analysis, and response development.[43]

The three dominant orientations of the model include philosophical orientation for the principles of social responsibility, institutional orientation for the processes of social responsiveness, and organizational orientation for social issues management.

Wood's Model

Donna Wood presented her model of corporate social performance as a configuration of principles of corporate social responsibility, processes of social responsiveness, and observable outcomes of corporate behavior.[44] The model is depicted in Exhibit 5.2. The principles of corporate social responsibility, including principles of legitimacy, public responsibility, and managerial discretion, are shown in Exhibit 5.3. The processes of corporate social responsiveness include environmental assessment aimed at organizational survival through adaptation to environmental conditions,[45] stakeholder management aimed at monitoring and maintaining the links between external stakeholders and company functions, and issues management arrived at developing policies to address social issues. Finally, the outcomes of corporate behavior fall in three categories: "The social impacts of corporate behavior, regardless of the motivation for such behavior or the process by which it occurs; the programs companies use to implement responsibility and/or responsiveness; and the policies developed by companies to handle social issues and stakeholder interests."[46] Examples of corporate social programs and policy are shown in Exhibit 5.4.

Exhibit 5.2
The Corporate Social Performance Model

Principles of corporate social responsibility

Institutional principle: legitimacy
Organizational principle: public responsibility
Individual principle: managerial discretion

Processes of corporate social responsiveness

Environmental assessment
Stakeholder management
Issues management

Outcomes of corporate behavior

Social impacts
Social programs
Social policies

Source: Donna J. Wood, "Corporate Social Performance Revisited," *Academy of Management Review*, 16, no. 4 (1991), p. 694. Reprinted with permission.

Exhibit 5.3
Principles of Corporate Social Responsibility

The Principle of Legitimacy: Society grants legitimacy and power to business. In the long run, those who do not use power in a manner which society considers responsible will tend to lose it.

Level of Application: Institutional, based on a firm's generic obligations as a business
                      organization.
               Focus: Obligations and sanctions.
               Value: Defines the institutional relationship between business and society
                      and specifies what is expected of any business.
             Origin: Davis (1973)

The Principle of Public Responsibility: Businesses are responsible for outcomes related to their primary and secondary areas of involvement with society.

Level of Application: Organizational, based on a firm's specific circumstances and rela-
                      tionships to the environment.
               Focus: Behavioral parameters for organizations.
               Value: Confines a business's responsibility to those problems related to
                      the firm's activities and interests, without specifying a too-narrow
                      domain of possible action.
             Origin: Preston & Post (1975)

The Principle of Managerial Discretion: Managers are moral actors. Within every domain of corporate social responsibility, they are obliged to exercise such discretion as is available to them, toward socially responsible outcomes.

Level of Application: Individual, based on people as actors within organizations.
               Focus: Choice, opportunity, personal responsibility.
               Value: Defines managers' responsibility to be moral actors and to per-
                      ceive and exercise choice in the service of social responsibility.
             Origin: Carroll (1979), Wood (1990)

Source: Donna J. Wood, "Corporate Social Performance Revisited," *Academy of Management Review*, 16, no. 4 (1991), p. 696. Reprinted with permission.

CONCEPTS OF SOCIAL PERFORMANCE

Nature of Social Performance

The measurement of social performance falls in the general area of social accounting.[47] Under this area there are four various activities that may be delineated: social responsibility accounting (SRA), total impact accounting (TIA), socioeconomic accounting, and social indicators accounting.[48] Exhibit 5.5 shows the characteristics of the various component parts of social accounting. One can see that the general concept and disclosure of social performance are products of SRA and TIA, and social accounting is appro-

Exhibit 5.4

Corporate Social Policy: Sample Outcomes of Acting on CSR Principles within CSR Domains

	CSR Principles		
Domains	Social Legitimacy (Institutional)	Public Responsibility (Organizational)	Managerial Discretion (Individual)
Economic	Produce goods & services, provide jobs, create wealth for shareholders.	Price goods & services to reflect true production costs by incorporating all externalities.	Produce ecologically sound products, use low-polluting technologies, cut costs with recycling.
Legal	Obey laws and regulations. Don't lobby for or expect privileged positions in public policy.	Work for public policies representing enlightened self-interest.	Take advantage of regulatory requirements to innovate in products or technologies.
Ethical	Follow fundamental ethical principles (e.g., honesty in product labeling).	Provide full and accurate product use information, to enhance user safety beyond legal requirements.	Target product use information to specific markets (e.g., children, foreign speakers) and promote as a product advantage.
Discretionary	Act as a good citizen in all matters beyond law and ethical rules. Return a portion of revenues to the community.	Invest the firm's charitable resources in social problems related to the firm's primary and secondary involvements with society.	Choose charitable investments that actually pay off in social problem solving (i.e., apply an effectiveness criterion).

Source: Donna J. Wood, "Corporate Social Performance Revisited," *Academy of Management Review*, 16, no. 4 (1991), p. 710. Reprinted with permission.

priately defined as "the process of selecting firm-level social performance variables, measures and measurements procedures; systematically developing information useful for evaluating the firm's social performance, and communication of such information to concerned social groups, both within and outside the firm."[49] A good conceptual framework for social accounting, proposed by K. V. Ramanathan, and comprising three objectives

Exhibit 5.5
The Characteristics of the Various Component Parts of Social Accounting

Division	Purpose	Area of Main Use	Time Scale	Measurements Used	Associated Areas
1. Social responsibility accounting (SRA)	Disclosure of individual items having a social impact	Private sector	Short term*	Levels I, II, mainly nonfinancial and qualitative	Employee reports, human resource accounting, industrial democracy
2. Total impact accounting (TIA)	Measures the total cost (both public and private) of running an organization	Private sector	Medium and long term	Financial AAA Level III	Strategic planning, cost-benefit analysis
3. Socio-economic accounting (SEA)	Evaluation of publicly funded projects involving both financial and nonfinancial measures	Public sector	Short and medium term	Financial, nonfinancial, Levels II and III	Cost-benefit analysis, planned programmed budgeting systems, zero-based budgeting, institutional performance indicators
4. Social indicators accounting (SLA)	Long-term nonfinancial quantification of societal statistics	Public sector	Long term	Nonfinancial quantitative AAA Level II	National income accounts, census statistics

*Normally short term to fit annual reporting patterns.

Source: Reprinted by permission of the publisher from "A Suggested Classification for Social Accounting Research," by M. R. Mathews, *Journal of Accounting and Public Policy*, 3, p. 202. Copyright 1984 by Elsevier Publishing Co., Inc.

and six concepts, is shown in Exhibit 5.6. This framework applies equally to SRA and TIA.

A question arises about who is "pushing" for corporate social reporting. Are they to the right or to the left of the political spectrum? R. Gray et al. presented corporate social reporting (CSR) as a dialectic between four positions: "(1) The extreme left-wing of politics ('left-wing radicals'); (2) the acceptance of the *status quo*; (3) the pursuit of subject/intellectual property rights; (4) the extreme right-wing of politics (the 'pristine capitalists' or 'right-wing radicals')[50] The major issues of discord in the development of corporate social reporting among these four groups are shown in Exhibit 5.7. The second group appears to represent those true advocates of corporate social reporting. They are represented by people

(1) who assume that the purpose of CSR is to enhance the corporate image and hold the, usually implicit, assumption that corporate behavior is fundamentally benign; (2) who assume that the purpose of CSR is to discharge an organization's accountability under the assumption that a social contract exists between the organization and society. The existence of this social contract demands the discharge of social accountability; (3) who *appear* to assume that CSR is effectively an extension of traditional financial reporting and its purpose is to inform investors.[51]

Rationale for Social Performance

Various arguments are used for the measurement and disclosure of social performance.

1. The first argument is that of *social contract*. Implicitly, it is assumed that organizations ought to act in a manner that maximizes social welfare, as if a social contract existed between the organization and society. By doing so, organizations gain a kind of organizational legitimacy vis-a-vis society. While the social contract may be assumed to be implicit, various societal laws may render certain covenants of the contract more explicit. These laws that constitute the rules of the game in which organizations choose to play become the terms of the social contract.[52] Through these implicit and explicit laws, society defines the rules of accountability for organizations.

The state, however, plays a primary role in the formulation of these laws and the specification of the rules of the game. In the U.S. contract, these laws and the general concern with social performance created a need for tracking environmental risk. With the 1989 SEC requirement that companies disclose any potential environmental cleanup liabilities they may face under the federal Superfund law, the 1990 annual reports of companies started the disclosure process. The 10K disclosures, added to the host of required filings with state and federal environmental agencies, led to the creation of data banks that provided information on companies specializing in the tracking of environmental risk. Examples of these companies include

Exhibit 5.6
Proposed Objectives and Concepts for Social Accounting

Objective 1

An objective of corporate social accounting is to identify and measure the periodic net social contribution of an individual firm, which includes not only the costs and benefits internalized to the firm, but also those arising from externalities affecting different social segments.

Objective 2

An objective of corporate social accounting is to help determine whether an individual firm's strategies and practices which directly affect the relative resource and power status of individuals, communities, social segments and generations are consistent with widely shared social priorities, on the one hand, and individuals' legitimate aspirations, on the other.

Objective 3

An objective of corporate social accounting is to make available in an optimal manner, to all social constituents, relevant information on a firm's goals, policies, programs, performance and contributions to social goals. Relevant information is that which provides for public accountability and also facilitates public decision making regarding social choices and social resource allocation. Optimality implies a cost/benefit-effective reporting strategy which also optimally balances potential information conflicts among the various social constituents of a firm.

Concept 1

A *social transaction* represents a firm's utilization or delivery of a socio-environmental resource which affects the absolute or relative interests of the firm's various social constituents and which is not processed through the marketplace.

Concept 2

Social overheads (returns) represent the sacrifice (benefit) to society from those resources consumed (added) by a firm as a result of its social transactions. In other words, social overheads is the measured value of a firm's negative externalities, and social returns is the measured value of its positive externalities.

Concept 3

Social income represents the periodic net social contribution of a firm. It is computed as the algebraic sum of the firm's traditionally measured net income, its aggregate social overheads and its aggregate social returns.

Concept 4

Social constituents are the different distinct social groups (implied in the second objective and expressed in the third objective of social accounting) with whom a firm is presumed to have a social contract.

Exhibit 5.6 (continued)

Concept 5

Social equity is a measure of the aggregate changes in the claims which each social constituent is presumed to have in the firm.

Concept 6

Net social asset of a firm is a measure of its aggregate nonmarket contribution to the society's well being less its nonmarket depletion of the society's resources during the life of the firm.

Source: K. V. Ramanathan, "Toward a Theory of Corporate Social Accounting," *The Accounting Review* (July 1976), p. 527. Reprinted with permission.

Ersite, based in Denver; Environmental Audits, in Lyonville, Pennsylvania; the Environmental Risk Information Center in Alexandria, Virginia; the Petroleum Information Corporation, Littleton, Colorado; Toxicheck, in Birmingham, Michigan; Vista Environmental Information in San Diego; Environmental Data Resources in Southport, Connecticut.[53] This new industry gives a glimpse of a future characterized by concerned shareholders regarding the social performance of firms and more accurate and reliable information on the environmental risks of U.S. corporations.

2. A second argument is that of *social justice.* Three theories of justice — John Rawls' theory of justice, as presented in his book *A Theory of Justice,*[54] Robert Nozick's "entitlement theory" as presented in his book *Anarchy, State, and Utopia,*[55] and A. Gerwith's theory of justice as presented in *Reason and Morality,*[56] — contain principles for evaluating laws and institutions from a moral standpoint. Both Rawls' and Gerwith's models argue for a concept of fairness favorable to social accounting (see Chapter 1).

3. The third argument is that of *users' needs.* Basically users of financial statements need social information for their revenue allocation decisions. An argument may be made by some that shareholders are conservative and care only about dividends. In fact, according to a recent survey of shareholders, they want corporations to direct resources toward cleaning up plants and stopping environmental pollution, and making safer products.[57] As a result, Marc Epstein advises corporations to do the following in order to manage expenditures on social concerns:

- Integrate corporate awareness of social, ethical and environmental issues into corporate decisions at all levels, and make sure such concerns have representation on the board of directors;

- Develop methods to evaluate and report on the social and environmental impacts of corporate activities;

- Modify the corporate structure to set up a mechanism to deal with social, environ-

Exhibit 5.7
Major Issues of Discord in the Development of Corporate Social Reporting

Societal Assumptions	Assumptions about CSR's Role in the Society/ Organization/ Relationship	Assumed and/or Imputed Purpose of CSR Activity	Criteria to be Applied in Selection of Information to be Reported	Form that the Social Report Should Take
Radical change (left wing)	Controlled and innocuous legitimation	None	Not relevant	External social audits (perhaps)
Marginal change	Element of the social contract	Discharge of accountability	Accountability	Compliance-with standard External social audits
	Demonstrates corporate beneficence	Enhance corporate image	Convenience, cost	Narrative disclosure Legally required disclosure
No change	None	Increase special interest groups' property rights e.g., accountants	User needs Total impact accounts "Truth"	Social income statements and balance sheets
Radical change (right wing)	Interferes with liberty	None	Not relevant	Legally required disclosure

Source: R. Gray, D. Owen, and K. Mauders, "Corporate Social Reporting: Emerging Trends in Accountability and the Social Contract," *Accounting, Auditing and Accountability*, 11, no. 1 (1988), p. 7. Reprinted with permission of MCB University Press Ltd.

mental and ethical crises. Then a company can be a crisis-prepared organization rather than a crisis-prone organization. Companies that do not prepare themselves for crises simply flounder;

- Create incentives for ethical, environmental and socially responsible behavior on the part of employees and integrate those incentives into the performance evaluation system and corporate culture. Unless this is institutionalized it never enters the corporate culture and significant, permanent change cannot occur;

- Recognize that if the environment is to be cleaned up, business must take a leadership role in the reduction of pollutants and the wise use of natural resources.[58]

There is, however, a lack of normative and/or descriptive models on the users' needs in terms of social information.

4. The fourth argument is that of *social investment*. Basically, it is assumed that an *ethical investor* group is now relying on social information provided in annual reports for making investment decisions. The disclosure of social information becomes, therefore, essential if investors are going to consider properly the negative effects of social awareness expenditures on earnings per share, along with any compensating positive effects that reduce risk or create greater interest from a particular investment clientele. Some argue that the risk-reducing effects will more than compensate for social awareness expenditures: "Between firms competing in the capital markets those perceived to have the highest expected future earnings in combination with the lowest expected risk from environmental and other factors will be most successful at attracting long term funds."[59]

Others believe that "ethical investors" form a clientele that responds to demonstrations of corporate social concern.[60] Investors of this type would like to avoid particular investments entirely for ethical reasons and would prefer to favor socially responsible corporations in their portfolios.[61] A survey by J. Rockness and P. F. Williams identifies an emerging consensus on the primary characteristics of social performance among fund managers.[62] The performance factors — environmental protection, treatment of employees, business relations with repressive regimes, product quality and innovation, and defense criteria — are considered investment criteria by most of the managers.

An emerging theory of social investment is provided by S. T. Bruyn who suggests that "social and economic values can be maximized together, and this creative synergism is the practical direction taken by social investors today."[63] Bruyn's investor is assumed to contribute to the development of a social economy design to promote human values and institutions, as well as self-interests. The social investor bases investment decisions on not only economic and financial considerations, but also on sociological grounded considerations. Both "social inventions" and technological inventions hold an expectation of profit and economic development. With regard to accountability, social investors, while concerned with the management of profits and scarce resources, are also interested in the corporations' accountability to other stakeholders in the environment besides stockholders.

THE NEED FOR AN EFFECTIVE PARADIGM

The Economic Paradigm

Corporate society relationships are governed by the economic principles espoused by the government and the nation. These same principles determine the role of the corporation in society and define the nature of its activities. The continuum of economic principles goes from the extreme right of libertarianism to the extreme left of radical economics. In between these views fall the institutional and the social economists.

Both libertarianism and radical economics center on extreme views concerning the preeminence of either the market or the state and present rigid solutions to complex economic and social problems. The social and institutional economists present a more reasoned approach to corporation-society relationships. The social economists may be identified by their deep commitment to human welfare and social justice. The institutionalists may be identified by their commitment to pragmatism and reliance on empirical observation and inductive logic as a way of analyzing economic and social problems. Both the social economists and the institutionalists work at the social level of generalization to analyze social organization and process and avoid the atomistic analytical units used by conventional microeconomics.

The interest in human and social welfare in social economics and the interest in a pragmatic approach to problems by the institutionalists may be strengthened by a synthesis of their approaches. Such a synthesis would serve to improve corporation-society relationships in a manner beneficial to both. The economic paradigm governing the relationships of corporation and society need not be the role or importance of the market and/or the state as in libertarianism or the radical economics but a clear statement of national and social goals based on a commitment to human welfare and social justice and experimentation with institutional arrangements to solve economic and social problems. This synthesis of social and institutional economics is at the heart and within the spirit of social accounting. It calls for every organizational unit, including the government, to define goals compatible with human welfare and social justice and to look for institutional arrangements suitable to their realization.

The Rectification Paradigm

We live at a time when there are increasing tensions about the nature of the social contract and the inadequate provision of public goods, economic inequality, and social injustice. Because the corporation is an active market and social agent, its activities can either worsen or correct some of these problems. Thus, the corporation's relationships with society are by definition affected by its role in dealing with the sources of those tensions. The options open to the corporation are on a continuum from complete indifference to an active role in rectifying some of these social problems. Complete indifference would definitely be harmful to the long-term interests of the firm. Involvement in some forms of rectification is a way of ensuring mutual acceptance by society and a role in securing social order and affluence. Social accounting is by definition compatible with a rectification paradigm.

It even implies that rectification is necessary to reassess and improve business' social conduct.

The Ethical Paradigm

The activities of business corporations have a tremendous effect on their environment in terms of both social costs and social benefits. Indeed, not only is a business corporation first a corporate citizen but it should be a *good* corporate citizen. This view of the world presents the business executive with a new set of choices. There are generally two opposite views on the role of management. One, the strict constructionism school, criticizes the social responsibility advocates and argues mainly that profit maximization is the only acceptable objective of business corporations. The other, the social responsibility school, argues that businessmen should be involved in correcting some of the social ills of society. Both views have generated a debate in the corporate-society literature.

Social accounting is by definition more favorable to the social responsibility school. It even implies ethical guidelines to reassess and improve business social conduct. It argues for an ethical paradigm of the corporate-society relationship more favorable to and supportive of social involvement by business in general and socioeconomic accounting in particular.

An Economic Remedy to Social Issues

For the market to produce an efficient level of output, the private marginal benefit must equal the social marginal benefit and the private marginal cost must equal the social marginal cost. With respect to both conditions, sources of market failure such as imperfect information, consumer ignorance, external economies and diseconomies, and monopoly render the market allocation unlikely to result in an efficient level of output. Similarly, the market fails to provide an equitable distribution of the level of output given the presence of poverty, inequality, and discrimination.

The failure of the market to provide an efficient and equitable level of output for most of the social issues requires some form of governmental intervention either by directly providing the good or service, by regulating the market, and/or by imposing a system of taxation/subsidization.

Government intervention has not necessarily met the criteria of efficiency and/or equity in most of the social issues. Experimentation may be needed before finding the type of economic organizations most adequate to deal with each of the social issues. For example, the voucher programs in education and housing, the negative income tax proposals for inequality, and the Health Maintenance Organization (HMOs) in health care are indicative of the type of experiments needed. *The controversy of market versus nonmarket solutions seems to obscure the real issue, which is to correct some of the social and unfair ills of society.* Experimentation in various forms of economic organizations coupled with the measurement and audit of the social costs and benefits is the key. Social accounting, with its emphasis on measurement and audit of costs and benefits, may help choose the type of economic organization needed to deal with each of the social issues.

Social Accounting

The previous calls for a synthesis of social and institutional economics, a rectification paradigm, an ethical paradigm, and an economic remedy to social issues may only be implemented by an effort at the micro and macro levels to identify, measure, and disclose the total performance, economic and social, of all the economic and social units of a nation. Such is the objective of micro and macro social accounting. Micro social accounting will deal with the measurement and disclosure of the social performance of microeconomic units, while macro social accounting deals with the same tasks for the macroeconomic units. Micro and macro social accounting will constitute an expansion of social accounting to deal with the effects of organizational behavior on the total environment. To accomplish these objectives, theories and techniques of social accounting need to be constructed, verified, and used by micro- and macroeconomic and social units.

Social Auditing

Public demand for socially oriented programs of one kind or another and measurement and disclosure of the environmental effects of organizational behavior will create pressure for a form of social auditing of the activities of corporations. Given the novelty of the phenomenon and the lack of generally accepted procedures, social auditing tends at present to take forms to accommodate the various views about the ways firms should respond to their social environment. However, as the need for social measurement and reporting increases with a greater acceptance of social accounting, social auditing may become as standard and as rigorous as financial auditing. The professional "social auditor" will be involved in the social audit and be asked to examine the validity of the social data prepared by the firm.

Social accounting relies heavily on social auditing for an appraisal of the total performance of profit and not-for-profit entities. These types of audits include social process/program management audit, macro-micro social indicator audit, social performance audit, social balance sheet and income statement, energy accounting and auditing, comprehensive auditing, environmental auditing, human resource accounting, and constituency group attitudes audit.

CONCLUSIONS

The concern with social responsibility and social performance in general and social accounting in particular is just another expression of the moral stand that accounting and accountants can take to fulfill their social contracts requirements and contribute to the public welfare. Failure to participate in the social accounting area will leave accountants in a moral dilemma about their just contribution to society in general.

NOTES

1. A. W. Clausen, "Toward an Arithmetic of Quality," *The Conference Board Record* (May 1971), p. 9.

2. U.S. Department of Health, Education and Welfare, *Toward a Social Report* (Ann Arbor: University of Michigan Press, 1970); Daniel Bell, "The Idea of a Social Report," *The Public Interest* (Spring 1969), pp. 78–84.

3. Daniel Bell, "Social Trends of the 70's," *The Conference Board Record* (June 1970).

4. Clausen, "Toward an Arithmetic of Quality," p. 9.

5. Peter F. Drucker, *Management: Tasks, Responsibilities, Practices* (New York: Harper & Row, 1973), p. 41.

6. Lee E. Preston and James E. Post, *Private Management and Public Policy: The Principle of Public Responsibility* (Englewood Cliffs, N.J.: Prentice-Hall, 1975), p. 30.

7. Milton Friedman, *Capitalism and Freedom* (Chicago: University of Chicago Press, 1962), p. 133.

8. Adam Smith, *The Wealth of Nations* (London: Cannan, 1930; originally published in 1776), p. 421.

9. Friedman, *Capitalism and Freedom,* p. 134.

10. Preston and Post, *Private Management and Public Policy,* pp. 31–34.

11. Adolf Berle and Gardiner Means, *The Modern Corporation and Private Property* (New York: Macmillan, 1932).

12. Frank X. Sutton et al., *The American Business Creed* (Cambridge, Mass.: Harvard University Press, 1956) pp. 5–58.

13. Committee for Economic Development, *Social Responsibilities of Business Corporations* (New York: CED, 1971), p. 22.

14. Ibid., pp. 27, 29.

15. *Business Week* (May 15, 1971), p. 63.

16. A. Belkaoui, *Conceptual Foundations of Management Accounting* (Reading, Mass.: Addison-Wesley, 1980), p. 61.

17. G. Steiner, *Business and Society* (New York: Random House, 1975), pp. 168, 169.

18. Stewart C. Easton, *The Heritage of the Past* (New York: Holt, Rinehart and Winston, 1964), p. 4.

19. Walter E. Friedlander and Robert Z. Apte, *Introduction to Social Welfare* (Englewood Cliffs, N.J.: Prentice-Hall, 1974), p. 4.

20. Harold L. Wilensky and Charles N. Lebeaux, *Industrial Society and Social Welfare* (New York: Free Press, 1965), pp. 60–62.

21. William R. Catton, Jr. and Riley E. Dunlap, "Environmental Sociology: A New Paradigm," *The American Sociologist* 13 (February 1978), p. 42.

22. Rachel Carson, *Silent Spring* (Boston: Houghton Mifflin, 1962); Barry Commoner, *The Closing Circle* (New York: Knopf, 1971); Paul R. Ehrlich and Anne H. Ehrlich, *Population, Resources, Environment* (San Francisco: Freeman, 1970); Garrett Hardin, "The Tragedy of the Commons," *Science* 162 (1968), pp. 1243–1248.

23. Catton and Dunlap, "Environmental Sociology," p. 42.

24. Lawrence B. Slobodkin and Anotol Rapoport, "An Optimal Strategy of Evolution," *Quarterly Review of Biology* (September 1974), pp. 181–200.

25. Anthony Wilden, "Ecology and Ideology," in Ahamed Idris-Solven, Elizabeth Idris-Solven, and Mary K. Vaughan (eds.), *The World as a Company Town* (The Hague: Mouton, 1978), p. 74.

26. Ibid., p. 76. Emphasis is mine.

27. D. H. Meadows et al., *The Limits to Growth* (New York: Universe Books, 1972).

28. Hardin, "The Tragedy of the Commons," pp. 1241–1248.

29. Ibid., p. 1244.

30. Ibid., p. 1243.

31. Daniel Bell, "The Corporation and Society in the 1970's," *The Public Interest* (Spring 1969).

32. Ibid., p. 10.

33. Ibid., p. 7.

34. Ibid., p. 23.

35. H. R. Bowen, *Social Responsibilities of the Businessman* (New York: Harper and Row, 1953).

36. T. Donaldson, "Constructing a Social Contract for Business," in T. Donaldson and P. Werhane (eds.), *Ethical Issues in Business,* 2nd ed. (Englewood Cliffs, N.J.: Prentice-Hall, 1983), pp. 153–165.

37. T. Donaldson, *Corporations and Morality* (Englewood Cliffs, N.J.: Prentice-Hall, 1982), p. 30.

38. A. B. Carrol, "A Three-Dimensional Conceptual Model of Corporate Social Performance," *Accounting of Management Review,* 4 (1979), pp. 497–506.

39. S. L. Wartick and P. L. Cochran, "The Evolution of the Corporate Social Performance Model," *Academy of Management Review,* 10, no. 4 (1985), pp. 758–769.

40. Friedman, *Capitalism and Freedom.*

41. Preston and Post, *Private Management and Public Policy.*

42. Carroll, "A Three-Dimensional Conceptual Model," p. 502.

43. Ibid.

44. Donna J. Wood, "Corporate Social Performance Revisited," *Academy of Management Review,* 16, no. 4 (1991), pp. 691–718.

45. Ibid., p. 704.

46. Ibid., p. 708.

47. See A. Belkaoui, *Socio-Economic Accounting* (Westport, Conn.: Quorum Books, 1984).

48. M. R. Mathews, "A Suggested Classification for Social Accounting Research," *Journal of Accounting and Public Policy,* 3 (1984), pp. 199–222.

49. K. V. Ramanathan, "Toward a Theory of Corporate Social Accounting," *The Accounting Review* (July 1976), p. 518.

50. R. Gray, D. Owen, and K. Maunders, "Corporate Social Reporting: Emerging Trends in Accountability and the Social Contract," *Accounting, Auditing and Accountability,* 1, no. 1 (1988), p. 8.

51. Ibid., p. 5.

52. Ibid., p. 13.

53. See D. B. Henriques, "Tracking Environmental Risk," *New York Times* (April 28, 1991), p. 13.

54. J. A. Rawls, *A Theory of Justice* (Cambridge, Mass.: Harvard University Press, 1971).

55. A. M. Nozick, *Anarchy, State, and Utopia* (New York: Basic Books, 1974).

56. A. Gerwith, *Reason and Morality* (Chicago: University of Chicago Press, 1978).

57. Marc J. Epstein, "What Shareholders Really Want," *New York Times* (April 28, 1991), p. 11.

58. Ibid.

59. See "Pollution Price Tag: 71 Billion Dollars," *U.S. News and World Report* (August 17, 1970), p. 41.

60. American Accounting Association, "Report of the Committee on External Reporting," *The Accounting Review,* 44 (Supplement, 1969), p. 41.

61. American Accounting Association, "Report of the Committee on Environmental Effects of Organization Behavior," *The Accounting Review,* 44 (Supplement, 1969), p. 88.

62. J. Rockness and P. F. Williams, "A Descriptive Study of Social Responsibility Mutual Funds," *Accounting, Organizations and Society* (1988): 397–411.

63. S. T. Bruyn, *The Field of Social Investment* (Cambridge: Cambridge University Press, 1987), p. 12.

SELECTED READINGS

Belkaoui, Ahmed. *Socio-Economic Accounting.* Westport, Conn.: Quorum Books, 1984.

Belkaoui, Ahmed and Philip Karpik. "Determinants of the Corporate Decision to Disclose Social Information." *Accounting, Auditing, and Accountability Journal,* 2 (1989).

Boal, K. B. and N. Peery. "The Cognitive Structure of Corporate Social Responsibility." *Journal of Management,* 11, no. 3 (1985), pp. 71–82.

Bruyn, S.T. *The Field of Social Investment.* Cambridge: Cambridge University Press, 1987.

Carroll, A. B. "A Three-Dimensional Conceptual Model of Corporate Social Performance." *Academy of Management Review,* 4 (1979), pp. 497–505.

Davis, K. "The Case For and Against Business Assumptions of Social Responsibilities." *Academy of Management Journal,* 16 (1973), pp. 312–322.

Post, J. E. *Corporate Behavior and Social Change.* Reston, Va.: Reston Publishing, 1978.

Preston, C. E. and J. E. Post. *Private Management and Public Policy: The Principle of Public Responsibility.* Englewood Cliffs, N.J.: Prentice-Hall, 1975.

Wartick, S. L. and P. L. Cochran. "The Evolution of the Corporate Social Performance Model." *Academy of Management Review* 10, no. 4 (1985), pp. 758–769.

Wood, Donna J. *Business and Society.* Glenview, Ill.: Scott, Foresman, 1990.

———. "Corporate Social Performance Revisited." *Academy of Management Review* 16, no. 4 (1991), pp. 691–718.

6

Truth in Accounting

The lack of concern in truth in accounting has always been a major issue in the accounting literature. Witness the following concern expressed by K. MacNeal in 1939:

For more than four hundred years since the publication of Paciok's book on double entry bookkeeping in 1454, accounting methods, and hence accounting reports, have been based on expediency rather than on truth. Financial statements today are composed of a bewildering mixture of accounting conventions, historical data, and present facts, wherein even accountants are often unable to distinguish between truth and fiction.[1]

MacNeal may have been a little bit too hard on accountants, given the possibilities and impossibilities of truth in accounting. They are examined in this chapter, showing that the idea of truth in accounting is at best a normative idea that has few chances of being applied in accounting.

NOTIONS OF TRUTH IN PHILOSOPHY

Knowledge of a proposition arises from its truthfulness. If we know of a proposition, we know it to be true. The question becomes: What makes a proposition a true one? In everyday life we encounter states of affairs occurring or existing in the world that we report using language. A true proposition relates to a state of affairs that occurs. The truth relates to the reporting of the occurrence or the existence of a state of affairs. The truth may be framed differently.[2]

- It can be *truth as correspondence* when the proposition is true if it corresponds to a fact. The notion of correspondence is best explicated as follows:

The word "correspondence" suggests that, when we make a true judgement, we have a sort of picture of the real in our minds and that our judgement is true because this picture is like the reality it represents. But our judgements are not like the physical things to which they refer. The images we use in judging may indeed in certain respects copy or resemble physical things, but we can make a judgement without using any imagery except words, and words are not in the least similar to the things which they represent. We must not understand "correspondence" as meaning copying or even resemblance.[3]

- It can be *truth as coherence* when the proposition is true because it is coherent with other propositions. The propositions must be mutually supporting.
- It can be *truth as what "works,"* implying that a true proposition is what works.

A distinction should be made between truth or falsity of propositions and the belief of people about them. Beliefs do not necessarily correspond to the state of affairs. A statement believed to be true or false still needs to be proven true or false. The proof will show that the truth of a proposition is not relative to time, space, or speaker although it might be about time, space, or speaker. As J. Hospers states, "Caesar's assassination occurred at only one point in space and time; and the burning of people as witches, though it occurred at different spaces and times, did not on that account occur at *all* spaces and times. States-of-affairs come and go, but truths are eternal."[4]

The truthfulness of propositions can be ascertained with different degrees of complexity. An analytical proposition, such as "all American accountants are American," is obviously true without further proof, since negation of it is self-contradictory. Synthetic propositions (propositions that are not analytic) need to be proven as true or false. The synthetic proposition, "Tunis is the capital of Tunisia," is a true synthetic proposition.

THE POSSIBILITIES OF TRUTH IN ACCOUNTING

Truth as Neutrality

To be able to report the truth, accounting needs to avoid injecting any bias. It may be difficult. Witness the following comment:

First, the difficulty is of knowing the facts. Secondly, the difficulty of describing them. It is well understood nowadays that the record of events cannot be dissociated from the recorder. There is no history without bias.[5]

. . . The other half of the problem is the right use of words. This is not a talent which everyone has, and these days one may justifiably conclude that fewer people have it than before. Many of the matters to be communicated in a set of accounts are of their nature difficult or obscure (e.g., most things to do with tax); some are highly delicate (e.g., liabilities under guarantee or contingencies); some are, as explained above, simply uncertain; and to convey an exact shade of uncertainty is a searching test of verbal skill.[6]

To avoid injecting bias in the knowledge, description, and communication of facts, accountants are expected to be neutral. The important characteristic of the information provided is to be "free from bias" or neutral. Neutrality is considered an important qualitative characteristic of accounting information.[7] Neutrality, in this context, refers to the absence of bias in the presentation of accounting information or reports. Thus, neutral information is free from bias toward attaining some desired result or inducing a particular mode of behavior. This is not to imply that the preparers of information do not have a purpose in mind when preparing the reports; it only means that the purpose should not influence a predetermined result. The accountant is expected to "tell it like it is" rather than the way any interest group might or would like to see it. This is generally stated as the criteria of "representational faithfulness and completeness." They refer to the correspondence between accounting data and the events those data are supposed to represent. If the measure portrays what it is supposed to represent, it is considered to be free of measurement and measurer bias. Therefore neutrality, representational faithfulness, and completeness establish truth in accounting as a correspondence. The accounting information is true because it corresponds to a fact.

Truth as Objectivity

To establish the accuracy of the attributes measured, accountants have relied on the principle of objectivity as a way of justifying their choice of procedures. Objectivity, however, has been given at least four possible meanings:

(1) measurements that are impersonal or existing outside the mind of the person making the measurement, (2) measurements based on verifiable evidence, (3) measurements based on a consensus of qualified experts, and (4) the narrowness of the statistical dispersions of the measurements of an attribute when made by different measurers.[8]

The first meaning of objectivity refers to the truth as neutrality examined earlier in the chapter. The second meaning refers to the need for evidence as a test of the accuracy of the information.[9] The third meaning refers to the need for evidence as a test of the accuracy of the information. The fourth meaning refers to the narrowness of the dispersion of the measurement values around a mean or average figure. This fourth meaning is the most interesting criterion of objectivity. It arises from the tendency of accounting theorists to give accounting information the characteristic of an average or expected value of a probability distribution. The average or mean is not considered as precise as other statistics. As Norton Bedford pointed out,

the main theoretical objection to the use of expected value as the accounting disclosure is the sin of omitting a measure of the dispersion around the expected value disclosed. In a sense, the theoretical objection is that accounting disclosures have been determined according to precise laws, when statistical laws are the relevant ones.[10]

As a result, variance and standard deviation are generally offered as a measure of objectivity and verifiability. The narrower the dispersion, the more objective is the measure. The variance is considered to be a function of the attribute measured (A), the object whose attribute is measured (O), the individual measurers making the measurement (M), the measurement rules they followed (R), and the constraints imposed on them (C), as follows:

$$\text{Variance } X_i = f(A, O, M, R, C)[11]$$

Its benefits are as follows:

An advantage of dispersion as an objectivity criterion is its applicability to predictions before they can be validated by correlation analysis. Second, dispersion can be expressed as a continuum. Another advantage of dispersion is its ability to test hypothesized relationships of changes resulting from modifying one of the measurement parameters such as the attribute, object, measurer, etc.[12]

Truth, Objectivity, and Reliability

An item of information could be considered verifiable based on the narrowness of the dispersion measurement values around a mean and yet be less reliable because of a bias factor.

Reliability refers to the "quality which permits users of data to depend on it with confidence as representative of what it proposes to represent."[13] Thus, the reliability of information depends on its degree of faithfulness in the representation of an event. Reliability will differ between users, depending on the extent of their knowledge of the rules used to prepare the information. Similarly, different users may seek information with different degrees of reliability. In the context of the conceptual framework, to be reliable, information must be verifiable, neutral, and faithfully represented.

The terms "bias" or "displacement" are the systematic difference between the mean of the sample estimates of a parameter and the true value of the parameter.

Y. Ijiri and R. K. Jaedicke define reliability as the degree of objectivity or verifiability plus the bias or displacement factor.[14] If the mean square error is used as the measure of reliability, then the relationship can be expressed as follows:

$$\text{Reliability} = \text{Objectivity} + \text{Bias}[15]$$

or

$$\text{Mean square error} = \text{Variance} + \text{Displacement}$$

or

Variance of observations = Variance of observations + (true − mean)²
about the true value of   about the mean of the
parameter   observations

$$\sum_{i=1}^{N} \frac{(X_i - X^*)^2}{N} = \sum_{i=1}^{N} \frac{(X_i - \overline{X})^2}{N} + (X^* - \overline{X})^2$$

where

X_i = ith observation used as an estimate of the true parameter X^*
$\overline{X}$ = mean of the X_i
X^* = the true value of the parameter being estimated

An evaluation of the relationship is stated as follows:

The greater dispersion of measures the more likely are incorrect decisions based on them because of the sampling errors they contain. The greater the displacement the more likely are incorrect decisions because the expected value of the measure is not equal to a more true measure of the attribute. Dispersion and displacement are undesirable to the extent wrong decisions have a high cost. To the extent resources must be consumed in reducing dispersion and displacement, poor measures can be accepted as long as the costs of improving them are greater than the cost of wrong decisions arising further.[16]

Another problem arises from the fact that the dispersion criterion is applicable to both assessments and predictors while the displacement criterion applies only to assessment measures, not to predictor measures.

Truth, Objectivity, and Hardness

The previous section on truth objectivity, and reliability focused on a comparison between what accountants do and what users of accounting measures expect them to do.[17] This section is a comparison among different groups of accountants. The relationship is between objectivity and hardness. Objectivity in this case is a high degree of consensus among diverse groups of accountants, in the sense that different groups of accountants produce a set of measures with the same mean u and the same variance 6^2, given their neutrality in terms of their interest in the outcome of the measurement.[18] Hardness, however, assumes a competitive environment such that different incentives may push the different groups of accountants to produce a different set of measures. The resulting distribution from all groups will have a wider distribution than in the original distribution. Ijiri shows that the degree of dispersion in the combined distribution by biased measurers is greater than the degree of dispersion by neutral measurers by an amount directly proportional to the size of the bias introduced by the incentive.[19]

More explicitly, assume the groups of accountants, one including m subjects and the other n subjects, produce a set of measures with the same mean u and the same variance 6^2.[20] Both groups are now induced to produce different numbers, one group induced to increase the measure by a constant c and the other induced to decrease the measure by a constant d. The distribution resulting from putting the two "biased" groups together produce a mean $\bar{z}$ and a variance h^2 as follows:

$$\bar{z} = u + z \frac{mc - nd}{m + n}$$

and

$$h^2 = 6^2 + pqs^2$$

where
  $s = c + d$ ("measurement slack")
  $p = m / (m + n)$
  $q = n / (m + n)$

The new relationship is that hardness (h^2) is equal to objectivity (6^2) plus the pqs^2 factor. Therefore, comparing two measures may lead to the result that one is more objective than the other but less hard. The hard measure is the one constructed in a way as to make disagreement arising among measurers difficult.

The measurement of truth in accounting is therefore best set in a competitive environment to allow the distinction between objectivity and hardness of the measure. As stated by Ijiri:

The outcome of the measurement under competitive circumstances is often far more revealing than the result in a neutral situation. This is because people may overlook many things when they are neutral and indifferent to the outcome of the measurement. They tend to tolerate ambiguities so long as their choice is not considered to be "out-of-line." In a competitive environment, not being "out-of-line" is not enough. One must justify his particular choice by stronger reasoning. Thus, the extent of ambiguity is highlighted by the difference in the measures produced by two parties with conflicting interests.[21]

Truth and Roles of Accounting

The kind of truth conveyed in accounting practices and discourses may be contingent on the roles accounting actually play in organizations. There is naturally the traditional role of a useful aid to rational decision making with a view of measuring organizational efficiency and effectiveness. The truth in accounting in this traditional context is to provide useful and known accounting numbers along technically based rules. But notwithstanding the evidence that accounting numbers may not be used as extensively as the traditional roles suggest, the literature presents a distinction between the traditional "real/actual" and nontraditional "espoused/articulated/intended" roles of accounting information that suggest different kinds of truths conveyed by accounting information.[22] In effect, examination of each of the roles of accounting will show a gradual move from accounting as a neutral portrayer of economic reality to accounting as an interpreter of the interplay of various sources of powers. For example, Lars Samuelson describes the coexistence of different expressions of the role of the budget at the same point in time as follows:

According to his view, senior management often articulate one role for the budget but budgeters then perceive that another very different role may be intended, with senior management actions following the course of the latter rather than the former role. Such conflicting expressions of the roles of the budgeting are here seen to be a major factor underlying both attitudes and behaviors orientated towards budgetary control systems.[23]

Similarly, Shahid Ansari and K. J. Euske classify different roles of accounting by emphasizing two dimensions: a traditional internal-external dichotomy of the use of accounting information, and a focus of organizational process congruent with either a rational or technical perspective.[24] These roles are depicted in Exhibit 6.1. One may early assume in terms of truth of accounting data that the reliability and objectivity of the data will decline as the roles of accounting move from cell 1 to cell 4. As Ansari and Euske state,

Exhibit 6.1
Roles of Accounting in Organizations

Focus of Organizational Process	User Group Location			
	Internal		*External*	
Technical-rational	1	Measuring technical efficiency	2	Resource allocations
Natural	3	Behavior changes politics	4	Gaining legitimacy

Source: S. Ansari and K. J. Euske, "Rational, Rationalizing and Reifying Uses of Accounting Data in Organizations," *Accounting, Organizations and Society,* 12 (1987), p. 553.

the foregoing analysis suggests that there are three alternative theoretical perspectives on the use of accounting data in organizations (1) technical-rational, which is driven by considerations of efficiency; (2) socio-political, which is the pursuit of power and influence; and (3) institutional, which stems from the need to put on an appropriate facade for the world to see. . . . Thus while the rational and natural distinction represents ideological and epistomological differences in the literature, the internal-external distinction underscores the organization-environment distinction.[25]

An appreciation of the different truths in accounting is provided by the diverse roles that accounting plays in practice. A review of literature revealed the following roles: rational/instrumental, symbolic, ritualistic, mythical, political/bargaining, legitimating/retrospective rationalizing, disciplinary, and repressive/dominating/ideological.[26]

The nature of truth in accounting in each of these roles evolves from truth as correspondence for a rational/instrumental role either to truth as coherence or a pragmatic view of truth in most of the other roles that recognize the social nature of accounting, and where accounting is used either to mystify or legitimize and/or discipline.

THE IMPOSSIBILITIES OF TRUTH IN ACCOUNTING

Truth and Measurement

Accounting is essentially involved in the measurement of financial performance, structure and conduct of a specific entity, and its related subaggregates. Whether the measurement will result in truth has been seriously questioned. Note the following statement:

The misconception held by some, that accountants should be able to present the one true measure, has hindered progress in the reporting of financial information. If accounting limited itself to presenting the amount of cash in the bank, a true measurement might be attainable, but when the scope of accounting is broadened from the limited objective of measuring cash, the possibility of finding a true measure falls out of reach.[27]

The failure of measurement in establishing the truth in accounting may be attributed to two factors.

The first factor relates to the accountant's understanding of the attribute that is being measured in financial statements.[28] As stated by Don Vickrey,

if accountants wish to represent economic facts about accounting entities by assigning monetary amounts to accounting phenomena and aggregating these amounts as they have done in the past, accounting is a measurement discipline if and only if at least one extensive economic property is identified which (1) is possessed by accounting phenomena, (2) is measurable in standard monetary units, and (3) is acceptable by accountants as appropriate for accounting measurement.[29]

The reality is that the identification of extensive accounting property is difficult given the absence of reliable instruments that can prove that accounting phenomena satisfy axioms of extensiveness with respect to economic properties.[30] One property suggested by Vickrey is purchasing power.[31] To reflect purchasing power changes, general price-level-adjusted historical cost statements are produced via extensive ratio scales and relative positive similarity transformations. The use of the ratio scale view is deemed invalid given the following seven problem areas referred to as objects, property, operations, and index difficulties:

1. Objects difficulty—In general-price-level-adjusted historical-cost statements (GPL statements), numerical values are assigned to claims, rights, promises, and future economic benefits (i.e., phenomena that do not have physical form—non-objects).
2. Property difficulty (first aspect)—The property that is supposed to be represented in the GPL statements has not been identified satisfactorily.
3. Property difficulty (second aspect)—The liabilities that are contained in GPL statements cannot be considered to possess service potential (i.e., the property that appears most likely to be that which is supposed to be measured using the historical cost system) under the conventional view of historical-cost accounting.
4. Operations difficulty—Empirical operations which can be used to show that the phenomena of historical-cost accounting satisfy axioms of extensiveness apparently do not exist.
5. Index difficulty (first aspect)—General-price indices are meant to compensate for changes in the purchasing power of the monetary unit as opposed to changes in the service potential of the monetary unit.
6. Index difficulty (second aspect)—General-price indices that actually reflect changes in the purchasing power of the monetary unit probably cannot be developed.
7. Index difficulty (third aspect)—At least some historical-cost values probably cannot be transformed via positive similarity transformations because these numerical assignments may be best interpreted as measures of numerosity (i.e., measures which are obtained via the absolute scale).[32]

Moustafa Abdel-Nagid, after reexamining the ratio-scale view from the standpoint of modern measurement theory, concluded that general price-level accounting is consistent with the rules of the ratio scale and conforms to the test of mathematical truth.[33] This debate in the ratio-scale view does not eliminate the problem of the identification of the right property to measure. It just focuses on how to measure what the accountant has decided to measure. As stated by Robert Sterling, this program is concerned with the discovery of the relevant properties. It appears that much of the previous accounting literature has not been concerned with that problem. Instead it has been concerned with "how" one measures and "what" one measures has been taken as given. My concern is with the discovery of what one ought to measure, i.e., what properties are relevant. "After" that has been established, then the question of how one goes about the measurement activity should be considered. Undoubtedly there will be a good many measurement problems, some of which may be unresolvable, but in regard to this interim program the measurement problems are of secondary concern.[34]

The second factor relates to the presence of both primary and secondary measures.[35] The primary measures result from the assignment of numbers to primary events or to the property of an object. The secondary measures result from the calculation or the combination of primary measures. Examples of primary measures include the following:

1. Counts of inflows, outflows, and balances on nonmonetary goods, which are made in terms of the physical quantities of such nonmonetary goods.
2. Entry and exit prices for nonmonetary goods, which may be past, present, or future prices.
3. Counts of inflows, outflows, and balances of monetary goods and obligations, which are made in terms of the dollar magnitudes or cash equivalents of such monetary items.[36]

The primary measure is essentially the result of a measurement process of a chosen property of the accounting object, while the secondary measure is essentially the result of calculation, including accrual accounting and matching. The differentiation between the measurement and calculation process in accounting is important. As stated by Abdel-Nagid,

the need to distinguish between measurement and calculation is essential for any valid analysis of conventional accounting numbers because there is a fundamental difference between measurement and calculation. While the operations involved in assigning numbers to properties in measurement are empirical, the operations involved in calculations are mathematical. The logical validity of calculated measures requires conformity with the rules of mathematical deduction.[37]

In addition, both primary and secondary measures are subject to measurement error in either the quantification or transformation processes. Because few primary measures are used in accounting, the accounting user ends up relying on the secondary measures as the true measure. Even in those cases where the accounting datum refers to a primary measure, the judgment process used by the accountant may lead to a divergence between the true measure and the estimated measure. It raises the question of what procedures should the accountant rely on to determine the measure of an accounting object. According to Harold Bierman, the choice comes down to

1. Conventional procedures which result in measures which will be independent of the accountant who is applying them, but which are not necessarily close to true measures of financial position or income.

2. Suggested procedures which attempt to come close to the unknown true measures of financial position or income, but which open up the possibility of wider differences among accountants since more judgment is being applied.[38]

Given that present-day accounting practices require both conventional and suggested procedures to be used, one should clearly expect that true measurement in accounting is seldom attainable. What's left for the accountant to do is minimize the differences between the unknown true state of the world and his estimate.

Truth and Income Smoothing

Does accounting stick to the truth? Pessimistic authors like I. Griffiths would comment that "every company in the country is fiddling with its profits. . . . Any accountant worth his salt will confirm that this is no wild assertion."[39] The general suspicion is that accountants rely on such practices as income smoothing that contribute to the impossibility of truth in accounting. The nature of, motivations for, dimensions of, and focus of smoothing are presented as evidence of the impossibility of truth in accounting.

The Nature of Income Smoothing

Income smoothing is the deliberate normalization of income numbers in order to reach a desired trend or level. As far back as 1953, S. R. Hepworth noted "some of the accounting techniques which may be applied to affect the assignment of net income to successive accounting periods . . . for smoothing or leveling the amplitude of periodic net income fluctuations."[40] What followed were arguments that corporate managers may be motivated to smooth their own income (or security), with the assumption that stability in income and rate of growth will be preferred over higher average income streams with greater variability.[41] The best definition of income smoothing is provided by C. R. Beidleman:

Smoothing of reported earnings may be defined as the intentional dampening of fluctuation about some level of earnings that is currently considered to be normal for a firm. In this sense smoothing represents an attempt on the part of the firm's management to reduce abnormal variations in earnings to the extent allowed under sound accounting and managed principles.[42]

The Motivations for Smoothing

Hepworth claims that motivations for smoothing include the improvements of relations with creditors, investors, and workers as well as dampening of business cycles through psychological processes.[43] Myron Gordon proposes that (1) the criterion corporate management uses in selecting accounting principles is to maximize its utility or welfare; (2) this same utility is a function of job security, the level and rate of growth of salary, and the level and growth rate of the firm's size; (3) satisfaction of stockholders with the corporation's performance enhances the status and rewards of managers; and (4) this same satisfaction depends on the rate of growth and stability of the firm's income.[44] These propositions culminate in the need to smooth as explained in the following theorem:

Given that the above four propositions are accepted or found to be true, it follows that a management should within the limits of its power, i.e., the latitude allowed by accounting rules, (1) smooth reported income, and (2) smooth the rate of growth in income. By smooth the rate of growth in income we mean the following: if the rate of growth in income is high, accounting practices which reduce it should be adopted and vice versa.[45]

Beidleman considers two reasons for management to smooth reported earnings.[46] The first argument rests on the assumption that a stable earnings stream is capable of supporting a higher level of dividends than a more variable earnings stream, and it has a favorable effect on the value of the firm's shares as overall riskiness of the firm is reduced. "To the extent that the observed variability about a trend of reported earnings influences investors' subjective expectations for possible outcomes of future earnings and dividends, management might be able to favorably influence the value of the firm's shares by smoothing earnings."[47]

The second argument attributes to smoothing the ability to counter the cyclical nature of reported earnings and thereby reduce the correlation of a firm's expected returns with returns on the market portfolio. "To the degree that auto-normalization of earnings is successful and that the reduced covariance of returns with the market is recognized by investors and incorporated into their valuation processes, smoothing will have added beneficial effects on share values."[48] This results from the need felt by management to neutralize environmental uncertainty and dampen the wide fluctuations in the operating performance of the firm subject to an intermittent cycle of good and bad times. To do so management may resort to organizational slack behavior,[49] budgetary slack behavior,[50] or risk-avoiding behavior.[51] Each of these behaviors necessitates decisions affecting the incurrence and/or allocation of discretionary expenses (costs) that result in income smoothing.

In addition to behaviors intended to neutralize environmental uncertainty, it is also possible to identify organizational characterizations that differentiate among different firms in their extent of smoothing. J. Y. Kamin and J. Ronen examine the effects of the separation of ownership and control on income smoothing under the hypothesis that management-controlled firms are more likely to be engaged in smoothing as a manifestation of managerial discretion and budgetary slack.[52] Their results confirm that a majority of firms behave as if they were smoothers and a particularly strong majority is included among management-controlled firms with high barriers to entry.

Management is assumed to circumvent some of the constraints of generally accepted accounting principles by attempting to smooth income numbers so as to convey their expectations of future cash flows, enhancing in the process the apparent reliability of prediction based on the observed smooth series of numbers.[53] Three constraints are presumed to lead managers to smooth: "(a) the competitive market mechanisms which reduce the options available to management; (b) the management compensation scheme which is linked directly to the firm performance; and (c) the threat of manager displacement."[54]

This smoothing is not limited to upper-level management and external accounting; it is also presumed to be used by lower-level management and internal accounting in the form of organizational slack and slack budgeting.[55] Recently the terminology has changed from income smoothing to earnings management. Earnings management is shown to be motivated by management's desire to increase annual compensation[56] and influence proxy contests,[57] and the likelihood of foreign trade regulation.[58]

The Dimensions of Smoothing

The dimensions of smoothing are basically the means used to accomplish the smoothing of income numbers. Paul Dascher and R. Malcolm distinguish between real smoothing and artificial smoothing as follows: "Real smoothing refers to an actual transaction that is undertaken or not undertaken on the basis of its smoothing effect on income, whereas artificial smoothing refers to accounting procedures which are implements to shift costs and/or revenues from one period to another."[59] These types of smoothing may be indistinguishable. For example, the amount of reported expenses may be higher or lower than previous periods because of either deliberate actions on the level of expenses (real smoothing) or the reporting methods (artificial smoothing). For both types an operational test is proposed to fit a curve to a stream of income calculated two ways: excluding a possible manipulative variable and including it. "If the variation of the observations around the curve is smaller in the latter case, income smoothing has been the consequence of transactions in the account."[60]

R. M. Copeland defines artificial smoothing as follows: "Income smoothing involves the repetitive selection of accounting measurement or reporting rules in a particular pattern, the effect of which is to report the stream of income with a smaller variation from trend than would otherwise have appeared."[61]

Besides real and artificial smoothing, other dimensions of smoothing are considered in the literature. A popular classification adds a third smoothing dimension, namely, classificatory smoothing. A. Barnea, J. Ronen, and S. Sadan distinguish among three smoothing dimensions:

1. *Smoothing through an event's occurrence and/or recognition.* Management can time actual transactions so that their effects on reported income would tend to dampen its variation over time. Mostly, the planned timing of an event's occurrences (e.g., research and development) would be a function of the accounting rules governing the accounting regulation of the event.

2. *Smoothing through allocation over time.* Given the occurrence and recognition of an event, management has more discretionary control over the determination of the periods to be affected by the event's quantification.

3. *Smoothing through classification (hence classificatory smoothing).* When income statement statistics other than net income (net of all revenues and expenses) are the object of smoothing, management can classify intraincome statement items to reduce variations over time in that statistic.[62]

Basically, real smoothing corresponds to the smoothing through an event's occurrence and/or recognition, while artificial smoothing corresponds to the smoothing through the allocation over time.

The Focus of Smoothing

The focus of smoothing is the smoothing variable that management chooses to change in order to reach a desired objective. They can choose net income, ordinary income, or per share figures or ratios because of the belief of investors' interests in those variables. G. White argues for the choice of earnings per share as an "appropriate surrogate for reported performance because of the heavy emphasis placed on this measure in annual report presentation and traditional security analysis."[63]

R. M. Copeland and Ralph Licastro choose as the focus of smoothing the dividends received from unconsolidated subsidiaries reported by the parent at cost.[64] They argue for their choice as follows: "The dividend-income variable was selected because it is an annually recurring item, and thus more open to management's manipulation if it wished to do so. Thus management could conceivably smooth with dividend income each period, rather than only in the periods when a particular decision situation availed itself."[65]

Income before and after extraordinary items may also be smoothed by the classification of an item as either extraordinary or ordinary, especially where the classification is subject to some managerial discretion. As stated by Barnea, Ronen, and Sadan,

non-recurring items could, within bounds, be classified as ordinary or extraordinary. Thus, if management wishes to impart a smoother appearance to the reported stream of "ordinary income before extraordinary items," it can use whatever discretion it has in the classification of nonrecurring items to achieve its objective. This is particularly true prior to Opinion 30 . . . because Opinion 9 . . . did leave management more flexibility in classifying nonrecurring items as either ordinary or extraordinary.[66]

The exhaustive list of smoothing variables cannot be compiled as long as there are various built-in flexibilities in the generally accepted accounting principles. It seems that each new Financial Accounting Standards Board standard includes built-in flexibility to allow in general the potential for management to fit their particular circumstances to the situation. Examples include FASB No. 13 on accounting for leases, which may allow management to structure leasing contracts so as to produce either an expensing or capitalization treatment. Another example is FASB No. 52, where management may produce a definition of functional currency that favors either a temporal method or a current rate method.

There is no clear consensus on what a good smoothing variable is. Copeland considers a perfect smoothing variable one that meets the following standards:

- Its use must not commit the firm to any particular future action.
- It should rest on professional judgement and be consistent with generally accepted accounting principles.
- It results in material shifts relative to year-to-year differences in income.
- It is merely a reclassification of internal account balances rather than a real transaction with other parties.
- Its use over consecutive periods of time can be in conjunction with other practices.[67]

Beidleman suggests the following two criteria as being necessary for an effective smoothing technique: (1) It must permit management to reduce the variability in reported earnings as it strives to achieve its long-run earnings (growth) objective; (2) once used, it should not commit the firm to any particular future action.[68]

Can income smoothing be eliminated? It can if all the flexibility in GAAP is eliminated, or if the accountant adopted an ethical attitude about truth in accounting. Witness the following comment:

From the accountant's point of view, attempting to eliminate all the differences in interpretations by users and preparers is not realistic. Passing legislation and accounting rules or guidelines framed in rigid terms may mean requiring endless rules for each specific situation. More importantly, it reduces the accounting function to a rule following exercise and removes the professional judgement aspect which is so important in a profession. Hence, given legislation and accounting rules or guidelines which are framed in broad terms, it is the professional duty and moral obligation of the accountant to present accounting numbers in a way that reflects a "true and fair" state of affairs of a company, to the extent of reflecting substance over the legal form of a transaction and departing from a ruling standard, if and when necessary. In this way, the amount and level of negative creative accounting existing at any one time are directly dependent on the ethical attitude of the accountant.[69]

Truth and Choice of Accounting Techniques

The general popular belief is that firms make accounting changes to mask performance problems.[70] The accounting literature explains the changes in accounting principles and estimates by management's desire to reach definite objectives such as income smoothing,[71] or the reduction of agency costs associated with a violation of debt covenants. A recent summary of existing research suggests that as the tightness of debt covenants increases, firms are more likely to loosen their tightness of covenant restrictions through appropriate accounting changes. In fact, two studies that examined the accounting changes of successful and unsuccessful firms[72] and firms facing or experiencing changes in their bond ratings[73] provide some evidence consistent with the assertion that managers can modify income through judicious accounting changes.

Accounting regulators have tried to limit management's ability to use accounting changes to increase or decrease net income. Since 1970, Accounting Principles Board No. 20 stipulated that the accounting changes should be accounted for as a cumulative change. It required reporting in the comparative income statements the cumulative effect of a change in the net income of the period of the change. It also required the disclosure in the notes of the effect of adopting the new accounting principles on income before extraordinary income and net income (and on related per share amounts) of the period of change. Similarly, the SEC's Accounting Series Release No. 177 required that accounting changes be made to more preferable accounting methods, using reasonable business judgment in the choice. While both pronouncements act as a control mechanism, they do not eliminate management's ability to increase and/or decrease income through accounting changes, and in the process they accentuate the impossibility of truth in accounting.

Truth and Asset Valuation

While there is no uniformly agreed or generally accepted definition of valuation, the following one is pretty much encompassing: "The assignment of money weights to an entity's past, present or future economic phenomena, on the basis of observation and according to rules, to facilitate informed judgements."[74]

The process of valuation requires a choice of an attribute to be measured and a unit of measure. The attributes of assets and liabilities refer to what is being measured and include the following:

1. *Historical cost,* which refers to the amount of cash or cash-equivalent paid to acquire an asset, or the amount of cash-equivalent liability.
2. *Replacement cost,* which refers to the amount of cash or cash-equivalent that would be paid to acquire an equivalent or the same asset currently, or that would be received to incur the same liability currently.
3. *Net realizable value,* which refers to the amount of cash or cash-equivalent that would be obtained by selling the asset currently, or that would be paid to redeem the liability currently.
4. *Present or capitalized value,* which refers to the present value of net cash flows expected to be received from the use of the asset, or the net outflows expected to be disbursed to redeem the liability.

Two units of measure are used in financial accounting: units of money or units of general purchasing power. Combining the four attributes and the two units of measures yields the following eight alternative asset valuation and income determination models:

1. Historical cost accounting measures historical cost in units of money.
2. Replacement cost accounting measures replacement cost in units of money.
3. Net realizable value accounting measures net realizable value in units of money.
4. Present value accounting measures present value in units of money.
5. General price-level accounting measures historical cost in units of purchasing power.
6. General price-level replacement cost measures replacement cost in units of purchasing power.
7. General price-level net realizable value accounting measures net realizable value in units of purchasing power.
8. General price-level present value accounting measures present value in units of purchasing power.

Each of these alternatives yields a different financial statement that imparts a different meaning and relevance to its users. In general, these models are evaluated in terms of interpretability and relevance and compared on the basis of whether they avoid timing and measuring-unit errors.[75,76] The analysis is summarized in Exhibit 6.2.[77] What appears is a set of results that includes some deficiencies but can be useful for different users for different purposes. It is therefore the usefulness criterion rather than the truth criterion that determines the appropriate asset valuation basis to be used in specific contexts.

Exhibit 6.2
Error-Type Analysis

Accounting Model	Timing Error — Operating Profit	Timing Error — Holding Gains	Measuring-Unit Error	Interpretation — NOD	Interpretation — COG	Interpretation — Relevance
1. Historical-cost accounting	Yes	Yes	Yes	Yes	No	No
2. Replacement-cost accounting	Yes	Eliminated	Yes	Yes (income statement)	Yes (asset figures)	Yes (asset figures)
3. Net-realizable-value accounting	Eliminated	Eliminated	Yes	Yes (income statement)	Yes (monetary assets and liabilities)	Yes (monetary assets and liabilities)
4. General price-level-adjusted historical-cost accounting	Yes	Yes	Eliminated	Yes	Yes	Yes
5. General price-level-adjusted replacement-cost accounting	Yes	Eliminated	Eliminated	Eliminated	Yes	Yes
6. General price-level-adjusted net-realizable-value accounting	Eliminated	Eliminated	Eliminated	Eliminated	Yes	Yes

This impossibility of truth in the process of valuation and reliance on relevance may be due to the lack of consensus on the users' needs of the output of financial accounting or, as sometimes stated, "generalized accounting." Witness the following comment:

Generalized accounting refers to situations in which the recipients of accounting numbers are not individually identifiable and, more importantly, there are no hierarchical relationships among the recipients and the accounting process that may be used in order to determine admissible valuation bases and select a valuation basis from among those deemed to be admissible. It seems to us that in these situations, the accounting process must (evidently) rely upon *aggregate* welfare criteria rather than an individual's welfare function or a hierarchically dictated welfare function.[78]

Given the absence of the impossibility of aggregate welfare criteria, the process of valuation falls then in the realm of subjective endeavors. This subjectivity of the process of valuation is stressed by Louis Goldberg as follows:

Clearly the process of valuation itself is often a complicated one, perhaps in some cases almost an unconscious one, and may frequently be affected by subjective considerations which could not be appreciated by anybody other than the person directly involved. In our present state of knowledge, it appears doubtful whether any calculus of satisfaction could ever be determined for consumption goods, at least for other than subsistence necessaries.[79]

Truth and Cost Allocation

The impossibility of truth in accounting is further aggravated by the subjective and unreliable process of matching and allocation.

Matching is an accounting procedure that requires first a determination of revenues and second a matching with expenses that represents the effort needed for the generation of the revenues. W. Paton and A. C. Littleton said:

The problem of properly matching revenues and costs is primarily one of finding satisfactory bases of association — clues to relationships which unite revenue deductions and revenue. . . . Observable physical connections often afford a means of tracing and assigning. It should be emphasized, however, that the essential test is reasonableness, in the light of all the pertinent conditions, rather than physical measurements.[80]

The problem is corrected by a reliance on three basic principles of matching: association of cause and effects, systematic and rational allocation, and immediate recognition.

The *association of cause and effect* requires that matching be made on the basis of some discernible positive correlation of costs with revenues. One expression of this principle is the "cost attach concept." As stated by Paton and Littleton,

ideally, all costs should be viewed as ultimately clinging to definite items of goods sold or services rendered. If this conception could be effectively realized in practice, the net accomplishment of the enterprise could be measured in terms of units of output rather than intervals of time. . . . In the more typical situation the degree of continuity of activity obtaining tends to prevent the basis of affinity which will permit convincing assignments, of all classes of costs incurred, to particular operations, departments, and — finally — items of product. Not all costs attach in a discernible manner, and this fact forces the accountant to fall back upon a time-period as the unit for associating certain expenses with certain revenues.[81]

As the statement indicates, the association of cause and effect constitutes a difficult principle, if not impossible.

The *allocation of costs* over time is another way of implementing the matching principle. It is a partitioning process to separate classifications or periods of time, so that the periods receive the correct benefits or series of the asset and in the process bear their share of the cost of the benefits received. A systematic and rational allocation is presumed to be used so that "the allocation method used should appear reasonable to an unbiased observer and should be followed systematically."[82]

To be theoretically justified, allocations are expected to meet the following three criteria:

1. *Additivity:* The total amount is allocated so that the sum of the allocated amounts is equal to the whole.
2. *Unambiguity:* The allocation method should result in a unique allocation — that is, should result in only one set of parts.
3. *Deferrability:* The allocation method selected is clearly superior to other methods on the basis of convincing arguments.[83]

The three criteria are generally difficult to meet, which renders most allocations to be arbitrary and impossible. They are incorrigible because they can't be verified or refuted by objective, empirical means. They do not correspond to anything in the real world. As Arthur Thomas states,

conventional allocation assertions do not refer to real-world partitioning; when an incorrigible allocation divides an accounting total, there is no reason to believe that this reflects the division of an external total into dependent parts. . . . Conventional allocation assertions do not refer to real-world economic phenomena, but only to things in asserter's and reader's minds.[84]

One solution to this dilemma is to use allocation-free financial statements based on cash-flow statements, exit-price systems, and certain types of replacement-cost systems. In spite of these criticisms and limitations, in practice costs continue to be allocated to serve a variety of needs, such as inventory value determination, income determination, pricing and production determination, and meeting regulatory requirements.

The *immediate recognition of expenses* is used for costs viewed in the current period or in previous periods that are assumed to no longer provide future benefits, or because there is a high degree of uncertainty about the existence of future benefits.

Truth and the Standard of Evidence

There is a general presumption that the accounting discipline is not well equipped to reveal the truth. Note the following comment:

Knowledgeable accountants realize that accounting cannot be a scientific investigation process directed to the disclosure of basic truth. Many aspects and methods of concern to the scientist must be omitted. Consequently, there must be recognition that for years to come, precise accurate observations of business activity cannot be made. Accountants and users alike must learn to be content with rough approximations of the philosophical ideal.[85]

In spite of these pessimistic pronouncements generally made in the literature, accounting is still presumed to generate truth and accuracy.

Evidence may be used to prove that an accounting observation is valid and/or to assist the auditor in forming a professional opinion as to the accuracy of the financial information being examined. The following types of evidence may be used to indicate that an event did in fact occur:

1. *Common knowledge* that the wear and tear of the elements of nature will ultimately destroy a piece of equipment is the objective evidence used to support the existence of the depreciation activity.
2. *Testimony* of both parties in an independent exchange transaction, to support the existence of most exchange transactions.
3. *Contractual agreement,* to support gradual performance of an activity as reflected in most accrual recognitions.
4. *Authoritative opinion,* to support the activity of creating goodwill, legal liability for damages, appraisals. This includes legal pronouncements. The assumption is that the authoritative opinion will be accepted.
5. *Accounting pronouncements,* to support such activities as the tracing and allocation of costs.
6. *Public recognition,* to support certain of the so-called public-cost activities of air, water, and land pollution. Illustrative of this activity is the 13-page insert, "Paper, People and Pollution," in the 1970 annual report of the Scott Paper Company.[86]

To obtain evidential matter, accountants use various methods—inspection, observation, inquiry, confirmation, and analytical tests. These methods, however, do not allow for an evaluation of the quality of the different types of evidence, given the absence of a method of designating different levels of proof as appropriate for different types of activities.[87] The same methods do not necessarily determine the truth but a perception of a real-world activity made by the accountant. The results of accounting measurement and disclosure reflect the perception of real-world activity made by the accountant. These perceptions are far from homogeneous and similar as they reflect the different judgment models and heuristics used by accountants with different backgrounds. As stated by Norton Bedford,

assuming . . . that an observation of any activity is a complex process involving both the immediate perception and the educational framework by which the initial perception is integrated into an observation, it appears that objectivity can be attached to an accounting observation only if accountants have a similar professional educational experience as background and a similar immediate view of the activity. Practically, this would never occur, so variations among accounting observations of value must be expected, unless precise operational rules are set forth.[88]

Narrative Truth and Historical Truth

Accounting relies on interpretation and narration of facts as an accounting phenomenon. It provides a narrative explanation of what really happened. What is provided is a "narrative truth" with its own special canons of truth embodied in the generally accepted accounting principles or on *what the process of constructing an accounting narrative itself imposes.* It is very much similar to the concept of narrative truth in psychoanalysis. As defined by D. Spence,

narrative truth can be defined as the criterion we use to decide when a certain experience has been captured to our satisfaction; it depends on continuity and closure and the extent to which the fit of the pieces takes on an aesthetic finality. Narrative truth is what we have in mind when we say that such and such is a good story, that a given explanation carries conviction, that *one* solution to a mystery must be true. Once a given construction has acquired narrative truth, it becomes just as real as any other kind of truth.[89]

The narrative truth contrasts, however, with the historical truth. Basically historical truth demands that all efficacious constructions be reconstructions. "Historical truth is time-bound and is dedicated to the strict observance of correspondence rules; our aim is to come as close as possible to what 'really' happened."[90] The historical truth of an event is tied to strict correspondence between the event and the statement about it. The correspondence may not be possible as true access to past events may not be either possible or plausible due to (1) fallibility of memory, (2) subjective interpretation of the events and even disinformation, and (3) secrecy.

Fallibility of Memory

Fallibility of memory as well as limitations in the human information processing capabilities of accountants is now well documented to present it as an obstacle to a perfect correspondence between narrative truth and historical truth in accounting.[91]

Subjective Interpretation and Disinformation

Subjective interpretation of the events as well as disinformation are related to the perceived role of accounting as a means of distortion. Because accounting is used to control or influence the actions of both internal and external users, it becomes an ideal target to those seeking to manipulate the nature of the message to be viewed by the user. Four groups of people may affect or be affected by accounting messages: those subjects whose behavior provides data for accounting messages, accountants who prepare the data, accountants who examine the data, and recipients of the data.[92] Each of these groups may then be tempted to engage in dysfunctional rather than normal behavior when it is involved with an accounting message. The dysfunctional behavior involves sending a dishonest or distorted message that is "one that managements expect to be interpreted in a manner inconsistent with their actual beliefs about the unobservable attributes of their decision."[93] The incentives to manipulate the message to be received by the internal or external user stem from the need to ensure or believe that certain messages will yield a particular behavior by the internal or external user. This dysfunctional behavior of manipulating data has been labeled as noise.[94] The methods used to distort the information system may be classified in the following six broad categories: smoothing, biasing, focusing, gaming, filtering, and "illegal" acts.[95]

Smoothing involves the process of altering the natural or preplanned flow of data without altering the actual activities of the organization. *Biasing* involves the process of selecting the signal most likely to be acceptable and favorable by the sender. *Focusing* involves the process of either enhancing or degrading certain aspects of the information set. *Gaming* involves the process of selecting activities by the sender so as to cause the desired message to be sent. *Filtering* involves the process of selecting certain favorable aspects of the information set as worthy of communication through overcollection, overrepresentation, aggregation, withholding, or delaying. *Illegal acts* involves the process of falsifying data and hence violating a private or public law.

All of these information-manipulation methods and behaviors are caused by low beliefs held by the sender in either the analyzability of the situation or the measurability and verifiability of data. Exhibit 6.3 illustrates the possible information-manipulating behavior.

All of these methods of information manipulation illustrate the belief that the information system may convey power to him or her given the ability to affect its output and consequently alter the resource-allocation process. M. L. Bariff and J. R. Galbraith have noted that "the design and operation of an organization's information system . . . will affect the distribution of intraorganizational power."[96] This is equivalent to the old maxim that information is power. It becomes important for organizational members to control the nature of information collected and conveyed and the choice of measures designed into accounting and control systems. This role of accounting as distortion raises serious questions about the limitations of narrative truth in accounting as compared to historical truth.

Exhibit 6.3
Possible Information-Manipulation Behavior

		High	Low
B E L I E F **I N** A N A L Y Z A B I L I T Y	H I G H	Very Little (1)	(2) Biasing Gaming Smoothing Illegal Acts
	L O W	(3) Filtering Focusing	(4) Biasing Falsifying Filtering Focusing Gaming Smoothing Illegal Acts

Source: Jacob G. Birnberg, Lawerence Turopolec, and S. Mark Young, "The Organizational Content of Accounting," *Accounting, Organizations and Society* (July 1983), p. 125. Reprinted with permission.

Secrecy

Truth in accounting implies the need to avoid secrecy. Secrecy is the act of concealing a fact or blocking information about it or evidence of it from reaching interested publics that can benefit from knowing it. Moral considerations argue against secrecy. As stated by Sissela Bok,

given both the legitimacy of some control over secrecy and openness, and the damages this control carries for all involved, there can be no presumption either for or against secrecy in general. Secrecy differs in this respect from lying, promise-breaking, violence and other practices for which the burden of proof rests on those who would depend on them. Conversely, secrecy differs from truthfulness, friendship, and other practices carrying a favorable presumption.[97]

Because accountants are not at liberty to disclose secrets that may benefit users, it raises questions about the limitations of narrative truth in accounting as compared to historical truth.

CONCLUSIONS

This chapter has clearly posited that truth in accounting is an elusive goal; it is not attainable. It is best stated by William Vatter as follows:

It is perhaps inevitable that the human mind should tend to view truth as an absolute or an ideal; such a view has merit in the attempt to make really precise explanations of scientific phenomena. But there are places where this ideal cannot be applied. The real world of business is nearly always too complicated for simple answers to questions, and accounting is no exception. Yet the search for single-valued truth persists in the notion that there should be some "right" or "best" way to present facts. This appears to some extent to underlie the general-purpose report, but it may be seen elsewhere. The search for "uniformity" or comparability in the presentation of financial data (even the idea that like things ought to be reported by the same methods, while unlike ones should not), the emphasis upon consistency, the pressure for conforming to specified forms of analysis and presentation, are all expressions of the single-valued truth idea. This conception affects the specification of accounting principles, supporting the view that there must be some basic formula or set of rules which, if established, could be depended upon to produce correct or proper results,. that some set of principles can be established as "the" basic way to report financial "facts." The trouble is that truth is not simple and unitary; facts arise only in context, and they must be abstracted and interpreted for communication.[98]

Accounting is reduced to scenarios where possibilities of truths are present if approximated by such criteria as neutrality, objectivity, reliability, and/or hardness and adapted to different roles of accounting and scenarios where impossibilities of truth are prevalent in cases involving measurement, income smoothing, choice of accounting techniques, asset valuation, cost allocation, relying on a standard of evidence, and using narrative truth.

The failure to capture the truth argues for the unscientific nature of accounting. The argument against the notion of accounting as a science capable of delivering the truth was made very early by A. C. Littleton as follows:

It is clear that accounting theory cannot justifiably be said to consist of scientific explanation. There are no immutable laws of accountancy comparable to the immutable laws of nature; there are no laboratory tests and controlled experiments to yield data which may be set up as mathematical formulas to express existing relationships.[99]

The accounting discipline is indeed socially constructed, and has no immutable laws or truths.[100] The man-made rules in accounting rely on judgment process for both the preparation and use of accounting information.

NOTES

1. Kenneth MacNeal, *Truth in Accounting* (Houston: Scholars Book Co., 1939), p. vii.

2. John Hospers, *An Introduction to Philosophical Analysis*, 2nd ed. (Englewood Cliffs, N.J.: Prentice-Hall, 1967), pp. 115–122.

3. A. C. Ewing, *The Fundamental Questions of Philosophy* (New York: Macmillan, 1951), pp. 54–55.

4. Hospers, *An Introduction to Philosophical Analysis,* p. 121.

5. A.M.C. Morison, "The Role of the Reporting Accountant Today," in W. T. Baxter and S. Davidson (eds.), *Studies in Accounting* (London: Institute of Chartered Accountants in England and Wales, 1977), p. 271.

6. Ibid., p. 272.

7. Financial Accounting Standards Board, Statement of Financial Accounting Concepts.

8. Eldon S. Hendriksen, *Accounting Theory*, 3rd ed. (Homewood, Ill.: Richard D. Irwin, 1977), p. 128.

9. W. A. Paton, and A. C. Littleton, *An Introduction to Corporate Accounting Standards* (Sarasota, Fla.: American Accounting Association, 1955), pp. 18–21.

10. Norton M. Bedford, *Extensions in Accounting Disclosures* (Englewood Cliffs, N.J.: Prentice-Hall, 1973), p. 158.

11. Committee on Accounting Valuation Bases, "Report of the Committee on Valuation Bases," *The Accounting Review*, Supplement to Vol. 47 (1972), p. 562.

12. Ibid., p. 563.

13. *Statement of Accounting Theory and Theory Acceptance* (Sarasota, Fla.: American Accounting Association, 1977), p. 16.

14. Y. Ijiri, and R. K. Jaedicke, "Reliability and Objectivity of Accounting Measurements," *The Accounting Review* (July 1966), pp. 480–483.

15. Committee on Accounting Valuation Bases, "Report of the Committee on Valuation Bases," p. 563.

16. Ibid., p. 567.

17. Yuji Ijiri, "Theory of Accounting Measurement," *Studies in Accounting Research No. 1* (Sarasota, Fla.: American Accounting Association, 1975), p. 39.

18. Ibid., p. 37.

19. Ibid.

20. Ibid., pp. 38–39.

21. Ibid., p. 40.

22. Wai-Fong Chua, "Accounting as Social Practice in Organizations: A Critical Review," paper presented at the Inaugural Management Accounting Research Conference, University of New South Wales, Australia, September 9–10, 1988.

23. Lars A. Samuelson, "Discrepancies Between the Roles of Budgeting," *Accounting, Organizations and Society*, 11, no. 1 (1986), p. 35.

24. Shahid Ansari, and K. J. Euske, "Rational, Rationalizing and Reifying Uses of Accounting Data in Organizations," *Accounting, Organizations and Society*, 12 (1987), pp. 549–570.

25. Ibid., p. 552.

26. Chua, "Accounting as Social Practice in Organizations," pp. 7–9.

27. Harold Bierman, Jr., "Measurement and Accounting," *The Accounting Review* (July 1963), p. 502.

28. Don W. Vickrey, "A Commentary on the Addition of Current Exit Values," *Journal of Business Finance and Accounting* (Winter 1978), pp. 413–423.

29. Don W. Vickrey, "Is Accounting a Measurement Discipline?," *The Accounting Review* (October 1970), p. 741.

30. Ibid.

31. Ibid.

32. Don W. Vickrey, "General Price-Level-Adjusted Historical Cost Statements and the Ratio Scale View," *The Accounting Review* (January 1976), p. 33.

33. Moustafa F. Abdel-Magid, "Toward a Better Understanding of the Role of Measurement in Accounting," *The Accounting Review* (April 1979), pp. 346–347.

34. Robert R. Sterling, "On Theory Construction and Verification," *The Accounting Review* (July 1970), pp. 444–457.

35. Committee on Foundations of Accounting Measurement, "Report of the Committee on Foundations of Accounting Measurement," *The Accounting Review,* Supplement to vol. 46 (1971), p. 11.

36. Ibid.

37. Abdel-Magid, "Toward a Better Understanding," p. 355.

38. Bierman, "Measurement and Accounting," p. 505.

39. I. Griffiths, *Creative Accounting* (London: Sidgewick and Jackson, 1986), p. 1.

40. S. R. Hepworth, "Periodic Income Smoothing," *The Accounting Review* (January 1953), p. 34.

41. R. J. Monsen, Jr., and A. Downs, "A Theory of Large Managerial Firms," *Journal of Political Economy*, 73 (1965), pp. 221–236; Myron J. Gordon, "Postulates, Principles and Research in Accounting," *The Accounting Review* (April 1964), pp. 251–263.

42. C. R. Beidleman, "Income Smoothing: The Role of Management," *The Accounting Review* (October 1973), p. 653.

43. Hepworth, "Periodic Income Smoothing," p. 34.

44. Gordon, "Postulates, Principles and Research in Accounting," pp. 251–263.

45. Ibid.

46. Beidleman, "Income Smoothing," pp. 653–657.

47. Ibid., p. 654.

48. Ibid.

49. R. Cyert, and J. March, *A Behavioral Theory of the Firm* (Englewood Cliffs, N.J.: Prentice-Hall, 1963).

50. M. Schiff and A. Lewin, "Where Traditional Budgeting Fails," *Financial Executive* (May 1968), pp. 57–62.

51. J. D. Thompson, *Organizations in Action* (New York: McGraw-Hill, 1967).

52. J. Y. Kamin, and J. Ronen, "The Smoothing of Income Numbers: Some Empirical Evidence on Systematic Differences among Management-Controlled and Owner-Controlled Firms," *Accounting, Organizations and Society*, 3, no. 2 (1978), pp. 141–153.

53. A. Barnea, J. Ronen, and S. Sadan, "Classificatory Smoothing of Income with Extraordinary Items," *The Accounting Review* (January 1976), pp. 110–122.

54. Ibid.

55. A. Belkaoui, *Behavioral Accounting* (Westport, Conn.: Greenwood, 1989).

56. See Maureen McNichols and G. Peter Wilson, "Evidence of Earnings Management from the Provision for Bad Debts," *The Accounting Review* (Supplement 1988), pp. 1–31; and Paul M. Healy, "The Effect of Bonus Schemes on Accounting Decisions," *Journal of Accounting and Economics*, 7 (1985), pp. 85–107.

57. L. DeAngelo, "Managerial Competition, Information Costs and Corporate Governance: The Use of Accounting Performance Measures in Proxy Contests," *Journal of Accounting and Economics* (January 1988), pp. 3–36.

58. J. Jones, "The Effect of Foreign Trade Regulation on Accounting Choices and Production and Investment Decisions," working paper, 1988.

59. Paul E. Dascher and R. Malcolm, "A Note on Income Smoothing in the Chemical Industry," *Journal of Accounting Research* (Fall 1970), pp. 253–254.

60. M. J. Gordon, "Discussion of the Effects of Alternative Accounting Rules for Nonsubsidiary Investments," *Journal of Accounting Research* 4 (Supplement 1966), p. 223.

61. R. M. Copeland, "Income Smoothing, Empirical Research in Accounting: Selected Studies," *Journal of Accounting Research,* 6 (Supplement 1968), p. 101.

62. Barnea, Ronen, and Sadan, "Classificatory Smoothing of Income with Extraordinary Items," p. 111.

63. G. White, "Discretionary Accounting Decisions and Income Normalization," *Journal of Accounting Research* (Fall 1970), pp. 260–274.

64. R. M. Copeland and Ralph D. Licastro, "A Note on Income Smoothing," *The Accounting Review* (July 1968), pp. 540–545.

65. Ibid., p. 542.

66. Barnea, Ronen, and Sadan, "Classificatory Smoothing of Income with Extraordinary Items," p. 111.

67. Copeland, "Income Smoothing, Empirical Research in Accounting," pp. 101–116.

68. Beidleman, "Income Smoothing," p. 658.

69. M. R. Mathews and M.H.B. Perera, *Accounting Theory and Development* (South Melbourne: Thomas Nelson, 1991).

70. *Wall Street Journal*, July 25, 1980, p. 41.

71. Andrew Christie, "Aggregation of Test Statistics: On Evaluation of the Evidence on Contracting and Size Hypothesis," *Journal of Accounting and Economics,* 12 (1990).

72. S. Lillien, M. Mellman, and V. Pastena, "Accounting Changes: Successful or Unsuccessful Firms," *The Accounting Review* (October 1988), pp. 642–656.

73. Ahmed Belkaoui, "The Effects of Bond Rating Changes in Accounting Changes," working paper, University of Illinois at Chicago, 1992.

74. Committee on Accounting Valuation Bases, "Report of the Committee," p. 535.

75. Robert R. Sterling, "Relevant Financial Reporting in an Age of Price Changes," *Journal of Accountancy* (February 1975), pp. 42–51.

76. S. Basu and J. R. Hanna, *Inflation Accounting: Alternatives, Implementation Issues and Some Empirical Evidence* (Hamilton, Ontario: The Society of Management Accountants of Canada, 1977).

77. Ahmed Belkaoui, *Accounting Theory* (London: Academic Press, 1992).

78. Committee on Accounting Valuation Bases, "Report of the Committee," p. 544.

79. Louis Goldberg, *An Inquiry to the Nature of Accounting* (Iowa City: American Accounting Association, 1965), pp. 316–317.

80. W. Paton, and A. C. Littleton, *An Introduction to Corporate Accounting Standards* (Iowa City: American Accounting Association, 1940), p. 71.

81. Ibid., p. 15.

82. Accounting Principles Board, *Statement No. 4* (New York: AICPA, 1966), para. 19.

83. Arthur L. Thomas, "The Allocation Problem in Financial Accounting Theory," *Studies in Accounting Research No. 3* (Sarasota, Fla.: American Accounting Association, 1969), pp. 6–15.

84. Arthur L. Thomas, "The Allocation Problem in Financial Accounting Theory," *Studies in Accounting Research No. 9* (Sarasota, Fla.: American Accounting Association, 1974), p. 3.

85. Bedford, *Extensions in Accounting Disclosures,* pp. 101–102.

86. Ibid., p. 3.

87. Ibid.

88. Ibid, p. 92.

89. D. Spence, *Narrative Truth and Historical Truth* (New York: W. W. Norton, 1982), p. 31.

90. Ibid., p. 32.

91. Ahmed Belkaoui, *Human Information Processing in Accounting* (Westport, Conn.: Quorum Books, 1989).

92. D. Green, Jr., "Evaluating the Accounting Literature," *The Accounting Review* (January 1978), p. 31.

93. N. J. Gonedes, "Corporate Signalling, External Accounting, and Capital Market Equilibrium: Evidence on Dividends, Income, and Extraordinary Items," *Journal of Accounting Research* (Spring 1978), p. 31.

94. C. E. Shannon and W. Weaver, *The Mathematical Theory of Communications* (Urbana: University of Illinois Press, 1949).

95. Jacob G. Birnberg, Lawrence Turopolec, and S. Mark Young, "The Organizational Content of Accounting," *Accounting, Organizations and Society* (July 1983), p. 120.

96. M. L. Bariff and J. R. Galbraith, "Interorganizational Power Considerations for Designing Information Systems," *Accounting, Organizations and Society* (Fall 1978), p. 15.

97. Sissela Bok, *Secrets: On the Ethics of Concealment and Revelation* (New York: Pantheon Books, 1982), pp. 26-27.

98. William J. Vatter, "Obstacles to the Specification of Accounting Principles," in R. K. Jaedicke, Y. Ijiri, and O. Nielsen (eds.), *Research in Accounting Measurement* (Sarasota, Fla.: American Accounting Association, 1966), p. 81.

99. A. C. Littleton, *Structure of Accounting Theory* (Columbus, Ohio: American Accounting Association, 1953), p. 153.

100. Ian Tilley, "Accounting as a Specific Endeavor: Some Questions the American Theorists Tend to Leave Unanswered," *Accounting and Business Research* (Autumn 1972), pp. 287-297.

BIBLIOGRAPHY

Abdel-Magid, Moustafa F. "Toward a Better Understanding of the Role of Measurement in Accounting." *The Accounting Review* (April 1979), pp. 346-347.

Ansari, Shahid and K. J. Euske. "Rational, Rationalizing and Reifying Uses of Accounting Data in Organizations." *Accounting, Organizations and Society,* 12 (1987), pp. 549-570.

Anton, Hector R. "Some Aspects of Measurement and Accounting." *Journal of Accounting and Research* (Spring 1964), pp. 1-9.

Bedford, Norton M. *Extensions in Accounting Disclosures.* Englewood Cliffs, N.J.: Prentice-Hall, 1973.

———. "Management Motives in Accounting Measurements." *Quarterly Review of Economics and Business* (Autumn 1963), pp. 35-45.

Belkaoui, Ahmed. *Accounting Theory.* London, Academic Press, 1992.

Bierman, Harold, Jr. "Measurement and Accounting." *The Accounting Review* (July 1963), pp. 501-507.

Chambers, R. J. "Measurement and Objectivity in Accounting." *The Accounting Review* (April 1964).

———. "Measurement in Accounting," *Journal of Accounting Research* (Spring 1965), pp. 32-62.

Churchill, Neil C. and Andrew C. Stedry. "Extending the Dimensions of Accounting Measurement." *Management Services* (March-April 1967), pp. 15-22.

Committee on Foundations of Accounting Measurement. "Report of the Committee on Foundations of Accounting Measurement." *The Accounting Review,* Supplement to vol. 46 (1971), pp. 1-49.

Homburger, Richard H. "Measurement in Accounting." *The Accounting Review* (January 1961), pp. 94-99.

Ijiri, Yuji. *The Foundations of Accounting Measurement.* Englewood Cliffs, N.J.: Prentice-Hall, 1967.

Ijiri, Y. and R. K. Jaedicke. "Axioms and Structures of Conventional Accounting Measurement." *The Accounting Review* (January 1965), pp. 36-53.

———. "Reliability and Objectivity of Accounting Measurements." *The Accounting Review* (July 1966), pp. 480-483.

Kemeny, G. "Measurement." In *A Philosopher Looks at Science* (New York: D. Van Nostrand, 1966), pp. 141-155.

Lim, R. S., "Mathematical Propriety of Accounting Measurements and Calculations." *The Accounting Review* (October 1966), pp. 642–651.

Tilley, Ian. "Accounting as a Specific Endeavor: Some Questions the American Theorists Tend to Leave Unanswered." *Accounting and Business Research* (Autumn 1972), pp. 287–297.

Vatter, William J. "Contributions of Accounting to Measurement in Management." *Management Science* (October 1958).

Vickrey, Don W. "Is Accounting a Measurement Discipline?" *The Accounting Review* (October 1970), pp. 731–742.

Willett, R. J., "An Axiomatic Theory of Accounting Measurement." *Accounting and Business Research* (Spring 1987), pp. 155–172.

Index

About the Author

AHMED RIAHI-BELKAOUI is Professor of Accounting at the University of Illinois at Chicago. He is the author of several accounting texts and more than 20 professional and scholarly books, mostly for Quorum, including *Multinational Financial Accounting* (1991), *Cost Accounting: Theory and Practice* (1991), and *Judgment in International Accounting* (1990).